Introducing Microsoft® Visual Basic 2005 for Developers

*Campbell, Swigart,
Horrocks, Hatchard,
Bernhardt, O'Brien, Rugless*

PUBLISHED BY
Microsoft Press
A Division of Microsoft Corporation
One Microsoft Way
Redmond, Washington 98052-6399

Library of Congress Cataloging-in-Publication Data pending.

Printed and bound in the United States of America.

3 4 5 6 7 8 9   QWE   9 8 7 6 5

Distributed in Canada by H.B. Fenn and Company Ltd.

A CIP catalogue record for this book is available from the British Library.

Microsoft Press books are available through booksellers and distributors worldwide. For further information about international editions, contact your local Microsoft Corporation office or contact Microsoft Press International directly at fax (425) 936-7329. Visit our Web site at www.microsoft.com/learning/. Send comments to *mspinput@microsoft.com*.

Microsoft, Active Directory, ActiveX, Authenticode, DataTips, DirectX, IntelliSense, Microsoft Press, MSDN, MS-DOS, Outlook, Verdana, Visual Basic, the Visual Basic logo, Visual Studio, Win32, Windows, Windows NT, and Windows Server are either registered trademarks or trademarks of Microsoft Corporation in the United States and/or other countries. Other product and company names mentioned herein may be the trademarks of their respective owners.

The example companies, organizations, products, domain names, e-mail addresses, logos, people, places, and events depicted herein are fictitious. No association with any real company, organization, product, domain name, e-mail address, logo, person, place, or event is intended or should be inferred.

This book expresses the author's views and opinions. The information contained in this book is provided without any express, statutory, or implied warranties. Neither the authors, Microsoft Corporation, nor its resellers or distributors will be held liable for any damages caused or alleged to be caused either directly or indirectly by this book.

Acquisitions Editor: Ben Ryan
Project Editor: Karen Szall
Technical Editor: Matt Stoecker
Copy Editor: Roger LeBlanc
Principal Compositor: Elizabeth Hansford
Indexer: Lynn Armstrong

Body Part No. X10-81699

Table of Contents

Acknowledgments

The creation of a book like this is possible only when the authors are supported by a team as good as the one we were privileged to work with.

We would first like to thank Ari Bixhorn and Christopher Flores, who were the initial supporters of the book, and without whose evangelism efforts this book would not have become a reality.

We also want to thank all of the folks at Microsoft Press who did what it took to deliver this book despite the significant obstacles inherent in writing about a product while that product is approaching Beta 1. Matt Carter, Karen Szall, Ben Ryan, Sally Stickney, and Danielle Bird Voeller were especially helpful in getting this book into your hands.

We would also like to thank Jay Roxe, who has been instrumental in ensuring that this book is targeted and timely, and Robert Green for providing the resources needed to ensure technical accuracy.

We would like to give a special thanks to Amy Strande, who will always hold a special place in our hearts because she was the first person at Microsoft willing to take a chance on 3 Leaf. Thanks, Amy.

Last—but absolutely not least—we would like to give thanks to our families and friends. Without your support, none of us would have found the time to write this book, nor would it have been as inspired.

Introduction

Developer productivity is the mantra for this release of Microsoft Visual Studio. Regardless of the application types you use or the languages you choose, Microsoft has focused its effort on building an integrated development environment (IDE), class library, and language suite that makes it as easy as possible to build and deploy applications.

It is obvious to us, the authors of this book, that Microsoft has looked at all aspects of coding—including the writing of the code itself, debugging, and deployment—and really examined how it could streamline each of these experiences. The enhancements are far reaching and include changes to the Microsoft Visual Basic .NET language itself, improvements to the IDE, simplification of data access and display, changes that increase developer productivity when constructing professional user interfaces, addition of a significant number of new classes to the framework to reduce the amount of code that you write, and an increase in the power and simplicity of deployment.

This book will examine each of these areas in depth. In addition, while this book focuses on building desktop applications, most developers are doing at least some Web development. For this reason, Chapter 6, "Building Web Applications," covers some of the most significant changes to ASP.NET.

This introduction briefly covers these topics and points you to the specific chapter where you can get more in-depth information. You can read this book from cover to cover or skip to the chapters of most interest to you.

Who Should Read This Book

This book is for Visual Basic developers. If you are a Visual Basic 6 developer, you should begin with Chapter 1, "Microsoft .NET Framework Primer for the Visual Basic Developer," which will bring you up to speed on development for the .NET Framework. The remainder of the book covers the significant enhancements to Visual Basic that will make you more productive when developing applications.

If you are an existing .NET developer, you can skip Chapter 1 and jump right into Chapter 2, "Language Enhancements for Visual Basic 2005."

What's in This Book

This book contains eight chapters. The first chapter, "Microsot .NET Framework Primer for the Visual Basic Developer," will be most helpful to developers currently working with Visual Basic 6. It provides the introduction to development for the .NET Framework.

This section describes each chapter and gives you some introductory information about each topic.

> **Important**   To run the samples in this book, you need two pieces of software installed: Visual Studio 2005 and SQL Server 2000 Desktop, Developer, Enterprise, or Desktop Engine edition. SQL Server 2000 should be installed with the Northwind sample database. The code samples and be found on MSDN at *http://msdn.microsoft.com/vbasic/VB6Migration*.

Chapter 2, "Language Enhancements for Visual Basic 2005"

This chapter introduces generics, The My Object, and new operators.

Generics   Possibly the most significant enhancement to the .NET Framework is the introduction of *generics*. Quite simply, generics let you create collections that are specific to the type of object that you're storing.

```
Dim customerDictionary As New Dictionary(Of String, Customer)
customerDictionary.Add(currentCust.FullName, currentCust)
```

In this example, the *customerDictionary* can store items only of type *Customer*. And the lookup is specifically a *String* value. Because the collection knows what it's storing (Customers vs. just Objects), it can provide full Microsoft IntelliSense, as shown in the following figure.

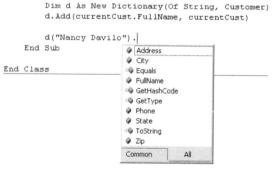

Figure I-1   IntelliSense on generic collections.

The My Object   Another significant enhancement to Visual Basic .NET is a feature simply known as "The My Object." This feature provides extremely quick and easy access to powerful functionality. For example, My.Application.Log.WriteEntry will let you write information to a text file, event log, or other destination. My.Computer.Audio.PlaySystemSound will let you play predefined operating system sounds, while My.Computer.Audio.Play will let you play any .wav file. The My Object also gives you default instances for items that are part of your project. For example, you can use My.Forms.MainForm.Show to display a form without first creating an instance of it.

New Operators   Visual Basic .NET also includes a number of new keywords. *IsNot* facilitates comparisons with *Nothing*. In the past, you often had to write **If Not X Is Nothing Then**. Now this can be written as **If X IsNot Nothing Then**. Visual Basic .NET also supports operator overloading, generics, and many other advanced programming features.

For more on these enhancements, see Chapter 2, "Language Enhancements for Visual Basic 2005."

Chapter 3, "Visual Studio 2005 Integrated Development Environment"

Visual Basic development has always been about productivity, and the key tool to provide this productivity is Visual Studio. With Visual Studio 2005, productivity has been enhanced across the board, with better and easier to navigate help content, easier customization of the development environment, and a more productive coding and debugging experience, including the reintroduction of Edit-And-Continue.

Coding and Debugging Enhancements   When you work with the new Integrated Development Environment (IDE), you will see that great effort was made to add "context" to your coding. Meaning that, in many cases, you don't have to navigate to some other window elsewhere in the IDE to get the information you need. In other cases, the IDE provides intelligent filtering of information so that the most likely choices are put front and center, and the rarely used options do not clutter the view. This functionality is apparent the first time you access a property of an object, as shown in the following figure.

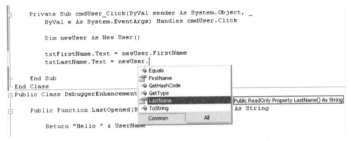

Figure I-2   Progressive disclosure of object members.

As you can see, Visual Studio 2005 can either show you all the members of an object or filter the list to show just the most commonly used members, making it easy to find the *Connection-String* property, for example.

Visual Studio 2005 also further extends familiar Visual Basic code expansions. You're used to typing in the beginning *Function* declaration and having the IDE automatically insert the *End Function* for you. Now this is expanded to such things as property declarations. Typing **public property UserName as String** and pressing Enter causes the automatic insertion of the following code:

```
Public Property UserName() As String
    Get

    End Get
    Set(ByVal value As String)

    End Set
End Property
```

Visual Studio 2005 also puts information at your fingertips when debugging, letting you drill into simple and complex types, without opening and navigating through the Watch window. The following figure shows how a complex type is displayed directly in the code editor.

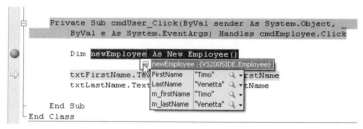

Figure I-3 Displaying the properties of a complex type, in-place.

One of the single biggest productivity enhancements provided by Visual Basic 6 was Edit-And-Continue. This functionality was a mainstay of the debugging experience and was unfortunately not available in Visual Studio .NET 2002 or 2003. Edit-And-Continue is back, allowing you to fix errors and continue execution without stopping and restarting.

IDE Customization and Help System Enhancements   Visual Basic developers highly value the ability to customize their development environment and place windows where they will be most useful to them. Visual Studio has always provided this capability, but with Visual Studio 2005, the capability has been significantly enhanced in several key areas. First, Visual Studio 2005 eliminates the "I wonder where this window will dock" problem, where you think you have a window positioned correctly, but when you let go of it, it either doesn't dock or doesn't dock the way you expected. In Visual Studio 2005, docking is a snap with "docking guides," as shown in the following figure.

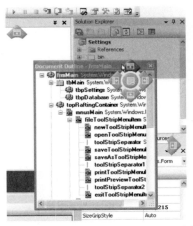

Figure I-4   Using the docking guides.

You simply drop the window on the appropriate arrow to dock it over, above, to the right of, below, or to the left of another window. No more guessing! Also, all your IDE customizations can be exported and imported.

In addition, the Help system has been greatly improved, providing you a better "F1" experience, but also letting you access the latest help available online. The help system even hooks into the "Code Wise" community of Web sites, providing access to such sites as CodeGuru, Net247, and ASP.NET right inside of the IDE.

For more information about the significant productivity enhancements provided in Visual Studio 2005, you can go directly to Chapter 3, "Visual Studio 2005 Integrated Development Environment."

Chapter 4, "Building Datacentric Applications"

Visual Studio 2005 brings with it a host of powerful tools for building datacentric applications. First, there are some new objects that build on top of ADO.NET 1.0. These include a typed *DataAdapter* class that makes calling a stored procedure as easy as calling a function. The toolbox also contains a new grid control that is very easy to customize and control. Finally, the IDE contains a new Data Sources window that helps you manage these objects and create your user interface at design time.

The Data Sources window is used to generate the typed *DataAdapters* and type *DataSets* that you will use throughout a given application. Once you have connected to the database and selected the tables and procedures that you want to use, you can simply drag objects from the Data Sources window to the design surface to create the user interface, as shown in the following figure.

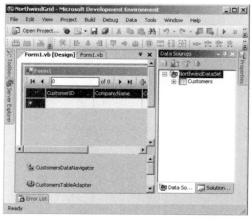

Figure I-5 Building a user interface with the Data Sources window.

You can see that by default, when the customers table is dropped on to the design surface, it renders it using the new *GridView* control. You can also have it render as individual fields, and you can determine the type of control that's used for each field.

You can also use the DataSet Designer to map methods to stored procedures. This makes calling a stored procedure as easy as the following code:

```
ds = MyDataSet.GetByCustomerID(customerID)
```

For more information on using data in Visual Studio 2005, see Chapter 4, "Building Datacentric Applications."

Chapter 5, "Constructing User Interfaces"

Visual Basic developers have never had any difficulty in rapidly building user interfaces. If there is one area where Visual Basic has always shined, it's the toolbox and form designer. However, a frequent refrain from Visual Basic developers has been, "Give us the user interface controls that Microsoft uses in its applications." And, more specifically, developers wanted many of the user interface elements, such as rafting toolbars, found in products such as Microsoft Office.

New Controls You will be happy to learn that this version of Visual Studio doesn't just focus on a toolbox full of stuff; this version really seeks to make it easy to build professional user interfaces without resorting to third-party components or extensive custom control development. The first control Chapter 5 examines is the *ToolStrip*, shown in the following figure.

Figure I-6 MenuStrip, StatusStrip, and ToolStrip.

You can see that a simple form has been created with two *ToolStrip* controls. This was literally done in a matter of seconds, but there are actually quite a few things to discuss. First, you can see that the *ToolStrip* controls support "rafting," which means that the user can drag the *ToolStrip* controls around and arrange them at run time. Second, the top *ToolStrip* contains the standard icons that you are familiar with. These were added with a single click. If there are any icons that you don't want, you can simply select them and press Delete. The *ToolStrip* also supports more than just buttons. It can contain text boxes, drop-down lists, labels, and more. Finally, the toolbars look just like the Microsoft Office toolbars, making it easy to build professional-looking applications that your users will natively understand how to use.

The menu bar and status bar build on the *ToolStrip* infrastructure, letting you have a wider variety of controls and capabilities in the menu or status bar.

In the toolbox, you'll also find a full .NET wrapper around the ActiveX Web browser control, making it simple to add Web functionality to applications. This control can be used to display Web-based help or take users to a page where they can purchase a product.

Changes to Existing Controls   One of the first things that you'll notice when you build forms is *snaplines*, which make it quick and easy to line up controls as you build the user interface, as shown in the following figure.

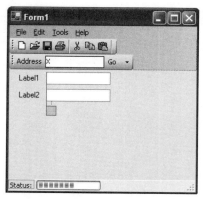

Figure I-7   Using snaplines to align controls.

When dragging controls around the design surface, rather than seeing the traditional grid, you have snaplines that appear and make it simple to perfectly align controls. The snaplines let you align the edges of controls and also recommend appropriate spacing between the controls. The spacing is controlled by a new *Margin* control property.

Many controls also contain new auto-complete properties that let the controls automatically provide suggestions for file names, URLs, custom lists, or other sources.

For more on building professional user interfaces, and the new application configuration infrastructure, see Chapter 5, "Constructing User Interfaces."

Chapter 6, "Building Web Applications"

Visual Studio .NET 2002 and 2003 brought revolutions to Web development, bringing an order of magnitude productivity enhancement to Web developers over classic ASP. ASP.NET 2.0 does it again. The goal for the product team was nothing less than a 70 percent reduction in the amount of code required to build Web sites. By all accounts, when Visual Studio 2005 is released, the product team will have easily met its target. Even now, many sites can be built with zero code.

With ASP.NET versions 1.0 and 1.1, you could declaratively create the user interface, but you had to write code to connect to the database, retrieve data, and bind the UI to the data. With ASP.NET 2.0, there are components that encapsulate the data source. This lets you declaratively wire a grid to a SQL Server data source, for example. The binding is quite sophisticated. You need to make changes to the data and push the changes back to the database. This new feature also isn't just "demoware" like design-time controls of the past. The controls have really been factored in such a way that the look and feel of the UI is completely customizable, and you can hook into the controls programmatically or declaratively.

Microsoft has also identified key scenarios and built the infrastructure for those scenarios right into the .NET Framework. For example, ASP.NET 2.0 has the concept of membership and personalization built in. Membership is a package of functionality that provides common controls for things such as logging in, changing your password, and so on. It also provides the infrastructure to automatically store and retrieve information from a back-end database. Finally, membership gives you APIs to work with a user programmatically.

ASP.NET also ships with a number of new controls to address key scenarios. For example, the *SiteMapPath* control provides built-in breadcrumb functionality, and the *SiteMapDataSource* can make it easy to build site navigation. Master Pages allow you to define common areas of the page in one place, with only the content area changing. Caching has been improved, and data can now be cached on a per-user basis.

For more information on ASP.NET 2.0, see Chapter 6, "Building Web Applications."

Chapter 7, "Microsoft .NET Framework Enhancements"

The enhancements are not just restricted to the development environment. The underlying framework itself contains significant improvements. Generics, a significant enhancement and a powerful language feature introduced in version 2.0 of the .NET Framework, are described in Chapter 2. This chapter covers Base Class Library, console, and security enhancements.

The .NET Framework contains a tremendous number of new classes to further reduce the amount of code that you need to write and make it easier to add functionality to your applications. *StopWatch* is a new class that makes it trivial to capture elapsed intervals. The *Trace-Source* class provides you with more flexibility over how event data is traced. The *System.Net* namespace contains significant enhancements, allowing you to Ping IP addresses, for example. There's now a fully managed wrapper for Internet Explorer. *System.XML* has been significantly enhanced both in terms of performance and functionality, and now includes support for XQuery.

For more information about these new classes and console and security enhancements, see Chapter 7, "Microsoft .NET Framework Enhancements."

Chapter 8, "Deploying Applications"

With Visual Basic 6.0, deploying an application generally involved building a Windows Installer package. This process was essential because Visual Basic 6.0 was COM based and applications generally required a number of DLLs to be registered before the application would function. The installer would also create Start menu shortcuts, install databases, or perform other needed tasks.

Versions 1.0 and 1.1 of the .NET Framework opened the door to more installation options. First, version 1.0 supported what was often referred to as the XCOPY Deployment. This meant that simple applications could just be copied to the hard drive and executed. This was possible because .NET DLLs do not need to be registered. Version 1.0 also supported what was known as No-Touch deployment—also sometimes called href-exes. In this method of deployment, an application executable was simply placed on a Web server. When you browsed to the URL for the application, it would download and run. The result was a full Windows application with the ease of deployment of Web applications. With .NET, even if you needed to create a Windows Installer package, the process of doing so was greatly simplified because you did not have to worry about DLL registration.

No Touch deployment was seen by many as an excellent approach for intranet applications. Through a simple portal, you could ensure that users were always running the latest version of the application. With Visual Studio 2005, Microsoft has significantly enhanced the capabilities of applications distributed through the Web. First, the applications can now download and fully install. This capability creates the appropriate Start menu shortcuts, and (more importantly) it lets the application function fully even when you're offline.

ClickOnce applications also do not require you to be an administrator to install them (as Windows Installer packages do). Finally, ClickOnce allows you to "bootstrap" other required software as part of the installation. For example, a ClickOnce application can install MDAC, or even the .NET Framework if needed, as part of the application installation.

For more information on ClickOnce, see Chapter 8, "Deploying Applications."

Support

Every effort has been made to ensure the accuracy of this book. If you run into a problem, Microsoft Press provides corrections for its books through the following Web site: *http://www.microsoft.com/learning/support/*.

If you have problems, comments, or ideas regarding this book or the companion CD-ROM, please send them to Microsoft Press.

Send e-mail to *mspinput@microsoft.com*

Send postal mail to

Microsoft Press
Attn: *Introducing Microsoft Visual Basic 2005 for Developers* Editor
One Microsoft Way
Redmond, WA 98052-6399

Please note that support for the software product itself is not offered through the preceding addresses. For product support, go to *http://support.microsoft.com*.

To connect directly to the Microsoft Knowledge Base and enter a query regarding a question or issue that you have, go to *http://support.microsoft.com*.

Chapter 1

Microsoft .NET Framework Primer for the Visual Basic Developer

The Microsoft .NET Framework and the corresponding versions of Microsoft Visual Studio that target the .NET Framework are major innovations for software developers. If you have been programming in Visual Basic 6 (or earlier), you will appreciate the advances in productivity, security, reliability, and "deployability" offered by these new development and execution environments.

Every program relies on its platform and other libraries to provide run-time services. Visual Basic 6 programmers know well the types of services provided by the Visual Basic Runtime. Java programmers use the Java Virtual Machine (JVM). Other programmers use the libraries for the technologies they develop with. The Microsoft .NET Framework class library provides a rich library for creating applications that run on the platform (or execution environment) known as the *common language runtime* (CLR). This chapter will introduce you to the basics of the .NET Framework, its class library, and the developer tools that make up Microsoft Visual Studio 2005. At the end of this chapter are some highlights of the new features in .NET Framework 2.0 and Visual Studio 2005 that are covered in more detail in the rest of this book.

The .NET Framework CLR is an execution environment that manages key platform services, including memory and security. Code that targets the .NET Framework is often referred to as *managed code* because it requires management services provided by the execution environment. All Visual Basic code you write for the .NET Framework is managed code. This includes Windows applications, Web applications, and all other types of applications.

The Applications You Can Build

You have probably heard a lot of hype about .NET and XML Web services. Much of that hype is well deserved because the .NET Framework and Visual Studio 2005 make building and consuming Web services so easy. But Microsoft .NET technologies are not just about Web services. Visual Studio 2005 and the .NET Framework are just as powerful for creating other types of applications including Windows and Web applications. At times, the hype around Web services has overshadowed the wide range of applications you can create with Microsoft .NET technologies and the many benefits of targeting the .NET Framework, including increased security, increased developer productivity, decreased deployment and maintenance costs, and an extensive pre-built library for many generic tasks.

Smart Client Windows Applications

You can, of course, create GUI-driven Windows applications that are similar to the Windows applications you create with Visual Basic 6. These .NET applications are often called Windows Forms applications, thick clients, or smart clients. The Microsoft .NET Framework offers many features for Windows GUI applications that have been enhanced beyond Visual Basic 6 capabilities, such as docking, anchoring, opacity, new controls, and more Windows messages exposed as events.

The term *smart client* refers to Windows applications that combine the processing power and rich user interface (UI) of desktop applications with the deployment and connectivity features more generally associated with Web applications. Smart clients are conventional Windows applications with features such as the following: consuming Web services; supporting offline modes; deployable from a central server; providing automatic updates (from a central server); or supporting multiple types of devices. Interest in smart clients has been growing steadily as Microsoft technology simplifies deployment and companies struggle with the limits of Web-based interfaces while looking for ways to use the processing power that sits at the edge of networks.

Web Applications

The .NET Framework has become an extremely popular technology for Web applications. The Web features in the .NET Framework, known collectively as ASP.NET, are embodied in a rich object model that provides power and scalability well beyond its predecessor ASP (now commonly known as *classic ASP*). Since its introduction, ASP.NET has been a highly effective set of technologies for creating and deploying everything from small to enterprise-scale Web applications.

Web Services

XML Web services are part of ASP.NET. A conventional Web page responds to HTTP requests with HTML output. By contrast, Web services are based on SOAP, an XML-based protocol that defines the syntax and rules for exchanging messages between two systems. SOAP messages can be transported over HTTP just like Web page requests, which means you can expose services (for example, Web services) that are accessible through most firewalls that allow traffic on port 80.

 Note   The term *dialect* refers to the rules for a version of XML used to represent certain types of data. SOAP is an XML dialect for message exchange. There are countless other dialects of XML defined for many different uses of XML, including standards and proprietary systems.

Windows Services

A long-standing lament among Visual Basic programmers was the difficulty in creating applications that could run as Windows Services (formerly NT Services). Windows Services are background applications that perform tasks or provide services to other programs. Windows Services are normally started automatically and run regardless of whether any users are logged on. They are controlled by a Windows subsystem called the Service Control Manager. Prior to the .NET Framework, Visual Basic developers had to use third-party tools to create applications that could be run as services. Creating Windows Services applications with the .NET Framework is as easy as creating any other type of application. The service can be written in any .NET-compliant language, including Visual Basic.

Console Applications

An often overlooked but powerful type of application is the console application. Console applications have streams for input and output data rather than the point-and-click interaction model used for GUI applications. Console applications are often called *command-line applications*. Visual Basic 6 does not offer an easy way to create console applications, but with the .NET Framework you can create console applications in Visual Basic or any .NET-compliant language.

Class Libraries

Maximizing code and binary reuse is a fundamental goal of professional developers. One way you work toward that goal is to design your software solutions so that code is generic and reusable. You then encapsulate that potentially reusable code in class libraries by generating DLL files. For Visual Basic 6 programmers, this process is somewhat analogous to creating a COM DLL project, except the DLL files created by Visual Studio 2005 are not COM components. They are assemblies that contain managed code. (Assemblies are covered later in this chapter.) The classes in these class libraries can be any sort of class, including controls and components (that you can then add to the toolbox in the Visual Studio 2005 IDE), classes that extend the Framework Class Library (for example, specialized forms), or your own classes that you implement completely (for example, classes for business rules).

Smart Device Applications

Windows, console, and Web applications (including Web services) target the .NET Framework. You can also write applications that target the .NET Compact Framework. The .NET Compact Framework is a subset of the full .NET Framework for smart devices. The .NET Compact Framework is optimized to run on devices with reduced resources like memory and screen size (for example, Smartphones and other handheld devices). Visual Studio 2005 includes a smart-device emulator to facilitate the development and debugging of smart-device applications.

Setup and Deployment Projects

You can create several types of setup and deployment projects with Visual Studio 2005. Setup and deployment projects are less important now than they used to be because many deployment issues have been simplified, including eliminating the need to register components used by a single application (that is, private assemblies). But there are still many situations in which you will want to have a robust and professional-looking installation program. Visual Basic 6 developers will find that the setup and deployment projects in Visual Studio 2005 are greatly improved over the Package And Deployment Wizard from Visual Basic 6. The power and flexibility of the development interface and the generation of MSI setup packages for Microsoft Installer gives Visual Basic developers access to features that were previously available only with third-party tools.

A Truly Integrated Development Environment

Visual Studio .NET introduced a unified development environment for all the types of applications you can build. Visual Studio 2005 is the latest offering in the evolution of that unified environment. It is a lot more than an integrated editor, compiler, and debugger. A common shell, shown in Figure 1-1, hosts the entire assortment of tools that makes up Visual Studio 2005, such as the Visual Basic code editor, the visual Windows Forms designer, the new visual Web designer, the Server Explorer, and much more. The shell is also extensible, allowing add-ins, new project types, and new designers to be plugged into the development environment.

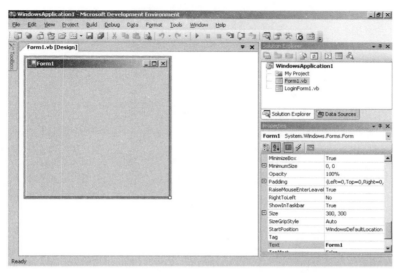

Figure 1-1   Visual Studio 2005 integrated development environment.

The Visual Studio 2005 IDE (integrated development environment) is a robust working environment in which you will probably spend most of your development time. For example, in this one environment you can write a Web application storefront, a Windows service for processing financial transactions, a Web service for exposing data to multiple back-office systems, and a smart client for retrieving data via the Web service in the back office. You can also use the IDE to debug all these applications, run unit tests (with third-party tools or the forthcoming tools from Microsoft), manage enterprise services (for example, MSMQ), manage SQL Servers, and more.

What Is .NET?

Understanding exactly what ".NET" means can be challenging. If you ask five experienced .NET developers "What is .NET?", you will probably get five different answers, just as you would get different answers if you asked "What is Microsoft Windows?" or "What is a computer program?" These differences arise because different types of users understand technologies from their own perspectives. From a developer's perspective, .NET is really three things: the .NET Framework, the .NET Framework SDK, and the development environment (first Visual Studio .NET, then Visual Studio .NET 2003, and now Visual Studio 2005).

The .NET Framework provides a core set of functionality for applications. It provides the services and other features necessary for code to run in a managed environment. The .NET Framework SDK is the set of base tools for creating managed applications and includes compilers along with a number of other useful tools. Visual Studio 2005 builds on the base tool set provided in the Framework SDK. Visual Studio is the premiere tool for developing applications that target the .NET Framework.

> **Note**   Some developers and IT professionals describe the .NET Framework as a platform, while others will insist that the .NET Framework is not a platform but a building block or ingredient in a broader platform, namely Microsoft Windows. Really the .NET Framework and the .NET Compact Framework are both platforms *and* building blocks of the broader platforms on which they sit, such as Windows Server 2003 or Windows CE. Those broader platforms run on hardware that is often referred to as a platform as well. To help reduce confusion with so many uses of the term *platform*, the .NET Framework is not referred to as a platform in this book.

The Common Language Runtime and Intermediate Language

Every program runs within a context. DOS programs ran within the context of the services provided by the 16-bit MS-DOS operating systems. Applications such as Microsoft Word run within the context of your current operating system and are subject to the constraints imposed and services provided by that operating system, such as the permissions granted to your user account. For example, on Windows XP and Windows Server 2003, applications have restricted access to the file system because the operating system runs applications within a security context and protects the file system with access control lists (ACLs).

The CLR is a core component of the .NET Framework that provides the context for managed code and executes that code. In some ways the CLR is a virtual machine, but the capabilities of the CLR extend beyond a simple virtual machine model. The CLR has a built-in understanding of its context and responds appropriately depending on the environment it finds itself in. For example, the CLR behaves differently in Windows 98 and Windows Me environments than it does in Windows XP or Windows Server 2003 because of fundamental differences between those two families of operating systems (MS-DOS-based versus Windows NT–based). The CLR also has the ability to behave differently in multiprocessor environments in order to leverage the benefit of multiple CPUs.

The CLR is an implementation of a standard known as the Common Language Infrastructure (CLI) that defines a machine-independent environment in which applications are executed. The CLR Virtual Execution System provides important services such as memory management (object lifetime management and garbage collection) and security. The CLR also provides a just-in-time (JIT) compiler for converting *Intermediate Language* into native code that can be executed by the physical CPU.

Intermediate Language (IL) is a new language designed to be efficiently converted into native machine code on different types of devices. IL is based on an abstract stack-based processor architecture. It is the lingua franca of the .NET Framework. The Visual Basic compiler, vbc.exe, generates IL. The C# compiler, csc.exe, generates IL. In fact, every .NET-compliant compiler generates IL. Intermediate Language is a lower level language than Visual Basic or C#. For programmers with a background in machine assembly languages, IL is reminiscent of assembly language but at a higher level of abstraction.

One of the tools included with the .NET Framework SDK is Ildasm.exe, the IL Disassembler. Ildasm is used to display the contents of a .NET program file in a human-readable form. Figure 1-2 shows part of the output from Ildasm for a simple Windows application.

Figure 1-2   Ildasm.exe showing a simple Windows application.

Ildasm can be used to view the IL within individual functions and subroutines (also known as *methods* in object-oriented languages). Figure 1-3 shows the IL listing for the *Form1_Load* method. The following code is the original Visual Basic source:

```
Private Sub Form1_Load(ByVal sender As System.Object, _
          ByVal e As System.EventArgs) Handles MyBase.Load
    Dim I As Integer
    Dim S As String
    For I = 1 To 20
        S += I.ToString() + " "
    Next
    MsgBox(S)
End Sub
```

```
/ HelloWorld.Form1::Form1_Load : void(object,class [mscorlib]System.EventArgs)              _|@|x|
Find  Find Next
.method private instance void  Form1_Load(object sender,
                                   class [mscorlib]System.EventArgs e) cil managed      ▲
{
  // Code size       44 (0x2c)
  .maxstack  3
  .locals init ([0] int32 I,
          [1] string S)
  IL_0000:  nop
  IL_0001:  ldc.i4.1
  IL_0002:  stloc.0
  IL_0003:  ldloc.1
  IL_0004:  ldloca.s   I
  IL_0006:  call       instance string [mscorlib]System.Int32::ToString()
  IL_000b:  ldstr      " "
  IL_0010:  call       string [mscorlib]System.String::Concat(string,
                                                              string,
                                                              string)

  IL_0015:  stloc.1
  IL_0016:  nop
  IL_0017:  ldloc.0
  IL_0018:  ldc.i4.1
  IL_0019:  add.ovf
  IL_001a:  stloc.0
  IL_001b:  ldloc.0
  IL_001c:  ldc.i4.s   20
  IL_001e:  nop
  IL_001f:  ble.s      IL_0003
  IL_0021:  ldloc.1
  IL_0022:  ldc.i4.0
  IL_0023:  ldnull
  IL_0024:  call       valuetype [Microsoft.VisualBasic]Microsoft.VisualBasic.MsgBoxResult [Micro ▼
◄|                                                                                      |►
```

Figure 1-3 IL listing for a simple subroutine.

The .NET Framework SDK also includes an assembler, Ilasm. You can type Intermediate Language in your favorite text editor and then use Ilasm to assemble it. The assembled IL could then be executed on the CLR. Although it would certainly be an educational exercise for some, most professional programmers find it more expedient to program in Visual Basic, C#, or another high-level programming language and then generate IL using a .NET-compliant compiler.

> **Note** Intermediate Language is sometimes called *Microsoft Intermediate Language* (MSIL) or *Common Intermediate Language* (CIL). MSIL is normally pronounced "missile."

If you consider for a moment that all .NET-compliant languages are compiled into IL and that the CLR executes IL, you realize that all managed code is the same to the CLR regardless of the original high-level programming language used. All languages are first-class languages. Every .NET-compliant language has access to the Framework Class Library. Every .NET programmer can reuse compiled IL created with any .NET-compliant language.

This is not to say that every .NET-compliant language is equal. Some languages are more appropriate than others for solving particular problems. Figure 1-4 shows a solution with a Windows application in Visual Basic that calls a method, *GetNumberListString*, from a class library in C#. Visual Basic and C# are both compiled into IL, so neither language is inherently faster than the other. However, different compiler settings can result in different IL for high-level code that is semantically equivalent. A *for* loop in C# will run faster than the equivalent loop in Visual Basic *if you use the default compiler settings* because the Visual Basic compiler includes overflow checks by default, but the C# compiler does not (a typical safety-versus-speed tradeoff). If you are writing code with high-iteration loops, you could use C# with the compiler's overflow checking option turned on and then wrap the high-iteration loops in *unchecked* statement blocks to turn off overflow checking for specific blocks of code for a small performance gain. Visual Basic does not provide an option for turning overflow checking on and off at such a granular level, so this is one of the rare scenarios in which C# could be more appropriate for solving a specific problem. (Visual Basic has its own set of unique features, such as the *My* namespace and optional method parameters.)

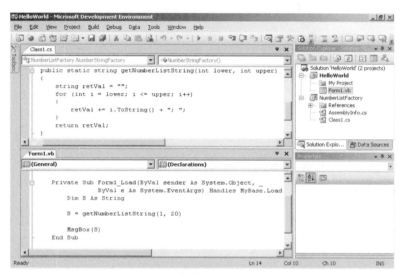

Figure 1-4 Visual Basic code calling a method written in C#.

The preceding example with a loop in C# is obviously a bit contrived. A loop body generally has to be unrealistically simplistic for the impact of integer overflow checking to be significant (unless, of course, the loop body contains mostly integer operations that would run faster without overflow checking). And unchecked integer operations are not exclusive to C#—you could factor the code out into a separate Visual Basic class library and disable overflow checking for that project only to obtain the same resultant IL. But even if this example is a bit contrived, there are many realistic scenarios in which you might use multiple .NET languages in the same solution. For example, you might have purchased third-party C# code that your Visual Basic project has to call into. Or your company might be like many development shops that have former ASP programmers building ASP.NET applications using Visual Basic while their COM programming colleagues with a C++ background build class libraries in C# for the ASP.NET applications to consume. In that case, it is matter of letting programmers use the .NET languages that are most comfortable for them given their programming backgrounds.

> **Note** Be careful when mixing multiple programming languages in your software solutions. Multiple languages can make it hard to refactor (restructure) code and can frustrate or confuse programmers who are not fluent in all the languages in use (especially junior-level coders). You should also beware of the difference between case-sensitive languages such as C# and case-insensitive languages such as Visual Basic. A public interface exposed by a C# component that differentiates between methods, properties, or fields by case only (for example, User-Name vs. username) cannot be used as intended from a Visual Basic program.

Common Type System

If you have spent much time writing Visual Basic 6 code that calls the Win32 API or functions exposed by a third-party DLL, you know that the built-in data types in Visual Basic 6 are different from the built-in data types in other languages (for example, C). If all .NET languages compile into IL that is callable from any .NET program, there has to be a common set of data types for representing integers, real numbers, dates, text, and so on in all those languages. The data types used by the .NET Framework are defined as part of the Common Type System, a set of rules for creating and using data types.

The Common Type System is fundamental in ensuring cross-language integration. A Visual Basic programmer can pass an *Int32* value or a *String* to a C# library with complete confidence because *Int32* and *String* are defined as part of the Common Type System. The Common Type System is also fundamental in ensuring type safety at runtime, which ensures that your code does not allow unauthorized memory access and is not vulnerable to certain types of security attacks.

Visual Basic has a number of primitive data types that map to predefined types in the Common Type System. For example, the Visual Basic primitive type *Integer* is an alias for *System.Int32*, a 32-bit integer. The Visual Basic primitive type *String* is an alias for *System.String*, a sequence of Unicode characters. C# and other languages have their own primitive data types that correspond to these same predefined types in the Common Type System.

> **Note** In Visual Basic 6, an *Integer* is a 16-bit value and a *Long* is a 32-bit value. In Visual Basic code targeting the .NET Framework, *Integer* is 32 bits and *Long* is 64 bits. If you use the Visual Basic 6 Upgrade Wizard to convert your code, your integer data types will be adjusted for you by the wizard.

Objects and Values

There are two kinds of data types in the Common Type System: reference types and value types. These two data types are fundamentally different in how they are created, passed around in memory, and finally destroyed. Value types hold the values you would normally think of as primitives: integers, floating point numbers, characters, and Boolean (true/false) values. Value types are generally simple to represent in memory, usually only requiring a few bytes. When value types are passed around in memory (for example, when they are passed as arguments to a method), the value itself is copied (by default).

Value types are simple and efficient. They do not require the same type of overhead required for creating objects (that is, reference types) and do not need special consideration for destruction. Values are stored directly on the stack and tied to a variable or constant (or literal). The lifetime of the value is the same as the lifetime of the variable used to access the value. A variable cannot be separated from its value, so a value type variable always has a value. Unlike reference types, value type variables cannot be null (*Nothing*).

The Common Type System defines the most useful value types (*Integer*, *Double*, *Date*, *Char*, and so forth) and allows you to define your own value types. You can also create enumerations, which are custom value types that contain symbolical aliases for a subset of the values of an integral type (normally *Integer*). Only the aliases specified in the enumeration definition are valid values for variables of the enumeration type. For example, the following code listing shows an enumeration for user types. A *UserType* variable can have only one of the three values specified (*Admin*, *Moderator*, or *User*).

```
Enum UserType As Integer
    Admin = 1
    Moderator = 2
    User = 3
End Enum
```

The .NET Framework Class Library makes extensive use of enumerations for everything from file I/O modes to colors.

Reference types are a very different kind of data type. The "value" of a reference type is the content of the memory location allocated to hold an instance of that reference type (that is, an object). The value of a reference type is always accessed via a reference to the memory location holding that value. Unlike value type variables, a reference type variable is not intrinsically tied to a fixed memory location that always has a value. A reference type variable can be a reference to any object in memory (of the appropriate data type). Or a reference type variable might not hold a reference to any object, in which case it is said to be a *null reference* or a reference to *Nothing*.

The CLR allocates space for objects (instances of reference types) in its runtime memory heap. Consider the following line of code:

```
conn = New SqlConnection(connectionString)
```

The variable *conn* is being assigned a reference to a new *SqlConnection* object. That object is created in the memory heap. The CLR allocates memory for the new object and calls a special method known as a *constructor* for the *SqlConnection* class. The CLR also takes on the responsibility of destroying that object and freeing its memory when the object is no longer in use. This is known as *garbage collection* and is one of the core services provided by the CLR.

When a reference type is passed as an argument to a method, the reference is passed by value. That means a copy is made of the reference, not the object value itself (in the memory heap). The original calling code and the method being called will both hold references to the same object in memory. If the method changes the content of that object, the change affects the calling code. Consider the following Visual Basic code:

```
Sub CreateDataSet()
    Dim ds As New DataSet
    AddTable(ds)
    '
    ' The message box displays "1" because the AddTable method
    ' has changed the DataSet object ds.
    '
    MsgBox(ds.Tables.Count.ToString())
End Sub

Sub AddTable(ByVal targetDataSet As DataSet)
    targetDataSet.Tables.Add("TableOne")
End Sub
```

The variable *ds* is a reference to a new *DataSet* object that is passed to the *AddTable* method. In the *AddTable* method, the variable *targetDataSet* is a reference to the same *DataSet* object. The *AddTable* method adds a new table to the *DataSet*. Then back in *CreateDataSet*, after calling *AddTable*, the *DataSet* object *ds* will have one table in its *Tables* collection. Both methods are working with the same *DataSet* object in memory even though there are two different variables in two different methods.

Classes, Methods, Properties, Fields, and Events

In object-oriented programming, objects are instances of classes. As a programmer, you define a class with data fields, properties, methods, and events. Then you create objects based on that class that have state (fields, properties) and behavior (methods, events). Consider the *Form* class as an example. The *Form* class defines the data and properties (for example, *Width*) for a window to be displayed in a Windows application. The *Form* class also defines behavior such as the *Show* method that displays a form. The *Form* class itself is not a form. The class defines what a *Form* object looks like and what it can do. An actual *Form* object would be a sequence of bytes at a specific memory location in the memory heap.

A class comprises four building blocks: fields, methods, properties, and events. A field is a value that a class holds. A field can hold a value directly (value type) or hold a reference to a value (reference type). A field in a class is somewhat analogous to a variable in a method. The value in a variable during a method call is part of the state of that method call, and the variable is tied to that "instance" of the method. Likewise, a field is part of the state of an object (that is, an instance of a class).

A method is a unit of functionality in a class. Subroutines (*Sub*) and functions (*Function*) in Visual Basic are methods. Methods are an important part of the behavior of an object. A method is something that an object can do. It is a block of programming logic that is executed within the context of an object, and it can access or manipulate the state of the object via its fields and properties.

A property is a hybrid between a field and a method. Like a field, a property is part of the state of an object. To other objects, a public property looks like a public field, and you use the same syntax for reading and writing property values. But internally, a property is actually two special methods: a *Get* procedure and a *Set* procedure. When you read the value of a property, the *Get* procedure is executed. When you set the value of a property the *Set* procedure is executed. Properties allow you to have logic associated with accessing values. More importantly, properties allow you to separate an object's public interface from the internal representation of its data.

Events are occurrences that objects can respond to. An event is the other kind of behavior an object can exhibit. If a method is something an object can do, an event is something an object says. Normally events are used to notify listening objects of a change in state. Listening objects are "notified" via *event handlers*. A listening object registers a method as an event handler for a specific event of a specific object. That method (the event handler) is then called automatically when the event occurs. Events occur when they are explicitly raised by an object. For example, a *Button* object raises a *Click* event when it receives a message from Windows indicating that the default mouse button was pressed while the mouse pointer was over the button. If you have programmed in Visual Basic 6, you are already familiar with event-driven programming. You'll find some differences in how event handlers work in managed code, but in many cases the code you write is very similar to the code you would write in Visual Basic 6.

When you write managed code in Visual Basic, you are always creating a class, which is the definition of a data type. The state and behavior of an object of that type is determined by your code. The following example is a class called *UserAddress*. This class contains four fields to hold the elements of a mailing address. In this example, the fields are all marked as *Private*, which means they are not accessible outside of the *UserAddress* class. Instead, the data is publicly exposed using four properties. The properties in *UserAddress* are simple wrappers around the private fields, but what is significant here is that the external (public) interface for the address is separate from the actual fields that hold the data. You could freely change the way the data is internally represented while continuing to expose the same external interface. This example also includes an event called *AddressChanged*. Each *Set* procedure in each property raises this event if the new value is different from the old value. Listening objects can register handlers for the *AddressChanged* event and execute code when the *UserAddress* state changes (that is, when some part of the address is changed). And finally, there is a *GetFormattedAddress* method that creates a new *String* object containing all the address data.

```vb
Public Class UserAddress

    Private _address As String
    Private _city As String
    Private _provState As String
    Private _postalCode As String

    Public Event AddressChanged()

    Public Property Address() As String
        Get
            Return _address
        End Get
        Set(ByVal Value As String)
            If _address <> Value Then
                _address = Value
                RaiseEvent AddressChanged()
            End If
        End Set
    End Property

    Public Property City() As String
        Get
            Return _city
        End Get
        Set(ByVal Value As String)
            If _city <> Value Then
                _city = Value
                RaiseEvent AddressChanged()
            End If
        End Set
    End Property

    Public Property StateProvince() As String
        Get
            Return _provState
        End Get
        Set(ByVal Value As String)
            If _provState <> Value Then
                _provState = Value
                RaiseEvent AddressChanged()
            End If
        End Set
    End Property

    Public Property PostalCode() As String
        Get
            Return _postalCode
        End Get
        Set(ByVal Value As String)
            If _postalCode <> Value Then
                _postalCode = Value
                RaiseEvent AddressChanged()
            End If
        End Set
```

```
End Property

Public Function GetFormattedAddress() As String
    Return _address + vbCrLf + _
           _city + ", " + _provState + vbCrLf + _
           _postalCode
End Function

End Class
```

The *UserAddress* class is a simple example of the kind of data types you can create in Visual Basic. Building applications for the .NET Framework is a process of turning requirements into classes that interact to achieve the desired functionality. Sometimes you have to code an entire class yourself, such as with the *UserAddress* class. Other times, the class is created for you automatically by a wizard or some other tool, such as when you add a new form to your application.

Anything you need to do in your application you will do with a class. Need something that represents a customer? Create a class. Need functionality to move data from a legacy system to a Microsoft SQL Server database? Create a class. If you design your classes with reuse in mind, you will end up with a set of classes you can copy into new applications. The .NET Framework itself includes a large library of classes designed to be reused in many types of applications. This collection of classes is known as the Framework Class Library and has been one of the most popular aspects of the .NET Framework since its introduction.

Note   In some object-oriented programming languages and abstract object models, the terms field, property, and attribute are used interchangeably. In the .NET Framework, properties and attributes are specific constructs that are distinct from fields.

Framework Class Library

A high-level programming language such as Visual Basic that targets an execution environment such as the CLR is a powerful concept, but it must be accompanied by an equally powerful set of libraries to be truly useful in the real world. The Framework Class Library (FCL), sometimes called the Base Class Library (BCL), is a set of DLLs that form an integral part of the .NET Framework. Each DLL contains a related set of classes for providing some specific functionality. For example, System.Drawing.dll provides classes for generating graphics; System.DirectoryServices.dll provides classes for interacting with Active Directory; and System.Xml.dll provides classes for working with XML documents. The Framework Class Library contains everything from basic file I/O to the classes that make up ASP.NET and ADO.NET.

Most developers seem to find that the biggest task in becoming a proficient .NET developer is learning the Framework Class Library. Part of that task is learning new ways to do familiar things. The larger part of the task is learning the many new capabilities in the Framework

Class Library that previously required a lot of custom code or third-party components. To ping a server, use the *Ping* and *PingReply* classes. To access a Web site programmatically, use the *WebClient* or *HttpWebRequest* classes. To validate the format of an e-mail address, use the *Regex* class. To transform an XML document, use the *XslTranform* class. To send an e-mail message programmatically, use the *SmtpMail* class.

The Framework Class Library is comprehensive enough that .NET developers will often confess that they spend an increased percentage of their time researching and finding the right classes from the Framework Class Library to accomplish general-purpose tasks (for example, converting a PNG image to a JPG image) and a decreased percentage of their time writing custom code to perform such tasks. Using the Framework Class Library for these tasks means having fewer lines of custom code to test, debug, and maintain as well as having prewritten documentation and support from other developers worldwide who are using the exact same classes to perform the same generic tasks.

This book focuses on the latest Framework Class Library features, which were introduced in version 2.0 of the .NET Framework. Many great sources are available for more in-depth information on the more established parts of the Framework Class Library, including the MSDN documentation that installs with Visual Studio 2005, information at the MSDN Web site (*http://msdn.microsoft.com/*), information that can be found by searching *http://www.google.com/*, and *101 Microsoft Visual Basic .NET Applications* (available from Microsoft Press).

Namespaces

The Framework Class Library is organized as a hierarchy of *namespaces*. Namespaces provide a way to organize classes to help avoid ambiguity, reduce naming collisions, and group related classes together. Without an organizational structure, naming collisions would be frequent and frustrating. If you were working on a page layout program, you might want to create a class to represent a block of text on a page, but if you tried to create a *TextBox* class you would collide with the *TextBox* class defined for Windows forms. If you were working on a tool for managing legal forms, you might want to create a class to represent a form, but if you tried to create a *Form* class you would collide with the existing *Form* class in the Framework Class Library. *Url*? Already used. *Semaphore*? Already used. *Ping*? *Timer*? *Thread*? All are used already in the Framework Class Library. The list would go on and on—the Framework Class Library is extensive. Fortunately, the Framework Class Library uses namespaces to prevent the frustration of naming collisions. In fact, the Framework Class Library itself repeats some class names in different namespaces. Most notable are the user interface controls—such as *TextBox*, *ListBox*, and *Button*—that appear in both the *System.Windows.Forms* and *System.Web.UI.WebControls* namespaces (although these two namespaces are not usually used together in the same application).

As mentioned previously, the Framework Class Library is extensive and mastering it is not a trivial task. Namespaces make using the Framework Class Library much easier because classes with related functionality are usually found under the same namespace. If you need to work with data, you look in the *System.Data* namespace. If you need to work with XML, you look in the *System.Xml* namespace. If you need to read or write a file, you look in the *System.IO* namespace. Familiarizing yourself with the namespaces immediately under the *System* namespace (including some of the most prominent classes) will make you a much more efficient .NET programmer because you will be able to quickly identify in which namespace to search when looking for classes that provide some specific functionality you need.

When you create an application with Visual Studio 2005, your classes are placed in a namespace with the same name as your application. You can change that default root namespace via the Visual Studio 2005 project properties window as shown in Figure 1-5. Namespaces can be nested, so you can create additional namespaces in your code that will be placed under your project's root namespace in the namespace hierarchy. As the number of classes in your application or class library grows, you will find that creating namespaces for related sets of classes is useful for keeping your classes organized. If the root namespace for your application is *ChooseYourOwnNamespace*, the following code would define a class named *Class1* in the *ChooseYourOwnNamespace.Namespace1* namespace:

```
Namespace Namespace1
    Public Class Class1

    End Class
End Namespace
```

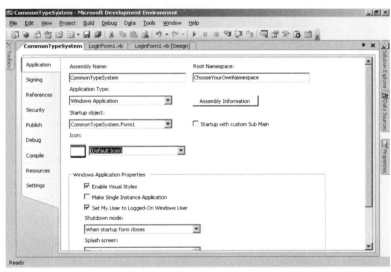

Figure 1-5   Project properties window showing the root namespace setting for the project.

Unless other information is provided for the compiler to resolve a class name, classes must be referred to using their fully qualified name. A fully qualified name is the class name preceded by its namespace. If the namespace is nested in another namespace, the full list of namespaces must be included in the fully qualified name. The fully qualified name for the class in the previous example is *ChooseYourOwnNamespace.Namespace1.Class1.* Of course, there are common namespaces you will use frequently and typing those fully qualified names over and over again would only serve to clutter your source code. As an alternative to typing fully qualified names, you can import namespaces into your entire project or into individual code files. Figure 1-6 shows namespaces imported into an entire project via the project properties window. Figure 1-7 shows several namespaces imported into a code file by using the *Imports* statement.

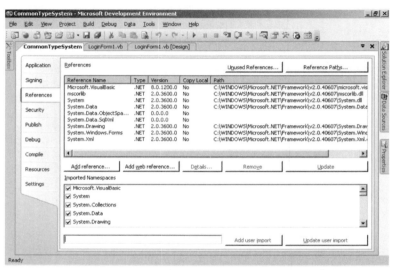

Figure 1-6   Namespaces imported for a project.

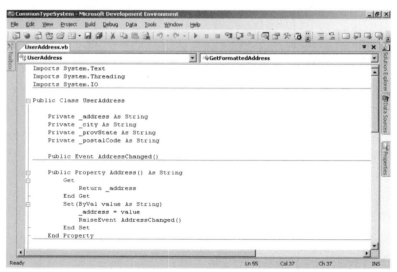

Figure 1-7   Namespaces imported for an individual code file.

Assemblies and Metadata

Applications are collections of functionality. Classes are the building blocks that contribute to the overall functionality of your applications. That functionality has to be bundled in such a way that it can be saved to storage media (for example, to hard disk or DVD), deployed to other computers, loaded by an execution environment (such as the CLR or the operating system for managed and unmanaged code, respectively), and in some cases reused by multiple applications. These "bundles" of functionality are called *assemblies* if they target the .NET Framework. In Windows-based environments there are two types of files that encapsulate functionality: executables (EXE files) and libraries (DLL files). An assembly is normally a single EXE or DLL file, although it is possible to create multifile assemblies. With Visual Studio 2005 (as well as Visual Studio .NET and Visual Studio .NET 2003), you can create both EXE and DLL assemblies.

Assemblies are the units of versioning and deployment for managed code. If an application is made up of one executable (EXE file) and one library (DLL file), you will have two assemblies, each with its own version number. You can deploy both files at the same time and then later deploy an updated DLL without deploying an updated executable.

Assemblies are made up of three things: Intermediate Language, metadata, and resources. As mentioned earlier, .NET compilers do not generate binary machine code, they generate Intermediate Language. The IL in an assembly is turned into binary machine code by the JIT compiler on a just-in-time basis—in other words, when the code is needed at runtime. The JIT compiled code is saved in memory so that it can be reused for subsequent executions of that code for the current process. JIT compilation is significantly different from interpreting code. IL is relatively easy to convert to native machine code, and it can be optimized for the hardware and resources available at runtime. The small upfront compilation cost yields optimized binary code for the current environment.

The metadata stored in the assembly file is called the *manifest*. The manifest includes the assembly version, references to other assemblies, supported cultures, type information, and other self-describing information about the assembly.

The resources in an assembly are content files embedded in the assembly itself that can be accessed at runtime. One of the most common uses of embedded resources is image files. The following code sample shows how to read an embedded JPG image from the current assembly and show it in a *PictureBox* control. In this example, the embedded resource is Image1.jpg. The root namespace of the assembly is *MyApp*.

```
Private Sub LoadResourceImage()
    Dim currentAssembly As System.Reflection.Assembly
    currentAssembly = System.Reflection.Assembly.GetExecutingAssembly()
    Dim img As System.IO.Stream
    img = currentAssembly.GetManifestResourceStream("MyApp.Image1.jpg")
    PictureBox1.Image = Image.FromStream(img)
    img.Close()
End Sub
```

Although all managed code gets packaged into assemblies, you get different types of applications depending on the type of the assembly (EXE or DLL) and how that assembly is loaded. Windows applications are EXE files that are loaded by the Windows shell. Web applications are DLL files that contain specific types of classes that are loaded by IIS (Internet Information Services). Later in this chapter, Windows and Web applications are discussed in more detail, including differences between versions of Visual Basic, COM, and ASP, and important new features introduced in the .NET Framework 2.0.

Data Access: ADO.NET

Data access is an essential aspect of many applications. When you first learned to program, you probably read or heard someone say that a program is useless (or least not very interesting) without input and output. One source of input for an application is a data source such as a SQL Server database, a Microsoft Access data file, or an XML document. Visual Basic programmers have seen several data access technologies over the years, including DAO, RDO, and ADO. If you have programmed in Visual Basic 6, you have probably used ADO to read and write data from an OLEDB data source such as a SQL Server database. ADO was designed to work with relational data in a connected environment. Although support was tacked on to ADO for disconnected recordsets, it was limited. The ADO.NET data access API was introduced as an integral part of the Framework Class Library to provide better support for disconnected scenarios as well as first-class support for XML.

Disconnected data is a central concept in ADO.NET. Instead of there being a *Recordset*, a number of classes in the *System.Data* namespace provide more options for working with data than a *Recordset* provides. The central class in ADO.NET is *DataSet*. A *DataSet* object contains a collection of *DataTable* objects (and can contain *DataRelation* objects to define relationships between *DataTable* objects). A *DataTable* contains a collection of *DataColumn* objects that define the structure of the *DataTable*. A *DataTable* also contains a collection of *DataRow* objects that hold the data for the *DataTable*. A *DataSet* and its contained objects are generic and completely disconnected from an underlying data source.

There are several ways to populate a *DataSet*, including the option of creating a *DataTable* and its *Columns* collection programmatically and then writing the code to add *DataRow* objects to the *Rows* collection. A more common approach in Visual Studio .NET 2003 is to use another object called a *data adapter* to create the *DataTable* objects based on the structure of the data returned from the data source. This is where ADO.NET starts to get specific about data sources. A data adapter is part of what is known as a managed provider, which is a set of classes for a specific type of data source. The *SqlClient* managed provider is for accessing SQL Server. The *OleDb* managed provider is for accessing any OLEDB data source. There are other managed providers available for other types of data sources (for example, ODBC and Oracle). A managed provider defines classes for a connection, a command, a parameter, database types, a data adapter, and several other useful classes. The following code shows how to populate a *DataSet* from a SQL Server database:

```
Dim conn As New SqlConnection
conn.ConnectionString = _
    "server=(local);database=Northwind;Trusted_Connection=True"

Dim adapter As SqlDataAdapter
adapter = New SqlDataAdapter("SELECT * FROM Products", conn)

Dim dsProducts As New DataSet

conn.Open()
adapter.Fill(dsProducts)

conn.Close()
```

To submit changes made in a *DataSet* back to the data source, you can use the *Update* method of a data adapter. To do updates, the data adapter must have command objects (such as *Sql-Command*, *OleDbCommand*, and so on) available for inserting, updating, and deleting data. You can create the command objects yourself, you can use a command builder object to auto-generate the command objects at runtime, or you can use a tool such as the Data Adapter Configuration Wizard in Visual Studio .NET 2003 to auto-generate the code to create the command objects.

Note   The Data Adapter Configuration Wizard is still available in Visual Studio 2005; how-ever, you should use it to edit only data adapters already present in code brought forward from Visual Studio .NET 2003. There are new tools and features for data access, which are discussed in Chapter 4, "Building Datacentric Applications."

After a *DataSet* object has been populated, it can be passed around to different parts of your application—even to distributed components—because the *DataSet* class is designed to be dis-connected and ignorant of any data source. The flexibility and disconnected nature of the *DataSet* makes it much easier to build distributed applications that pass data around and to support important smart client scenarios such as offline use.

Visual Studio 2005 and .NET Framework 2.0 introduce some new options for data access tasks such as populating a *DataSet*. In most cases, you will not use a data adapter when writ-ing data access code in Visual Studio 2005. Instead, you will use data sources and populate a *DataSet* object by using table adapters. These new features and the new tools that support them, such as the Data Source Configuration Wizard, are discussed in detail in Chapter 4.

Windows Applications

Windows application development has been a hallmark of Visual Basic since its introduction. Although much has changed about how a Windows application developed with Visual Basic compiles and executes, most of your development skills from Visual Basic 6 will transfer to Windows development with Visual Studio 2005.

Similarities and Differences Between Visual Basic 6 and Visual Basic 2005

If you have built applications with Visual Basic 6 (or earlier), you are well acquainted with the visual design and event-driven features that have made Visual Basic so popular. Visual Studio 2005 carries on the tradition of an easy-to-use visual design experience coupled with an event-driven model.

The Visual Studio 2005 designer for Windows applications maintains enough of the look and feel of the visual designer from Visual Basic 6 that moving forward is quite easy. Figure 1-8 shows an example of a form in design view in Visual Studio 2005. You can position controls visually, add new controls from the toolbox, edit properties in the Properties window, and double-click a control to write an event handler.

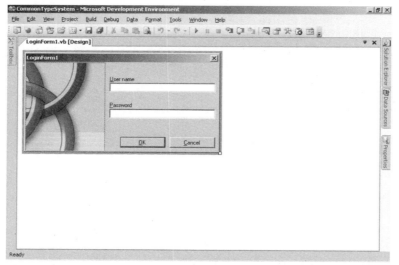

Figure 1-8   Visual Studio 2005 visual Windows Forms designer.

Although the designer is very similar at first glance, many enhancements make Windows Forms development easier while giving you more power and flexibility. One of the most significant changes from Visual Basic 6 is that all controls and other UI components are actually classes in the Framework Class Library. When you drag a *TextBox* onto a form, Visual Studio 2005 auto-generates a field to hold a reference to a *TextBox* object and writes the code for instantiating a *TextBox* object when the form is initialized. The visual designer also writes the code for setting the properties of the control. If you change the *BackColor* property of the *TextBox* in the Properties window, Visual Studio 2005 generates a line of Visual Basic code that sets the *BackColor*. Figure 1-9 shows some of the auto-generated code for the login form shown in Figure 1-8.

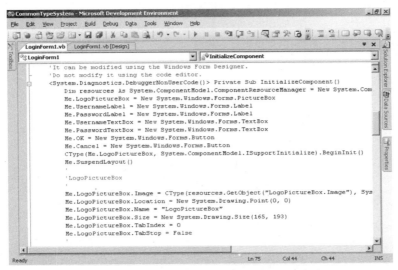

Figure 1-9 Code generated by the Visual Studio 2005 designer.

Another important change from Visual Basic 6 is that every form and every control is an instance of a class. When you create a new form with the visual designer, you are defining a new class. But you are not left to implement all the features required for a form yourself. There is an existing class, *Form*, in the *System.Windows.Forms* namespace, that provides the base functionality of a form with properties such as *Size* and *BackColor*. When you create a new form, you inherit the functionality from the base *Form* class. The first two lines of LoginForm1.vb (from Figure 1-9) are an example of how you create a class that inherits the functionality of another class:

```
Public Class LoginForm1
    Inherits System.Windows.Forms.Form
```

When you place a button on a form called *btnOK*, you are actually creating a field for your specialized form class that will hold a reference to a *Button* object at runtime. The visual designer also generates code that manipulates the state of that *Button* control to properly position it on the form, set its caption (that is, its *Text* property), and so on. When you double-click the *Button* control in the visual designer to write some code, the designer creates an event handler that is registered with the *Click* event of *btnOK*. You can also add your own events and properties to the form class. In fact, anything you can do with a class you can do with a form because a form is a class.

All the details for forms are contained within .vb code files. Visual Studio 2005 provides an excellent design environment for creating and editing these .vb files visually. You can also code .vb files by hand, even in a bare-bones text editor such as Notepad.

There is an important difference in how you open a form in Visual Basic .NET. In Visual Basic 6, you create a .frm file such as Form1.frm. The name of the form is *Form1*, and you open this form by typing *Form1.Show*. In Visual Studio 2005, the filename is irrelevant. What is important is the name of the class defined in the .vb code file. Suppose the class name is *Form1*. If you want to open *Form1*, you have to create an instance of that class and call the *Show* method of that instance, as in the following code block:

```
Dim f As New Form1
f.Show()
```

The .NET Framework changed the Windows development landscape dramatically. Version 2.0 of the .NET Framework introduces new features to make you more productive and give you access to a richer set of functionality when building your Windows applications.

Important New Features in Visual Basic 2005

There are a number of new features in Visual Basic 2005, such as options for setting padding within a control (specifically, in the internal margin of a control) and margins around a control. These properties are inherited from the base *Control* class, so they are available for every type of control. There are new controls and settings for creating user interfaces with the professional look and customization support of products such as Microsoft Office. There are also new panel controls that support flow and table layouts. These and other enhancements are discussed in more detail in later chapters, including Chapter 5, "Constructing User Interfaces."

An extremely useful and popular new RAD feature is *snap lines*, a feature of the visual form designer in the IDE (rather than a language or Framework Class Library feature). If you have spent much time building user interfaces in Visual Basic 6 or Visual Studio .NET 2003, you know how difficult it can be to properly align controls without resorting to editing property values by hand. The visual designer in Visual Studio 2005 includes new visual alignment guides (snap lines) that help you line up controls both horizontally and vertically when placing them on a form. Figure 1-10 shows an example of the alignment guides helping a developer line up an OK button with some other controls vertically *and* another button horizontally.

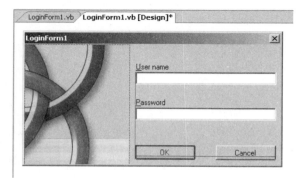

Figure 1-10   Control alignment guides in Visual Studio 2005.

Web Applications

Before the release of Visual Studio .NET, building Web applications with Visual Basic required multiple tools and multiple development languages. Visual Studio .NET introduced a unified development environment and a new Web programming model that allowed Visual Basic programmers to transfer their Windows development skills to Web development. Visual Studio 2005 introduces a number of significant enhancements to Web development using .NET technology.

Similarities and Differences Between ASP, ASP.NET 1.0, and ASP.NET 2.0

If this is your first exposure to ASP.NET, welcome to the new world of Web development! ASP.NET is an integral part of the Framework Class Library. ASP.NET provides an object-oriented, event-driven infrastructure for your applications that enables them to be hosted by a Web server so that they can respond to Web requests (that is, serve content to Web browsers). ASP.NET 2.0 is an especially exciting release because of the opportunities for incredible productivity boosts and dramatically reduced lines of code.

ASP.NET 1.0 replaced ASP/COM development, which was cumbersome at best. Classic ASP, as it has come to be known, is difficult to debug and maintain. Everything is interpreted script, so performance is lackluster unless you move intensive processing into COM components. If you do use COM components, you have to use multiple development environments and write in multiple programming languages—usually VBScript and either Visual Basic 6 or C++ for the COM components. Using COM components, of course, requires components to be registered on the Web server, adding a layer of complexity to deployment. And in shared hosting and virtual host environments, you are often not allowed to register COM components at all, leaving many developers with scripting as their only option. And VBScript, as you might know, does not allow for strong typing, which means even simple syntax errors have to be discovered and diagnosed at runtime as the script is interpreted rather being discovered during compilation.

In contrast to ASP, ASP.NET Web applications are compiled to IL, which is then JIT-compiled into native binary code. As with Windows applications, the JIT compilation happens up front and the native code is cached for subsequent reuse. There is a small latency associated for the first Web request as the code is JIT compiled. After the first request, ASP.NET Web applications show an impressive performance benefit over script-based Web technologies. That feature alone is compelling enough to move to ASP.NET. But there are also many other benefits.

ASP.NET provides an object-oriented, event-driven framework for Web applications. Web pages are classes that inherit basic functionality from a base *Page* class in the same way that a Windows form inherits functionality from the base *Form* class. When you request a Web page, an instance of the class is loaded in memory, a series of methods are called, and a series of events are raised. You write event handlers for events such as *Page.Load* and *Page.PreRender* to inject your own custom logic into the page processing. When the processing is finished, the resulting HTML output is sent to the user.

The processing model of ASP.NET is fundamentally different from ASP. In classic ASP, HTML and script are intermingled and processed sequentially (from top to bottom). Dynamic content is injected using *Response.Write* statements or render blocks (for example, *<%= Now %>* displays the current date and time). The resulting HTML and script combination can be difficult to read and hard to debug. By contrast, ASP.NET uses objects, methods, and events to generate output. The result is a better separation of code from content and a richer programming model.

An ASP.NET Web page, or ASPX page, comprises page directives, HTML content, server control tags, and code. Page directives are special ASP.NET instructions for controlling things such as output caching, turning on *Option Strict*, referencing components, and importing namespaces. Server controls are special markup elements (that is, tags) that map to classes in the Framework Class Library. When an ASPX page is compiled into a class, server controls become fields of that class. Instances of the appropriate control classes are created at runtime, and references to those objects are assigned to the class fields for the various server controls on the page. The object referenced by each field is then asked to produce its HTML output via its *Render* method. The resulting HTML output from an ASPX page is the HTML output from the page itself plus the HTML output generated by each server control.

> **Note** Output can also be generated in ASP.NET by using *Response.Write*, but the event-driven processing model makes it difficult to use *Response.Write* unless all content is generated with *Response.Write* (ASP style), which would negate the benefit of the object-oriented, event-driven model.

The following ASPX markup shows a simple Web page that includes a *TextBox* server control.

```
<%@ page language="VB" %>

<html>
<body>
    <form id="form1" runat="server">
        <asp:TextBox ID="txtName" Runat="server" />
    </form>
</body>
</html>
```

When this Web page is rendered, the *TextBox* control renders itself as an HTML *<input>* tag as shown here:

```
<html>
<body>
    <form method="post" action="Default.aspx" id="form1">
<div style="display:none">
<input type="hidden" name="__VIEWSTATE"
value="/wEPDwULLTIwNDAwODk2OTNkZLcvFD+nrIIdGTNg9IaMLK9y8exu" />
</div>
        <input name="txtName" type="text" id="txtName" />
    </form>
</body>
</html>
```

One of the great benefits of server controls is that complex behavior can be encapsulated in a server control and then used on a Web page with a single tag. Controls such as *Calendar*, *Grid-View*, and *SiteMapPath* are all examples of complex server controls that can generate considerable amounts of HTML output but only require a line or two of ASPX markup to use. This concept is of course very familiar to Visual Basic 6 programmers who are used to working with controls that encapsulate complex functionality. For this and other reasons, many Visual Basic 6 programmers have discovered that the level of skill transfer between Windows development and Web development with the .NET Framework is remarkably high.

The ASP.NET programming and processing models are similar to the Windows Forms programming and processing models, making it easier than ever for Windows programmers to also be Web programmers. For example, the *Page.Load* event is analogous to the *Form.Load* event in Windows programming. There are, of course, some additional considerations when working with Web pages, but they are not difficult to master. (For example, form-level field values do not survive after a request.) In fact, a Web programmer using Visual Studio 2005 can be quite productive using the same skills used for Windows programming while knowing very little HTML (or even no HTML).

Important New Features of ASP.NET 2.0

The .NET Framework 2.0 introduces a considerable number of new features for Web applications. There are new Membership and User Profile subsystems that provide significantly enhanced support for managing and authenticating users, doing role-based authorization, and storing user information (for example, address information). There are also new security controls such as the *Login* and *LoginView* controls that tie into the new Membership system. With ASP.NET 2.0, you can actually create a Web site with built-in authentication, including a users database, without writing any code! Just add a few lines of markup and that's it!

New data source controls let you declaratively specify data source settings instead of having to write common data access code. There are also a number of new data controls and enhancements to existing data controls—most notable is the ability to bind a data control to a data source control to create rich, data-driven, zero code Web sites.

All Web server controls are now device-aware. The .NET Framework 1.1 had separate mobile controls specifically for limited devices such as phone-based browsers. As a Web developer, you no longer have to use different controls to support different types of devices. You might, however, have to give some consideration to the types of devices you are going to support when you design your interfaces.

There are still more new features in ASP.NET 2.0. You will see more about these enhancements later in this book, particularly in Chapter 6, "Building Web Applications."

Enhancements in Visual Studio 2005 and the .NET Framework 2.0

There are many good reasons for writing code that targets the .NET Framework, including those mentioned at the beginning of this chapter such as productivity, security, and "deploy-ability." Developers have found that they can write better code faster when they target the .NET Framework and develop with Visual Studio. Visual Studio 2005 is the next step in the evolution of Visual Studio. Visual Studio 2005 and the .NET Framework 2.0 contain many interesting and exciting enhancements that are detailed in the rest of this book. The following sections provide some examples.

Visual Basic Enhancements

There are a number of changes in Visual Basic, including the much-anticipated introduction of *Generics*, the new *Using* statement, the new *IsNot* keyword, and operator overloading. Edit-and-continue debugging is now supported for Visual Basic .NET projects, a feature missed by many former Visual Basic 6 programmers.

The Visual Basic code editor includes additional features, such as symbolic rename, which intelligently renames all occurrences of an identifier (for example, a variable). Also new in Visual Studio 2005 are code snippets, which are blocks of code for common tasks that you can insert into the code editor from the context menu. Visual Studio 2005 includes a number of predefined snippets for common tasks, and you can define your own snippets.

A new feature unique to Visual Basic 2005 is the *My* namespace, which acts as a wrapper or "speed dial" for common tasks. One of those common tasks is showing a default instance of a form. Instead of explicitly creating a new *Form1* variable and instantiating it, you can just call *My.Forms.Form1.Show*. The *My.Forms* collection exposes a default instance of each form class in your project. You can even leave off the *My.Forms* prefix and simply call *Form1.Show*, giving you the same syntax as Visual Basic 6, although with a very different underlying implementation.

IDE Enhancements

Each successive version of Visual Studio introduces new IDE features to help make you more productive. Just a few of the new IDE features in Visual Studio 2005 are the Exception Helper, new debugger data visualizations for HTML and XML, window docking guides, and syntax error assistance.

The Exception Helper is a new feature that gives you better access to exception details when debugging and provides troubleshooting tips to help you correct your code to avoid fatal exceptions.

There are new visualizations for viewing HTML and XML data in string variables at runtime. In debug mode, when you hover over a string variable you can choose to view the string as XML or HTML. When you select one of these views, the data is rendered appropriately in a pop-up window.

If you have ever been frustrated trying to reposition windows within the Visual Studio IDE, you will love the new docking guides that make it easy to dock a window exactly where you want it.

The Visual Studio IDE has long provided design-time syntax checking for your code. Visual Studio 2005 enhances that design-time experience with new syntax error assistance that not only identifies the syntax error but provides suggestions for correcting the error based on what your code appears to be intended to do.

These new IDE features and more are covered in Chapter 3, "Visual Studio 2005 Integrated Development Environment."

New Visual Web Developer

Visual Studio 2005 includes a completely revamped Web development tool called the Visual Web Developer. Although some of the improvements over Visual Studio .NET 2003 will not be immediately evident, many become quickly apparent. One of the noticeable changes is that the designer does not reformat your markup on you when you switch between design and markup views of your Web pages.

The new Visual Web Developer in Visual Studio 2005 includes a new lightweight Web server that listens for requests on an arbitrary port (for localhost only) when you run your Web applications. Figure 1-11 shows an example of a Web page being served by the built-in Web server. The Visual Web Developer Web Server is meant for development purposes only. It allows developers to create and test ASP.NET Web applications without requiring IIS (Internet Information Services). It also makes it easier for Web developers to work without elevated permissions (for example, running as Domain User instead of local Administrator) because rights are not needed for administering IIS or debugging other users' processes.

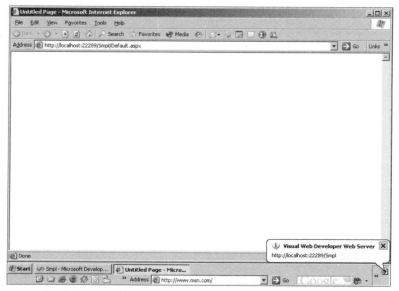

Figure 1-11 Visual Web Developer Web Server running on port 22289.

ClickOnce Deployment

The difficulties associated with deploying Windows applications in the past have driven many organizations toward Web applications for the sake of simplified deployment. This leaves computing resources on the edge of the network underutilized and constrains applications to a very limited user interface. Although the .NET Framework 1.1 solves some of the problems of deployment, such as DLL versioning conflicts, and makes possible a Web-based deployment strategy known as "No-Touch" deployment, there is room for improvement. The new ClickOnce deployment features in the .NET Framework 2.0 make it easy to deploy self-updating Windows or console applications that do not require administrative rights to install and can run in an offline mode.

For more details on how ClickOnce deployment works, see Chapter 8, "Deploying Applications."

Conclusion

The Microsoft .NET Framework provides a managed environment for running many types of applications. The .NET Framework is a platform for Windows, Web, console, and smart device applications. Services provided by the .NET Framework include object lifetime management (also known as garbage collection), security, type safety, and interoperability with COM. The .NET Framework also provides a rich class library that you can use to reduce the amount of code you have to write (and therefore test and maintain). This results in better productivity and safer code because the class library has already been field-tested on computers around the world.

The .NET Framework has brought about a radical shift in the way developers build software. The services provided by the Common Language Runtime and the functionality provided in the Framework Class Library take care of a lot of the plumbing and utility type of programming that can be so time-consuming. By targeting the .NET Framework, developers are able to spend more time solving their domain-specific problems instead of solving generic problems such as how to pass messages between a client application and a server (Web services).

The rest of this book introduces Visual Studio 2005, the latest version of the premiere development tool for targeting the .NET Framework. You will see many of the improvements made to the .NET Framework in version 2.0 and the new features in Visual Studio 2005 that will help make you a more productive developer.

Chapter 2

Language Enhancements for Visual Basic 2005

Visual Basic 2005 introduces a number of enhancements designed to make your coding simpler and more efficient. In this chapter, you're introduced to four of those enhancements. *Generics* provide a means for you to design classes that can handle objects of different kinds efficiently and in a type-safe way. *The My Object* offers convenient shortcuts for accessing Base Class Library classes that refer to the currently running application, the local machine, the application's collection of forms, the logged-on user, and Web services associated with the application. By overloading operators such as = (equal to) and > (greater than), you can now define what happens when two instances of your class are compared. And finally, you'll review some new keywords.

Application: Generics

This application illustrates the new Microsoft Visual Basic 2005 support for generics.

New Concepts

Before getting into the implementation of generics, it's worth spending a minute to analyze why this feature has been added to Visual Basic 2005. Generics come from the need to deal with potentially any type of object in a "generic" way. For example, you might want to create a class that can accept only *Employee* objects or *Customer* objects, and can process each one differently by distinguishing between them.

Even without generics, Visual Basic has always provided some mechanisms for dealing with objects, regardless of their type. For example, with Visual Basic 6.0, you can store objects of any type in a *Collection* object. This technique has some disadvantages, which are described in the next section. Generics provide an efficient alternative to *Collections*, enforcing type safety, providing better performance, and integrating tightly with the Microsoft IntelliSense technology.

Visual Basic 6.0 Collections

Visual Basic 6.0 really lets you store just about anything in a *Collection*. However, the *Collection* class has a number of limitations. For example, let's say that you want to store the following *Employee* class in a *Collection*:

```
' Visual Basic 6.0
Public SSN As String
Public FirstName As String
Public LastName As String
Public Salary As Currency
```

Storing this in the collection is relatively straightforward:

```
Dim employees As New Collection

Dim emp As Employee
Set emp = New Employee
emp.SSN = "111-11-1111"
emp.FirstName = "Scott"
emp.LastName = "Swigart"
emp.Salary = 50000

employees.Add emp, emp.SSN
```

This code first creates an instance of a *Collection* named *employees*. An *Employee* object is then created and populated with data. Finally, this *Employee* object is added to the *Collection*. The following code shows how the *Employee* object could then be retrieved from the *Collection*:

```
Dim emp2 As Employee
Set emp2 = employees("111-11-1111")
```

Now let's examine the limitations of the Visual Basic 6.0 *Collection*. First, it's likely that you want to store only *Employee* objects in the *employees* collection. However, there is nothing to prevent anyone from storing any other type of object in the *Employees* collection. In addition, when you attempt to retrieve an item from the *Employees* collection, there's nothing to let you know what type you're retrieving. For example, the following code will compile just fine:

```
Dim s As String
s = employees("111-11-1111")
```

Although it's obvious to the developer that this can't work, there's no way the compiler can catch this. This will show up as the worst kind of error, a run-time error. *Collections* also limit the ability of IntelliSense. Consider the following code:

```
employees("111-11-1111").LastName = "SomeoneElse"
```

This code shows that you can directly edit an item while it is in a *Collection*. However, you won't have any IntelliSense support when selecting the *LastName* property. Again, from the perspective of Visual Basic, that *Collection* could be storing anything. With Visual Basic 6.0, there's no way to say "Create a collection *of employees.*"

Two final limitations of the collection class are performance and flexibility. Even though it's easy to use, a collection class performs poorly when used as a dynamic array. A collection class is also designed to work like a dictionary, so if you need something more like a Stack or Queue, it's not a good fit.

Framework Collections

The .NET Framework versions 1.0 and 1.1 solved some of the problems with collections by simply offering more types of collections. By importing the *System.Collections* namespace, your code gained access to such collections as the *ArrayList*, *BitArray*, *HashTable*, *Queue*, *SortedList*, and *Stack*. The usage scenario for these types of collections is shown in Table 2-1.

Table 2-1 Collection Classes

Collection Name	Use
ArrayList	The *ArrayList* makes it easy to create arrays that grow dynamically.
BitArray	The *BitArray* class is optimized to store an array of Boolean (true/false) values.
HashTable	The *HashTable* is most like the Visual Basic 6 *Collection* class. This class allows you to look up values by using a key. However, the key and the value can be any type.
SortedList	A *SortedList* is similar to a *HashTable*, except that the keys are always sorted. This means that if you use For...Each to iterate through the collection, you will always retrieve the items in a sorted order.
Queue	A *Queue* is a collection that supports a "first in, first out" model.
Stack	A *Stack* is just the opposite of a *Queue*, providing "first in, last out" functionality.

The .NET Framework 1.0/1.1 did much to solve the flexibility limitations of Visual Basic 6.0; however, these collections are still loosely typed. This means that you can store anything in an *ArrayList*, even if, for a given application, it makes sense to store only a specific type.

What you really want is a collection where you can specify that every key must be a *string* and every value must be an *Employee*. With the .NET Framework 1.0/1.1, you would have been required to create your own class that wrapped the *Hashtable* and provided this functionality. With the .NET Framework 1.2, this problem is solved with far less code, using generics.

Walkthrough

As the "generics" application shows, generics provide strict type checking, better IntelliSense functionality, and better performance. In other words, they address pretty much all the issues encountered with collection classes of the past.

Consuming Generic Types

First, it's worth mentioning that the .NET Framework 1.2 provides generic collections *in addition* to the existing .NET Framework 1.0/1.1 collection classes. The .NET Framework 1.2 in no way forces you to use generics.

If you do want to use the new generic types, you begin by importing the *System.Collections.Generic* namespace. This grants access to *Dictionary*, *List*, *Queue*, *SortedDictionary*, and *Stack* classes. An example of using the generic *Dictionary* is shown in the *btnConsumeGenerics_Click* event:

```
Private Sub btnConsumeGenerics_Click(ByVal sender As System.Object, ByVal e As
System.EventArgs) Handles btnConsumeGenerics.Click
    Dim employees As New Dictionary(Of String, Employee)
    Dim emp As Employee
    emp = New Employee
    emp.SSN = "111-11-1111"
    emp.FirstName = "Scott"
    emp.LastName = "Swigart"
    emp.Salary = 50000

    employees.Add(emp.SSN, emp)

    txtOutput.Text = "Consuming generics" & vbCrLf & vbCrLf

    Dim emp2 As Employee
    emp2 = employees.Item("111-11-1111")

    Dim s As String
    's = employees.Item("111-11-1111")   ' This is now a syntax error

    employees.Item("111-11-1111").LastName = "SomeoneElse"
    txtOutput.Text &= "Employee last name:" & vbCrLf & _
        employees.Item("111-11-1111").LastName
End Sub
```

If you walk through the code, you will notice a few interesting facts about generics. First, the generic type is instantiated as follows:

```
Dim employees As New Dictionary(Of String, Employee)
```

This code translates to "Create a *Dictionary* where the keys will be *strings* and the values will be *Employees*." Note the use of the new *Of* keyword to specify the desired data type for the keys. Any attempt to store a value other than an *Employee* object will result in a compile-time error. That's worth repeating. With generics, if you use the wrong type, it's a compile-time error, not a run-time error. In fact, the following line must be commented out or the application will not run, as the compiler knows that the *Dictionary* holds *Employee* classes, not *strings*:

```
's = employees.Item("111-11-1111")   ' This is now a syntax error
```

In addition, you now have full IntelliSense for the types in your collection. If you examine Figure 2-1, you can see that Microsoft Visual Studio knows that this *Dictionary* holds only *Employee* classes, and the properties of the *Employee* class are available through IntelliSense.

Figure 2-1   IntelliSense for items in a generic collection.

As you can see, generics are simple to use, they result in strongly typed code (which reduces the possibility for run-time errors), and they allow IntelliSense to be more functional. Those would be reasons enough to use generics, but generics have a number of additional advantages as well, including performance and code reuse.

One of the main reasons for including generics in the .NET Framework is performance. Simply put, they're faster than the previous collection classes because the compiler optimizes them specifically for the types they store. An example can be seen in the following code, which compares the performance of an *array*, *ArrayList*, and generic *List*:

```
txtOutput.Text = "Performance" & vbCrLf & vbCrLf

Const iterations As Integer = 5000000
PerfTime.Start()
Dim myArray(iterations) As Integer
For i As Integer = 0 To iterations - 1
    myArray(i) = i
Next
Dim elapsed As Integer = PerfTime.Stop
txtOutput.Text &= "Array time: " & elapsed & vbCrLf
myArray = Nothing
GC.Collect()

PerfTime.Start()
Dim myArrayList As New ArrayList
For i As Integer = 0 To iterations - 1
    myArrayList.Add(i)
Next
elapsed = PerfTime.Stop
txtOutput.Text &= "ArrayList time: " & elapsed & vbCrLf
```

```
myArrayList = Nothing
GC.Collect()

PerfTime.Start()
Dim myList As New List(Of Integer)
For i As Integer = 0 To iterations - 1
    myList.Add(i)
Next
elapsed = PerfTime.Stop
txtOutput.Text &= "List time: " & elapsed & vbCrLf
myList = Nothing
GC.Collect()
```

This code stores 5 million values into a fixed-size *array*. The values are also stored in an *Array-List*, which grows automatically, and a generic *List*, which also grows as needed. The performance numbers (on the computer where this code was developed) tell an interesting story:

```
Array time: 344
ArrayList time: 4656
List time: 797
```

Nothing is faster than an array that stores a specific type and never needs to resize. (Your numbers will vary from those shown.) However, for a collection class that grows dynamically, its performance compared to the static array is pretty good. And look at the *ArrayList*. Not good. It's less than one-tenth the speed of the static array. The problem is that the *ArrayList* is designed to store objects. *Integers* are not objects; they're value types. Before they can be stored into the *ArrayList*, they have to go through a process called "boxing," which converts the *integer* to an *object*. Boxing is expensive, and if you are storing value types (*integer, DateTime, boolean*, your own structures, and so on), you will notice a significant performance improvement using generic collections rather than the *Object*-based collections.

Note   For more information about boxing and unboxing, see "Boxing Conversions" and "Unboxing Conversions" in the MSDN library.

Creating Generic Types and Methods

You are not limited to simply consuming generic types with Visual Basic 2005. You have the ability to also create your own generic types and methods.

Generic Methods   You might want to create a generic method if there is some common algorithm you want to perform that is independent of any type. For example, a typical bubble sort walks through all the items in an array, comparing one item with the next and swapping the values as needed to sort the array.

If you know in advance that you're going to be sorting only integers, you could simply hard-code the *Swap* method for *integer* types. However, if you wanted to be able to sort any type, you could code a generic *Swap* as follows:

```
Private Sub Swap(Of ItemType) _
    (ByRef v1 As ItemType, ByRef v2 As ItemType)

    Dim temp As ItemType
    temp = v1
    v1 = v2
    v2 = temp
End Sub
```

Notice the "*Of ItemType*". When the *Swap* method is called, in addition to the standard arguments, a data type must also be passed. This data type will be substituted for every instance of *ItemType*. The following is an example of a call to *Swap*:

```
Swap(Of Integer)(v1, v2)
```

This code tells the *Swap* method that it will be swapping *integer* types, causing every instance of *ItemType* in the original listing of *Swap* to be replaced with *integer* by the JIT compiler. The *Swap* method is essentially rewritten by the JIT to the following:

```
Private Sub Swap(ByRef v1 As Integer, ByRef v2 As Integer)
    Dim temp As Integer
    temp = v1
    v1 = v2
    v2 = temp
End Sub
```

This is the code that's actually executed. The JIT generates a version of the method to handle *integer* types. However, if you later wanted to sort *string* types, you could have another call to *Swap* as follows:

```
Swap(Of String)(v1, v2)
```

When this method executes, the JIT will write another version of *Swap*, this one specialized for *string* types:

```
Private Sub Swap(ByRef v1 As String, ByRef v2 As String)
    Dim temp As String
    temp = v1
    v1 = v2
    v2 = temp
End Sub
```

A full example of a bubble sort that uses *Swap* is as follows:

```
Private Sub btnSortIntegers_Click(ByVal sender As System.Object, ByVal e As System.EventArgs)
Handles btnSortIntegers.Click
    Dim ints(9) As Integer
    Dim r As New Random
    For i As Integer = 0 To 9
        ints(i) = r.Next(1, 100)
    Next
```

```
' Bubble sort
For j As Integer = 0 To 9
    For k As Integer = 9 To 1 Step -1
        If ints(k) < ints(k - 1) Then
            Swap(Of Integer)(ints(k), ints(k - 1))        End If
    Next
Next

txtOutput.Text = "Sort Integers" & vbCrLf & vbCrLf
For i As Integer = 0 To 9
    txtOutput.Text &= ints(i) & vbCrLf
Next
End Sub
```

Generic Types   As a final point, you can create entire generic classes. In this case, *Of ItemType* is used with the class declaration as follows:

```
Public Class SomeClass(Of ItemType)

    Private internalVar as ItemType
    Public Function SomeMethod(ByVal value As ItemType) As ItemType
    End Function

End Class
```

The same rules apply to classes as methods. The JIT compiler will simply replace every instance of *ItemType* with a specific type when the class is instantiated.

Constraints

Generics also support a feature known as constraints. This feature lets you ensure that when you specify types, they implement certain minimum functionality. For example, if you are implementing a generic sort algorithm, you might want to ensure that the type that you're sorting implements *IComparible*. You can accomplish this with a constraint:

```
Public Class SomeClass(Of ItemType As IComparible)

    Public Function SomeMethod(ByVal value As ItemType) As ItemType
    End Function

End Class
```

Conclusion

Generics offer a number of advantages over *Object*-based collection classes. First, generic classes are strongly typed, which allows many errors to be caught at compile time rather than at run time. The strong typing also lets IntelliSense provide more information. Generics also allow you to reuse your code, creating generic algorithms that work with a variety of types. Finally, generic collections are just faster than *Object*-based collections, especially when dealing with value types.

Application: The My Object

Visual Basic 2005 introduces a speedy way to access many important classes relating to the computer on which your application is running, the user who is running it, the application itself, its forms, and any associated Web services. They are all accessible by using the new My Object.

New Concepts

When building applications with Visual Basic 6, you have access to the Visual Basic Run time, a wide variety of COM objects, and a Win32 API for whichever version of the Microsoft Windows operating system you're running on. The first versions of the .NET Framework unified much of this functionality into a single mammoth set of classes known as the Base Class Library. Within the Base Class Library, there are classes to support accessing information about the underlying operating system. There are classes that allow you to easily access information about the hardware on the machine. There are also classes that allow you to easily communicate across the network between different applications, encrypt data, provide access to the registry, and more.

Understanding the Base Class Library, and the wealth of functionality it offers, is important if you want to become a competent .NET developer. A lack of knowledge about the Base Class Library can cause developers to reinvent the wheel and construct classes that already exist. In some cases, the functionality provided by the .NET Framework is so hidden or obscured by the size of the .NET Framework that things are overlooked. Numerous articles have been written that include a home-brewed algorithm to support actions that you could perform simply by knowing about such Framework classes as *Path* or *PasswordDeriveBytes*. In fact, many people will tell you that learning .NET isn't so much about learning Visual Basic .NET or C#, but that it is really about learning the Base Class Library.

However, learning the Base Class Library is also a mammoth challenge, simply because it is so large. The classes that are used every day are mixed in with other classes that you might never need. To make the common classes in the .NET Framework more discoverable, Visual Basic 2005 now provides a "speed dial" called The My Object. By using The My Object, you have the ability to easily access computer, application, and user information, as well as obtain access to Web services and forms. It is important to understand that The My Object is accessible to you only when writing Visual Basic .NET applications and is not directly available to you when using C#.

It is important to note that The My Object goes beyond being a simple speed dial. In some cases, the classes in The My Object provide more functionality than you easily find by simply searching through the various namespaces that make up the Base Class Library. For example, the *Folder* object provides additional properties, such as *Drive*, that are not available on the

System.IO.DirectoryInfo class. The My Object also forced Microsoft to think of the computer, application, and user as complete entities and ask "What should you be able to do with a computer?" The result was methods such as *My.Computer.Network.Ping*. You will now find that functionality previously available only by calling into COM libraries, or the Win32 API, are now easily accessible and discoverable through The My Object.

The My Object is broken down into a few areas of focus, as detailed in Table 2-2.

Table 2-2   The My Object Model

Object	Description
My.Application	Contains information about the running application, such as the title, working directory, version, and the common language runtime (CLR) version in use. It also gives access to environment variables, allows you to easily write to the local application log or to a custom log, and so on.
My.Computer	Contains information about the underlying platform and the hardware on the local machine that the application is running on.
My.Forms	A collection of all the instances of the forms in your current project. Allows you to easily show and hide forms without having to explicitly create an instance of the form in code.
My.User	Contains information about the current user, including his display name, domain name, and so on.
My.WebServices	Allows you to easily access Web services that are added as Web References in your project.

As you can see, The My Object gives you easy and direct access to functionality that you can use on a daily basis when building applications.

Walkthrough

In this section, you'll gain a good understanding of The My Object by looking at a small sample application that explores it in some depth. The application has three tabs, as shown in Figure 2-2, each of which focuses on a particular subsection of The My Object.

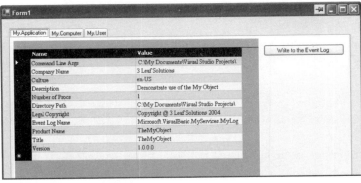

Figure 2-2   My.Application tab.

My.Application

The first tab with the text *My.Application* displays a data grid that exposes the values for many of the properties that are part of the *My.Application* object. The code that populates this grid with data is as follows:

```
Dim cmds As String = ""
For Each cmd As String In My.Application.CommandLineArgs
    cmds &= ", " & cmd
Next
AddnewRow("Command Line Args", Mid(cmds, 2))
AddnewRow("Company Name", _
    My.Application.AssemblyInfo.CompanyName)
AddnewRow("Culture", _
    My.Application.CurrentCulture.ToString())
AddnewRow("Description", _
    My.Application.AssemblyInfo.Description)
AddnewRow("Number of Procs", _
    My.Application.GetEnvironmentVariable("NUMBER_OF_PROCESSORS"))
AddnewRow("Directory Path", _
    My.Application.AssemblyInfo.DirectoryPath)
AddnewRow("Legal Copyright", _
    My.Application.AssemblyInfo.LegalCopyright)
AddnewRow("Event Log Name", _
    My.Application.Log.ToString)
AddnewRow("Product Name", _
    My.Application.AssemblyInfo.ProductName)
AddnewRow("Title", My.Application.AssemblyInfo.Title)
AddnewRow("Version", _
    My.Application.AssemblyInfo.Version.Major & "." & _
    My.Application.AssemblyInfo.Version.Minor & "." & _
    My.Application.AssemblyInfo.Version.Revision & "." & _
    My.Application.AssemblyInfo.Version.Build)
```

The preceding code is intentionally somewhat verbose. The code could have used reflection to iterate through the properties, but by listing them out in code, you can look at the application and get a better idea of what information is returned by a specific property. The individual value retrieved from a given property is added to the DataTable, *dt*, which is then bound to the *Datagrid* on the My.Application tab. You can gather a great deal of information about your application simply by accessing properties that make up the *My.Application* object. Table 2-3 lists the properties and methods of the *My.Application* object.

Table 2-3   My.Application

Property/Method	Description
ApplicationContext	Gives you access to the context associated with the current thread
AssemblyInfo	Allows you to easily access data from the AssemblyInfo.vb file, including CompanyName, Description, FolderPath, LegalCopyright, LegalTrademark, Name, ProductName, Title, and Version
ChangeCurrentCulture	Lets you change the culture in which the current thread is running, which affects such things as string manipulation and formatting

Table 2-3   My.Application

Property/Method	Description
ChangeCurrentUICulture	Lets you change the culture that the current thread uses for retrieving culture-specific resources
CommandLineArgs	Returns a collection of command-line arguments
CurrentCulture	Returns an instance of the culture object, which lets you determine the current culture of the application, among other things
CurrentDirectory	Returns the folder where the application resides
CurrentUICulture	Returns the culture that the current thread is using for retrieving culture-specific resources
DoEvents	Causes all messages in the message queue to be processed
GetEnvironmentVariable	Returns a specific environment variable on the local machine
IsNetworkDeployed	Returns True if the application was network-deployed and returns False otherwise
Log	Allows you to write to the application log on the local machine
MainForm	A read-write property that lets you set or get the form that the application will use as its main form
OpenForms	Returns a collection representing all the application's currently open forms
Run	Sets up and starts the Visual Basic Startup/Shutdown Application model
SplashScreen	Lets you set or get the application's splash screen

Scenarios for Using My.Application When Developing Applications

The *My.Application* object provides you with a great deal of functionality with much less code than when building applications with the .NET Framework 1.0/1.1, Visual Basic 6, or both. In this section, we'll look at some ways you can use *My.Application*. For example, the code required to write to an Event Log has now been shortened to the following:

```
My.Application.Log.WriteEntry("Application Starting", _
    EventLogEntryType.Information, Nothing)
```

By default, this code will write an entry to debug output, as well as to your assembly's log file. You can see the result either by running the application in Debug mode in Visual Studio and reading the output in the Output window, or by accessing the log file. This file, by default, is called *assemblyname.log,* and is located in the application's data directory, which is available as a property of *My.Computer.*

```
Dim AppLogLocation As String = _
    My.Computer.FileSystem.SpecialDirectories. _
        CurrentUserApplicationData & "\" & _
    My.Application.AssemblyInfo.Title & ".log"
MsgBox("Successfully wrote to log." & vbCr & _
    "Log is located at: " & AppLogLocation)
```

Previously, if you wanted to write to the *EventLog* in the .NET Framework 1.0/1.1, you would need multiple lines of code to do so. With Visual Basic 6, you had some limited logging functionality through the *App* object, but you could not specify an event ID and you could not write to the System or Security log or create your own custom logs.

In addition, *My.Application* gives you direct access to a wealth of application-level information in a single line of code. Some examples of where you could use these aspects of *My.Application* follow:

- To quickly determine the folder in which your application is placed by using the *Current-Folder* property

- To get quick access to assembly metadata such as the Product Name, Company Name, and so on

My.Computer

The next piece of The My Object is the *Computer* object. The *My.Computer* object gives you access to information about the underlying platform and hardware that your application is running on. The My.Computer tab (shown in Figure 2-3), which is the second tab in the sample application, extracts some of the more interesting property values you can retrieve from the *My.Computer* object.

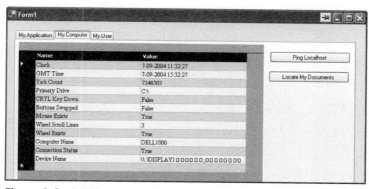

Figure 2-3   My.Computer tab.

The code that populates this grid with data is as follows:

```
AddnewRow("Clock", _
    My.Computer.Clock.LocalTime)
AddnewRow("GMT Time", _
    My.Computer.Clock.GmtTime)
AddnewRow("Tick Count", _
    My.Computer.Clock.TickCount)
AddnewRow("Primary Drive", _
   My.Computer.FileSystem.Drives(0).ToString())
AddnewRow("CRTL Key Down", _
    My.Computer.Keyboard.CtrlKeyDown.ToString())
AddnewRow("Buttons Swapped", _
    My.Computer.Mouse.ButtonsSwapped)
AddnewRow("Mouse Exists", _
```

```
    My.Computer.Mouse.Exists.ToString())
AddnewRow("Wheel Scroll Lines", _
    My.Computer.Mouse.WheelScrollLines.ToString())
AddnewRow("Wheel Exists", _
    My.Computer.Mouse.WheelExists)
AddnewRow("Computer Name", _
    My.Computer.Name)
AddnewRow("Connection Status", _
    My.Computer.Network.IsAvailable)
AddnewRow("Device Name", _
    My.Computer.Screen.DeviceName)
```

The code is similar to the code used to populate the grid on the My.Application tab in the application. A DataTable, *dt*, is populated with values from properties of the *My.Computer* object, and then bound to a grid.

The properties and methods of the *My.Computer* object are listed in Table 2-4.

Table 2-4   My.Computer

Property/Method	Description
Audio	Lets you play sound files on your local machine.
Clipboard	Gives you access to the system's clipboard.
Clock	Allows you to access the current GMT time, local time, and a Tick Count.
FileSystem	Allows you to perform a variety of input/output (IO) operations, such as copying files and directories, moving files and directories, and reading and writing to files, typically in one line of code.
Info	Lets you access information about the local machine, including its name, operating system, memory, and loaded assemblies.
Keyboard	Allows you to determine the state of the keyboard and the state of various keys on the keyboard. You can determine whether the CTRL key, SHIFT key, or ALT key are pressed, whether the CAPS lock is on, or whether SCROLL LOCK is on.
Mouse	Lets you determine the state and specific hardware characteristics of the attached mouse, such as the number of buttons, whether a mouse wheel is present, and so on.
Name	Gives you the name of the local machine the application is running on.
Network	Gives you access to the IP Address information for the local machine, the local machine's current connection status, and the ability to *Ping* addresses.
Ports	Lets you access the serial ports on the local machine, as well as creating and opening a new serial port object.
Printers	Lets you access the printers on the local machine.
Registry	Gives you easy access to the registry and the ability to read and write to registry keys.
Screen	Gives you access to all the monitors attached to the system and properties of those displays, such as *BitsPerPixel*, *WorkingArea*, and so on.

Scenarios for Using My.Computer When Developing Applications

The *My.Computer* object gives you a great deal of access to the underlying platform that you can use in a variety of scenarios. For example, you can easily ping network addresses using the *Network* property and its associated *Ping* method.

```
Dim pingResult As Boolean = _
    My.Computer.Network.Ping("localhost")
If pingResult = True Then
    MessageBox.Show("Ping of localhost succeeded")
Else
    MessageBox.Show("Ping of localhost was not successful")
End If
```

The simple *Ping* method of the *My.Computer.Network* property returns True if the ping was successful, and False otherwise. Being able to ping an address such as this makes it easy to determine whether your application is able to communicate with a particular server. You can also easily determine the network connection status by simply using *My.Computer.Network. IsAvailable*. The *IsAvailable* property returns a value of true or false, depending on whether the computer has a current network connection.

Another good use of *My.Computer* in your applications is when you need access to the file system. *My.Computer. FileSystem* gives you better access to the file system with fewer lines of code than in previous versions of Visual Basic. With *My.Computer. FileSystem*, you can perform the following actions in one line of code:

- Read all the text in a file.
- Copy a folder while creating all the parent folders necessary to complete the path.
- Move a folder while creating all the parent folders necessary to complete the path.

If you wanted to read all the text from a file, you could accomplish this with the following code:

```
My.Computer.FileSystem.ReadAllText(filePath)
```

Copying and moving folders has also been made much easier:

```
My.Computer.FileSystem.CopyDirectory(sourcePath, targetPath, True, True)
```

The preceding code will take the folder that is the *sourcePath* and copy it to the *targetPath*. The last two Boolean arguments specify that the *targetPath* will be overwritten if it is found and that all the parent folders needed to create the *targetPath* will be created as necessary.

With one line of code, you can determine the location of the My Documents folder.

```
MessageBox.Show(My.Computer.FileSystem.SpecialDirectories.MyDocuments)
```

It is also easy to work with individual files and folders using the *FileIO* object. For example, with one line of code you can easily rename the file you are working with:

```
My.Computer.FileSystem.RenameFile(sourceFilePath, targetFilename)
```

My.User

The next piece of The My Object is the *My.User* object. The *My.User* object allows you to obtain information about the currently logged-in user, such as her username, display name, and the roles she belongs to. The My.User tab is shown in Figure 2-4.

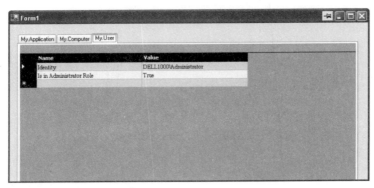

Figure 2-4   My.User tab.

The code that populates this grid with data is as follows:

```
AddnewRow("Identity", My.User.Identity.Name)
AddnewRow("Is in Administrator Role", _
    My.User.IsInRole("Administrators").ToString())
```

The code used to access current user information is quite simple. All you do is access the appropriate property of the *User* object. The user object is composed of the properties and methods shown in Table 2-5.

Table 2-5   **My.User**

Property/Method	Description
Identity	Returns the identity of the current user
IsInRole	Allows you to query whether the user is a member of a specific role

Scenarios for Using My.User When Developing Applications

The *My.User* object gives you a good deal of information about the currently logged-on user. In many ways, *My.User* is an excellent example of the speed dial that The My Object provides for the developer learning or using the .NET Framework.

In previous releases of the .NET Framework, if you wanted to get access to information similar to that provided by The My Object, you had to write code similar to the following:

```
Imports System.Security.Principal
Imports System.Threading.Thread
...
Dim winPrin as WindowsPrincipal = Thread.CurrentPrincipal
MessageBox.Show(winPrin.Identity.Name)
```

You also had the option of writing the following code:

```
MessageBox.Show(System.Threading.Thread.CurrentPrincipal.Identity.Name)
```

But with The My Object, you get the much more intuitive:

```
My.User.Identity.Name
```

This code is a classic example of how The My Object performs the function of a speed dial for the .NET Framework. Most developers when first exposed to the .NET Framework would not natively assume that to get access to the currently logged-on user account name they would have to either access *Principal* objects or access the current process's identity from the executing thread for the application. Many developers would expect this information to be exposed at a higher level of abstraction. With The My Object, this type of information is easily and quickly accessible.

My.WebServices, My.Forms

As you'll learn in later chapters, two other significant areas of functionality make up The My Object. These are *My.WebServices*, and *My.Forms*. Let's take a quick look at each of these before concluding this section of the chapter.

My.WebServices gives you the same easy access to Web services that are referenced in your project that you have when accessing data sources:

```
dgOrders.DataSource = _
   My.WebServices.Northwind.GetOrders().Tables("Orders")
```

In this code, you can see that you do not have to create an instance of the proxy class for the Web service as you would have with the .NET Framework 1.0/1.1. In this way, *My.WebServices* provides an easy speed dial to all the Web References that are part of your project.

Last but definitely not least, *My.Forms* gives you access to a collection containing the application's forms. This restores a significant programming enhancement for Visual Basic desktop application development that was lost temporarily with the advent of .NET. If you programmed previously in Visual Basic 6, you know that the following code could be used to show one of the forms in your project:

```
Form2.Show
```

With the advent of the .NET Frameworks 1.0/1.1, you were unable to do this as easily. The following code was required when you attempted to show a form in the .NET Framework 1.0/1.1:

```
Dim frm1 As New Form1()
frm1.Show()
```

With *My.Forms*, all the forms in your project are easily accessible as part of this collection. In addition, you also have access to a default instance for all the forms in your project without even using *My.Forms*. Therefore, the following lines of code are equivalent:

```
My.Forms.Form2.Show()
Form2.Show()
```

You'll see many more uses of this method of displaying forms throughout the book. You'll also see *My.WebServices* and *My.Forms* covered in more detail later in the book.

Conclusion

The My Object has four main uses to you as a developer. First, it contains additional functionality that was not available to you in previous releases of the .NET Framework. Second, it provides a valuable speed dial to let you more quickly find and use .NET Framework Base Class Library functionality in your applications. Third, it fills in some gaps and lets you think of things, such as the computer, as logical entities. Fourth, it brings back some familiar coding syntax, such as *Form1.Show*.

Application: Operators

This application introduces the new operator overloading features and the new *IsNot* operator that was added to the Visual Basic language.

New Concepts

Operator overloading allows you to define the behavior of your classes when used with intrinsic language operators such as +, -, <, >, =, and <>. The concept of using an operator such as + to operate on objects is not new in Visual Basic. For example, the following line of code operates on two string objects using the + operator:

```
str = "Hello, "  +  "world"
```

When applied to strings, the + operator concatenates two strings to produce a new string. Concatenation is an appropriate outcome for an addition operation on strings. Operator overloading in Visual Basic allows you to define the appropriate outcome for operations, such as addition, when applied to instances of your own classes.

Consider a scenario where you need to determine whether one employee has more seniority than another:

```
Dim emp1, emp2 As Employee
emp1 = Employee.GetFromID(123)
emp2 = Employee.GetFromID(155)
```

Seniority is the natural comparison between two *Employee* objects in this application, so the semantics of the next line of code should express "if emp1 is greater than emp2." With operator overloading, you can actually define how the > (greater than) operator works when used with two *Employee* objects. Once the > operator is defined, the following code would be valid:

```
If emp1 > emp2 Then
  ' Add code here
End If
```

Walkthrough

This application populates two list box controls with *Employee* objects. The user can then select two employees to see which employee has more seniority. For this application, seniority is determined solely on the basis of date hired.

Operator Overloads

Overloading operators is as simple as creating new methods. In fact, operator overloads are really just methods created with the *Operator* keyword. The definition of the > operator for the *Employee* class would look like this:

```
Public Shared Operator >(ByVal lhs As Employee, _
                         ByVal rhs As Employee) As Boolean
  ' Add code here
End Operator
```

The operator must be marked *Shared* and at least one of its parameters must be of the enclosing type (*Employee*). The > operator is a binary operator, which means that it requires two operands: the left-hand side of the operator and the right-hand side of the operator. Only one of these operands has to be of the enclosing type. The other operand can be another type if you want to define how an *Employee* object is compared against something else (for example, an integer). A typical result of this code is shown in Figure 2-5.

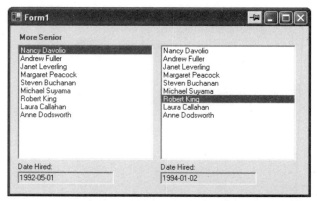

Figure 2-5 Employee objects can be compared based on the hire date of the employees.

The arguments passed to an operator method can be *Nothing* (null references), so you need to check them before attempting to access properties or methods. The full implementation of the > operator for the *Employee* class includes logic for handling null references:

```
Public Shared Operator >(ByVal lhs As Employee, _
                        ByVal rhs As Employee) As Boolean
    If rhs Is Nothing Then
        If lhs IsNot Nothing Then
            Return True
        Else
            Return False
        End If
    End If

    If lhs Is Nothing Then
        Return False
    End If

    If rhs.HireDate > lhs.HireDate Then
        Return True
    Else
        Return False
    End If
End Operator
```

When you define certain operators, Visual Basic requires that you also define the operator for the inverse operation. If you define the = (equal to) operator, you must define the <> (not equal to) operator. If you define the >= (greater than or equal to) operator, you must define the <= (less than or equal to) operator. If you define the > (greater than) operator, you must define the < (less than) operator. Fortunately, you can usually leverage the first operator to define the inverse operator. So instead of writing the inverse logic for the < operator, you simply reverse the operands and use the > operator:

```
Public Shared Operator <(ByVal lhs As Employee, _
                        ByVal rhs As Employee) As Boolean
    Return rhs > lhs
End Operator
```

Similarly, the <> operator returns the logical inverse of the = operator:

```
Public Shared Operator <>(ByVal lhs As Employee, _
                          ByVal rhs As Employee) As Boolean
    Return Not lhs = rhs
End Operator
```

IsNot Operator

The > operator overload method in this application makes use of the new *IsNot* operator. In previous versions of Visual Basic, determining that an object reference was not *Nothing* required applying the *Not* keyword to an *Is* keyword:

```
If Not obj Is Nothing Then
```

Although this syntax is perfectly logical, it can be awkward to use, especially when trying to read or verbalize the logic. With the new *IsNot* operator, the following *If* statement is possible:

```
If obj IsNot Nothing Then
```

This statement is logically identical to the previous *If* statement but reads more naturally: *if the object is not nothing, then....*

IsTrue, IsFalse, and Not Operators

Operator overloading in Visual Basic includes the ability to overload two special operators named *IsTrue* and *IsFalse*. These operators cannot be called explicitly from your code, but they can be used by the compiler to compute a true or false value for an object in expressions from which a Boolean value is expected (such as an *If* statement). Consider the following use of an *Employee* object:

```
Dim emp As New Employee()
If emp Then
    ' Add code here
End If
```

This use of *emp* is valid only if the class definition of *Employee* contains a way for a Boolean value to be computed. This can be done by defining an *IsTrue* operator or a *CType* operator (described in the next section). The *IsTrue* operator for *Employee* returns the value of the Employee.IsActive field or false for a null reference:

```
Public Shared Operator IsTrue(ByVal emp As Employee) As Boolean
    If emp Is Nothing Then
        Return False
    Else
        Return emp.IsActive
    End If
End Operator
```

When you define *IsTrue*, Visual Basic requires you to also define its inverse operator, *IsFalse*. In a simple case such as the *Employee* class, defining this inverse operator is very simple:

```
Public Shared Operator IsFalse(ByVal emp As Employee) As Boolean
    Return Not emp
End Operator
```

However, the luxury of using the *Not* operator on the *Employee* class does not come for free. You must define that operator as well:

```
Public Shared Operator Not(ByVal emp As Employee) As Boolean
    If emp Then Return False Else Return True
End Operator
```

CType Operator

Another special operator that you can overload in Visual Basic is the *CType* operator. *CType* is used to convert an expression from its original data type to a new data type. For example, *CType("100", Integer)* converts a *string* to an *integer*. By overloading the *CType* operator for your classes, you are able to define exactly how an instance of your class is converted to another data type. Three possible conversions for the *Employee* class in this application are *Employee* to *string*, *Employee* to *date*, and *Employee* to *boolean*. For each conversion, you must provide a separate overload of the *CType* operator.

```
Public Shared Widening Operator CType(ByVal emp As Employee) As String
    Return emp.FirstName + " " + emp.LastName
End Operator

Public Shared Widening Operator CType(ByVal emp As Employee) As Date
    If emp Is Nothing Then
        Return Nothing
    Else
        Return emp.HireDate
    End If
End Operator

Public Shared Widening Operator CType(ByVal emp As Employee) As Boolean
    If emp Is Nothing Then Return False Else Return emp.IsActive
End Operator
```

CType operator overloads can be marked as either *Widening* or *Narrowing*. A conversion is narrowing if the target data type cannot express all possible values of the original data type. That is not the case with any of the conversions defined for *Employee*, so they have all been marked as *Widening*.

> **Note**   The Visual Basic compiler does not allow implicit narrowing conversions when using *Option Strict On*.

In the *Employee* class, the *ToString* method is overridden so that the employee's first and last names are returned rather than the class name. The *Employee* class has a *CType* operator that defines a widening conversion from an *Employee* to a *string*, so the code required in the *ToString* method is minimal. A conversion from *Employee* to *string* is implicit because the function has an explicit return type (*string*) and a widening conversion is defined from the *Employee* object to that return type:

```
Public Overrides Function ToString() As String
    Return Me
End Function
```

> **Note**   Unless *ToString* is redefined (overridden), an object uses the *ToString* method inherited from *System.Object*, which returns the fully qualified class name of the object.

You can use operator overloading to create an effective and natural interface for working with your classes. However, poor choices for parameter and return types can make an application programming interface (API) confusing. For example, the greater than (>), less than (<), equal to (=), and not equal to (<>) operators should normally return *Boolean* values. A > operator that returns *DateTime* would be confusing and unnatural in most situations. The binary + operator should normally return the enclosing type, as should the unary + and − operators:

```
Dim var1 As New MyCustomClass
Dim var2 As New MyCustomClass
Dim var3 As MyCustomClass = var1 + var2
var3 = -var3
```

For operators such as the binary − operator, you might want to return a different data type. For example, the difference between two *Employee* objects in this application could be an integer value that represents the difference in months between the hire dates of the two employees.

Conclusion

Operator overloading lets you determine how operators such as = and > work when used with two instances of an object you've defined. To overload an operator, you simply have to create a method in your class that includes the *Operator* keyword. When overloading operators, be sure to define their inverses. For example, for an overload of the = (equal to) operator, define a corresponding <> (not equal to) operator overload.

A well-planned set of operator overloads with appropriate parameter and return types can make your classes easier to use and promote more concise source code.

Application: Keywords

This application introduces the new Visual Basic keywords *Using*, *Global*, and *Continue*.

New Concepts

Language designers are generally conservative about adding new keywords to a programming language. A language has to be expressive enough to be useful, but adding too many keywords makes the language too complex to master. The new keywords being added to Visual Basic with the release of Visual Studio 2005 are designed to clarify or simplify your code in some common programming scenarios.

Global Keyword

Visual Basic allows you to create your own namespaces to organize the classes in your applications and libraries. Meaningful namespaces can greatly increase the intuitiveness of your class hierarchy and the readability of your source code. But if you name one of your namespaces the same as a top-level namespace from the .NET Framework Base Class Library, the top-level namespace will be inaccessible. For example, you would be unable to declare a variable as *System.String* within the custom namespace *Util.System* because *String* is not defined in *Util.System*. The *Util.System* namespace eclipses the top-level *System* namespace.

The new *Global* keyword in Visual Basic allows you to access the root of the namespace hierarchy when your namespace hierarchy eclipses part of it. So a string variable inside the *Util.System* namespace can be declared as *Global.System.String*. See the "Walkthrough" section for an example.

Using Keyword

The .NET Framework common language runtime contains a sophisticated memory management subsystem that deals with allocating and releasing memory for managed applications. Memory is reclaimed from unused objects by the garbage collector at appropriate times. The garbage collector will automatically call a special cleanup method known as a *finalizer* when it is freeing memory. However, there is no guaranteeing when objects will be finalized. This non-deterministic approach to cleaning up objects can be problematic when your objects are using unmanaged resources such as a file handle.

To work around the nondeterministic nature of garbage collection, your classes that use unmanaged resources should include some way for a programmer to explicitly clean up unmanaged resources before abandoning an object. The conventional way to do this is to implement the *IDisposable* interface, which requires a *Dispose* method. The programmer simply calls your *Dispose* method when an object is no longer needed. This approach requires the programmer to ensure that a call to *Dispose* is made at the end of every possible path of execution.

The new *Using* keyword in Visual Basic simplifies the use of *Dispose* methods by automatically calling *Dispose* for an object. In the following code segment, the *Dispose* method of *obj1* is called automatically at the end of the *Using* block:

```
Dim obj1 As New MyCustomClass
Using (obj1)
    ' Add code here
End Using
```

The *Using* keyword can be applied to any object that implements the *IDisposable* interface. *Using* keywords can be nested so that *Dispose* is called automatically for any number of objects.

Continue Keyword

Most Visual Basic programmers have encountered a situation when certain iterations of a loop can be skipped. Previous versions of Visual Basic did not have an easy way to simply skip to the next iteration of a loop. This meant that you had to wrap the entire body of the loop inside conditional blocks. The *Continue* keyword in Visual Basic now allows you to skip to the next iteration of a loop without processing the rest of the loop body. The following *While* loop uses the *Continue* keyword to skip to the next iteration if the first column of the current record (in a *SqlDataReader*) is *Nothing*:

```
While dr.Read()
    If dr(0) Is Nothing Then Continue While
    ' Process current record in SqlDataReader
End While
```

The *Continue* keyword can be used in a nested loop to skip to the next iteration of an outer loop:

```
While I < 1000
    For J As Integer = 1 To 5
        If I Mod J = 0 Then
            Continue While
        End If
    Next
    I += 1
End While
```

When an inner loop is the same type of loop as an outer loop, such as a *For* loop nested inside a *For* loop, the *Continue* keyword applies to the innermost loop.

Walkthrough

The Keywords application is built around the *FileWriter* class defined in the *Util.System.IO* namespace:

```
Namespace Util.System.IO

    Public Class FileWriter
        Implements IDisposable

        Private _outWriter As Global.System.IO.StreamWriter

        Public Sub New(ByVal filename As String)
            _outWriter = Global.System.IO.File.CreateText(filename)
            _outWriter.WriteLine("Output started at " + Now.ToString())
        End Sub

        Public Sub WriteLine(ByVal message As String)
            _outWriter.WriteLine(Now.ToString().PadRight(30) + message)
        End Sub

        Public Sub Dispose() Implements IDisposable.Dispose
            _outWriter.Close()
            MsgBox("StreamWriter closed by Dispose()")
            GC.SuppressFinalize(Me)
        End Sub

        Protected Overrides Sub Finalize()
            _outWriter.Close()
            MsgBox("StreamWriter closed by Finalize()")
        End Sub

    End Class

End Namespace
```

The *FileWriter* class is a simple wrapper around the *StreamWriter* class. A *FileWriter* object adds the current date and time to each line it writes to the file. The *StreamWriter* is closed either when the *FileWriter.Dispose* method is called by the consumer or when the *Finalize* method is called by the .NET Framework garbage collector.

The *Dispose* and *Finalize* methods contain *MsgBox* calls to tell you when each method is called. These calls are for illustrative purposes only in this application. You should not normally display message boxes from non-UI classes such as *FileWriter*.

As you can see in Figure 2-6, the user interface for the Keywords application is a single Windows form with two buttons. The click event handler for one button uses the *Using* statement with a *FileWriter* object. The click event handler for the second button does not use *Using* nor does it call *Dispose*—it relies on the garbage collector to call *Finalize*:

```
Private Sub Button1_Click(ByVal sender As System.Object, _
                          ByVal e As System.EventArgs) _
                          Handles Button1.Click

    Dim fw As New _
        Util.System.IO.FileWriter( _
        System.Environment.CurrentDirectory + "\button1.txt")

    Using (fw)
        For I As Integer = 1 To 100
            If I Mod 3 = 0 Then
                Continue For
            End If
            fw.WriteLine(CStr(I))
        Next
    End Using

End Sub

Private Sub Button2_Click(ByVal sender As System.Object, _
                          ByVal e As System.EventArgs) _
                          Handles Button2.Click

    Dim fw As New _
        Util.System.IO.FileWriter( _
        System.Environment.CurrentDirectory + "\button2.txt")

    For I As Integer = 1 To 100
        If I Mod 3 = 0 Then
            Continue For
        End If
        fw.WriteLine(CStr(I))
    Next

End Sub
```

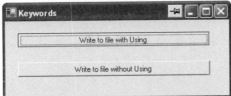

Figure 2-6   Keywords application user interface.

In both cases, the click event handlers use the *FileWriter* class to write to file every integer from 1 to 100 except values that are evenly divisible by 3.

Using the Global Keyword

The *FileWriter* class uses a *StreamWriter* from the Base Class Library *System.IO* namespace. But *System.IO* cannot be accessed directly from the class definition because *FileWriter* is defined inside a *System.IO* namespace (*Util.System.IO*) that eclipses the *System.IO* namespace at the root of the namespace hierarchy. To work around this naming collision, the *Global* keyword is used to access *System.IO* from the Base Class Library:

```
Private _outWriter As Global.System.IO.StreamWriter
```

The *Util.System.IO* namespace does not contain a *StreamWriter* class, so declaring the variable as *System.IO.StreamWriter* or *IO.StreamWriter* would not compile. But using the *Global* keyword allows the compiler to resolve the class to the proper type from the .NET Framework class library.

Using the Using Keyword

A *FileWriter* object opens its internal *StreamWriter* when the object is created (that is, in its constructor) and keeps the *StreamWriter* open until *Dispose* or *Finalize* is called. In the *Button1_Click* event handler, the *Using* keyword is applied to the *FileWriter* object *fw*. At the end of the *Using* block, *fw.Dispose* is called automatically, which closes the underlying *Stream-Writer* object. The result is shown in Figure 2-7.

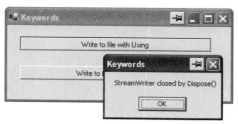

Figure 2-7   Message box displayed after Dispose is called automatically.

Dispose is called immediately after the *Using* block, so in this example the message box from *Dispose* is displayed immediately. By contrast, the second button creates a *FileWriter* but does not call *Dispose*. The message box from the *Finalize* method will appear at some seemingly arbitrary time when the garbage collector is cleaning up the object. For this simple application, the message box is most likely to appear when you close the program.

Using the Continue Keyword

The click event handlers for the buttons in this application both write to file the integers from 1 to 100 that are not divisible by 3:

```
For I As Integer = 1 To 100
    If I Mod 3 = 0 Then
        Continue For
    End If
    fw.WriteLine(CStr(I))
Next
```

The *For* loop that generates the numbers illustrates a simple use of the new *Continue* keyword. If *I* Mod 3 is 0, the current value of *I* is evenly divisible by 3. When this condition is true, *Continue For* moves execution to the next iteration of the loop without processing the remaining body of the *For* loop. If, for example, *I* is 6, *Continue For* would execute, which would move iteration back to the top of the loop with *I* equal to 7. A partial listing of the output would look like the following (note the absence of 3, 6, 9, and 12):

```
Output started at 12/12/2003 8:06:42 AM
12/12/2003 8:06:42 AM      1
12/12/2003 8:06:42 AM      2
12/12/2003 8:06:42 AM      4
12/12/2003 8:06:42 AM      5
12/12/2003 8:06:42 AM      7
12/12/2003 8:06:42 AM      8
12/12/2003 8:06:42 AM      10
12/12/2003 8:06:42 AM      11
12/12/2003 8:06:42 AM      13
```

Conclusion

The new keywords demonstrated in this application—*Continue*, *Global*, and *Using*—add extra convenience and flexibility to the Visual Basic language. The *Continue* keyword can help alleviate awkward logic in loops to deal with special cases that you do not want to process. The *Global* keyword gives you the flexibility to use any namespace names for your class hierarchy without making namespaces from the .NET Framework class library inaccessible. And the *Using* keyword relieves you of the responsibility of calling *Dispose* explicitly at the end of every path of execution in your program. These new keywords are incremental changes to the Visual Basic language. They will not dramatically change the way you write code, but in some situations they will serve to simplify or clarify your source code.

Chapter 3
Visual Studio 2005 Integrated Development Environment

Before .NET, there was Microsoft Visual Basic 6, one of the most popular and easy-to-use programming languages of all time. The simple reason for its success was that it allowed developers to be more productive than their counterparts working with other programming languages and development tools. Certainly the productivity benefits enjoyed by Visual Basic 6 developers came at the expense of limited language support. When Visual Basic .NET came along, it introduced a new programming architecture and features, such as full access to the platform, for building state-of-the-art applications. Visual Basic .NET was thus established as a first-class programming language. However, the promise of all that functionality and language support came at the expense of some productivity benefits Visual Basic developers had come to love and expect.

Microsoft Visual Studio 2005 contains a number of new enhancements, innovations, and advances to the development environment, offered with the singular objective of making Visual Basic .NET developers more productive than ever before. This chapter explores some of these features, and explains how you can make use of them as a developer to write code faster and more accurately.

Tip Among other "improvements" to the IDE, Visual Studio 2005 reintroduces Edit and Continue, which will be good information for experienced Visual Basic developers.

Application: IDE Enhancements

This application demonstrates the Class Designer in the Visual Studio 2005 IDE, a tool for visually designing the class hierarchy in a Visual Basic .NET application. Before examining the details of the application, let's first take a more general look at features that are either new or improved in the Visual Studio 2005 IDE.

Configuration Settings

If you have used previous versions of Visual Studio, you have probably spent some time customizing the development environment. You might have learned through some experimentation that you can specify the position of tool windows, or you might have found that menus and toolbars in Visual Studio are fully customizable. You can also configure keyboard mappings, project template types, Help filters, and so on. In fact, Visual Studio has always been designed for you to arrange elements of the IDE to best suit your individual development style.

The Options Dialog

The Options dialog shown in Figure 3-1 provides a broad array of settings categories for customizing the Visual Studio development environment. By default, the Options dialog displays the most common settings. To display all of the available settings, select the Show All Settings check box.

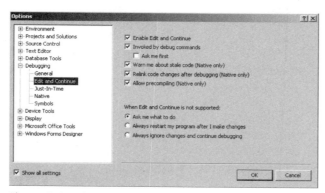

Figure 3-1   The Options dialog box.

Before the release of Visual Studio 2005, the main drawback with IDE customization was that you had no way to save your preferences in a portable format, which would come in handy if you had to re-create those settings on another machine. With Visual Studio 2005, you can now quickly and easily restore your personal settings at a later time or on another machine. Visual Studio 2005 allows you to use customized settings in the following ways:

- Make a copy of your current settings for use on a second machine.
- Distribute your settings to other developers.

■ Allow teams to use the same settings for certain elements of the IDE (such as the code editor, for example), while preserving individual customizations in other areas of the IDE.

As shown in Figure 3-2, the Options dialog Environment settings include an Import/Export Settings item. The file specified in the Always Save My Settings To This File text box is updated every time you close Visual Studio. This can be a local file or a network file. In a scenario where you regularly work on two machines, set this file to a network location accessible by both machines; this will ensure that you enjoy the same Visual Studio "look and feel" on both machines. In addition, every time you change a setting on one machine, it will automatically show up on the other machine.

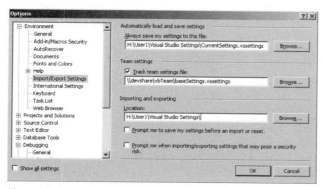

Figure 3-2   Import/Export Settings options.

Under the Team Settings section, you can specify a .vssettings file containing settings to be shared among a team of developers. To understand how this would be useful, consider a situation in which a development team's members must all use the same indenting and formatting options for Visual Basic .NET code files. The lead developer can configure the formatting options in Visual Studio 2005, and then use the Import/Export Settings dialog to save only those formatting settings to a .vssettings file on a network share. Other members of the development team would then update their Visual Studio configuration to use that team settings file. If the team later decides to change the defaults, the lead developer can export new settings to that same file location and everyone on the team will automatically receive the new settings the next time they launch Visual Studio.

In the Location text box under the Importing And Exporting section, specify a default location where settings can be exported or imported. The following section describes how to import and export settings files.

Note   Your active settings consist of two parts: predefined customizations from the installed .vssettings file you selected the first time you started Visual Studio 2005, and any subsequent IDE customizations you have made. Active settings are saved automatically to the currentsettings.vssettings file every time you exit Visual Studio.

The Import/Export Settings Dialog

The Visual Studio 2005 Tools menu includes an Import/Export Settings menu item that opens a dialog box for managing settings files. The dialog provides three basic areas of functionality:

- Exporting your current IDE settings to a file
- Importing IDE settings from a file
- Resetting your environment to a work style predefined in a default file

Depending on whether you are exporting or importing settings, the dialog lets you choose which settings to export to a .vssettings file, or which settings to import from an existing .vssettings file, respectively.

Note A settings category generally defines a logical grouping of settings for a tool window, an options page, or an IDE feature.

Figure 3-3 shows the Import/Export Settings dialog box with the Export IDE settings to a file option selected. Under Choose The Settings To Export, select or clear individual settings or an entire category of settings for export.

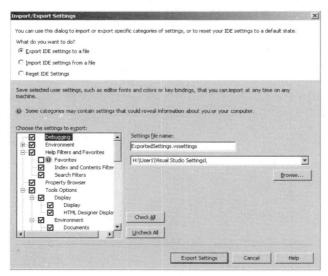

Figure 3-3   Export IDE settings.

An obvious downside of a highly customizable development environment is the opportunity for developers to accidentally (of course) remove necessary features from the IDE. For example, you might remove necessary items from a toolbar or a menu. Or, through innocent experimentation, rearrange tool windows into an unusable layout. In earlier versions of Visual

Studio, you could restore individual items within the IDE (for example, by going to the Window menu and choosing the Reset Window Layout command). Most of these reset tools are carried forward in Visual Studio 2005. However, individual reset tools encompass just a small portion of IDE functionality, and the fact that they are scattered throughout the IDE can sometimes make it difficult to find the appropriate one.

As shown in Figure 3-4, select the Reset IDE settings option to change the IDE environment to a work style defined in a number of predefined settings files, which are listed under the Available Installed Settings Files section. These files are installed with Visual Studio 2005, and include specific customizations for window layouts, toolbars, and menu commands that reflect the common preferences related to specific programming orientations, such as VB.NET, C++, C#, Web, or J#.

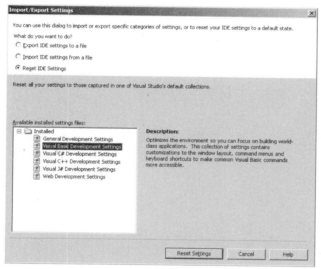

Figure 3-4   Reset IDE settings.

Tip   If your settings reach a state where you can't use the IDE, or they prevent you from accessing the Import/Export Settings dialog, restore the default settings by restarting Visual Studio 2005 from a command prompt using a reset switch, as follows: devenv / resetsettings

If you need to reset only certain settings categories, use the Import IDE Settings From A File option. You can select settings from one of the default settings files or a local settings file. You can also browse to a file located in a folder other than the Visual Studio 2005 default folder. For example, in a situation where your development team shares a settings file, the file might be located on a network share. As shown in Figure 3-5, once you have selected the file, the tree view titled Settings Available To Import lists the settings stored in the file. By selecting or clearing items displayed in the list, you can choose which settings to import. The Import IDE Settings From A File option allows you to change all or a portion of your settings from a .vssettings file.

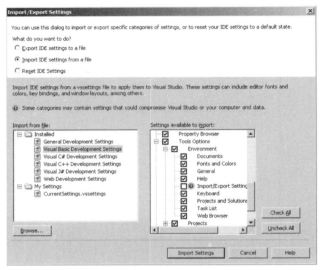

Figure 3-5 Import IDE settings.

Help and Community Integration

Visual Studio 2005 represents significant advances both in the content of Help information and in the tools for accessing that information. These improvements also include more comprehensive integration with community-based resources.

Then and Now

Before reviewing what is new and improved in the Help system, for some perspective let's review how previous versions of Visual Studio provided ways to get help, highlighting the limitations of each:

- **F1** This was at best a "hit or miss" tool. Sometimes F1 returned the right answer. Other times, it showed the Dynamic Help window—that provided help on the "Code and Text Editor"—which was rarely the area in which you needed assistance.

- **Table of Contents (TOC)** You can browse the content tree of a TOC to look for topics unrelated to a current topic. Yet, while this may sometimes yield useful information, it can also be time consuming and fruitless.

- **Index** In certain situations, the Help Index is still a good option for locating useful information. For example, if you already know the .NET Framework class name in which you are interested, the Index works well. It falls short, however, when you are looking for conceptual information.

- **Search**   The major drawback of searching was that it could return up to five hundred results in a random order.

- **Web-based search**   While results vary depending on your preferred search engine, this remains the help tool of choice for many developers. It not only avoids the shortcomings of earlier Visual Studio help tools, but it also provides access to information on the Internet.

Visual Studio 2005 offers the following significant updates to these tools to allow you to access help content more efficiently:

- **F1**   Improvements to the metadata on Help topics make F1 more consistently helpful, even if you're not in the context of a project.

- **Search**   The filtering mechanism is improved over earlier versions of Visual Studio, thereby delivering results that include topics that more closely match your search criteria. Another important improvement is that the results include a dynamically generated abstract of each returned item.

- **How Do I**   This is a new tool, shown in Figure 3-6, for accessing the help system that presents a hierarchical organization of common developer tasks. For Visual Basic .NET developers, the tool provides hundreds of tasks, and each task contains technical instruction content and sample code that a developer can easily paste into the code editor.

- **Help Favorites**   Earlier versions of Visual Studio included an integrated Favorites tool, but only for Internet Explorer links. The updated Help Favorites tool lets you save help-specific favorites, including the parameters of search queries.

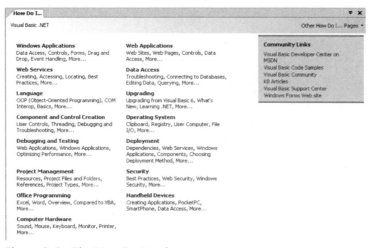

Figure 3-6   The How Do I tool.

Using Online Help Content

As with earlier versions of the development environment, Visual Studio 2005 provides direct access to content found at Web sites like CodeGuru and Net247. These and other .NET-focused Web sites are members of a group known as the *.NET CodeWise Community*. The CodeWise Community is a Microsoft-sponsored community of Web sites providing independent expertise in Microsoft developer tools and technologies. If you have accessed these sites in the past, you already know that contributions from members of the developer community expand and enrich static help resources. While MSDN content provides breadth of coverage, community content complements this with depth and context for areas important to real-world developers. In addition to extending help content and providing additional code samples, community-based Web sites also provide other resources, like message forums.

In a step forward from previous versions of the IDE, Visual Studio 2005 integrates content from CodeWise Community member sites directly into the help system. When you search for help on a topic such as generics from Visual Studio 2005, for example, the search might return a list of local MSDN topics, a list of MSDN online topics, and a list of links to relevant pages on CodeWise Community sites. This innovative feature gives you easy-to-use, direct access to the newest and most popular code samples and technical articles in the community, presented alongside the comprehensive static content available from MSDN. Moreover, this represents a significant advantage over performing ad hoc Web-based searches, where you need to validate for yourself whether the information you find is technically accurate. Configure online help resources, including CodeWise Community providers, in the Help category of the Options dialog box as shown in Figure 3-7.

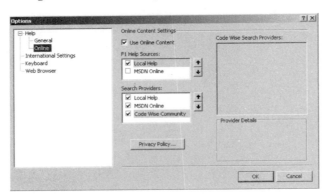

Figure 3-7   Configuring online help resources.

Project Enhancements

The most immediate productivity enhancement you'll encounter with Visual Studio 2005 is the ability to create new projects without having to specify a storage location. The inspiration for this change came from the common experience of developers who create projects for testing code or building prototypes that they will use only once. Rather than committing these projects to disk as a new solution, the IDE gives you control of whether or not to save the project.

This enhancement works in a way similar to creating a new document in Microsoft Word, where you can open a document, type some text, print it, and then exit Word without saving the document. The same process applies to projects created in Visual Studio 2005; you can build a new application, run it in the debugger, add project items and resources, and even compile the application before saving. (The New Project dialog box is shown in Figure 3-8.) As with Word, Visual Studio 2005 holds the unsaved files in temporary file storage until you choose to either save them to a permanent location or discard them when you close the project. If you choose to discard them, Visual Studio 2005 removes the project and all its associated files from temporary storage. These are also known as "zero-impact" projects.

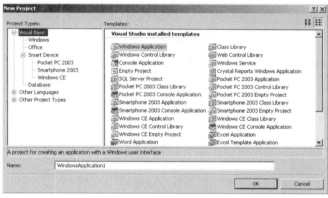

Figure 3-8 Visual Basic project templates.

Visual Studio 2005 also introduces a number of new project item types. Many item types provide templates for common user interface elements, including a Login Form, an About Box, and an Explorer Form template, which is shown in Figure 3-9.

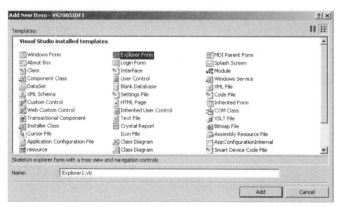

Figure 3-9 Project item types.

Project Designer

In prior versions of Visual Studio, you could manipulate project properties by using a dialog box accessible from the project menu. Because dialog boxes are modal, you needed to first open the properties dialog box, change a setting, close the dialog box, and then continue working on your code. Throughout the course of a typical development cycle, you likely returned to the project properties many times. Perhaps you wondered to yourself, "Wouldn't it be nice if I could leave these properties open all the time for easier access?"

The Project Designer addresses the need for easier, more consolidated access to project properties. When you create a new project in Visual Studio 2005, you'll find an additional project element, named My Project, listed in Solution Explorer. (See Figure 3-10.) Opening this item displays the Project Designer in the main editing window of the IDE.

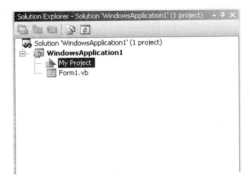

Figure 3-10   My Project.

The Project Designer provides nonmodal access to project properties, making them as easy to get to as code files or form designers. If you're familiar with earlier versions of Visual Studio, you'll notice that the Project Designer panes consolidate properties that used to be contained in the properties dialog box and other areas of the IDE, while other panes provide configuration tools for features introduced with the .NET Framework 2.0 (such as Click-Once publishing).

> **Note**   For details on the Publish and Security panes, see Chapter 8, "Deploying Applications."

Application Pane

The Application pane, shown in Figure 3-11, is one of the places where the designer incorporates settings from the properties dialog of prior versions of Visual Studio. This pane also introduces new items for defining the behavior of your application. Once you open the Project Designer, the Application pane is available as a tab in the Visual Studio 2005 document window. (Alternatively, you can open the Project Designer by right-clicking the project in Solution

Explorer and selecting the Properties menu command, or select the Project | *<Project Name>* Properties menu command.)

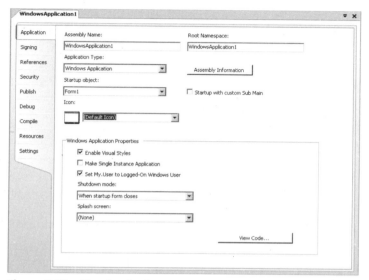

Figure 3-11   The Application pane.

Here are a few of the new and updated settings:

- **Startup Object**   You can still specify a form or Sub Main procedure as the startup object for an application. Project Designer also includes a Startup With Custom Sub Main check box to allow you to design your own startup routine. In addition, Visual Studio 2005 supports an application event model for Visual Basic that includes two types of startup events (see Table 3-1).

- **Enable Visual Styles**   This setting is enabled by default, and it allows your applications to use the Windows XP themes present on the host operating system. However, you might encounter certain situations where your applications use controls from a previous version of Windows XP themes, in which case you should disable Windows XP themes to preserve the desired look and feel of the application.

- **Make Single Instance**   When you click a particular Windows application several times (Media Player, for example), the application is launched only one time. Other applications (Calculator, Notepad, and so forth) launch separate instances of the program each time you click the icon. Selecting this setting allows you to set the launch behavior of the application as a single instance; if this setting is not selected, the application will launch multiple instances.

- **Shutdown Mode**   This option determines what event signals the shutdown of the application. For a Windows Forms application, for example, you can choose to shut down the application when the startup form closes or when the application exits.

- **Splash Screen**   This setting allows you to select a form in the project to serve as a splash screen.

- **View Code**   Clicking the View Code button opens the *MyEvents.vb* code module. *MyEvents.vb* contains a partial *MyApplication* class (defined within the *My* namespace). The *MyApplication* class exists for the express purpose of containing handlers for application events, described in Table 3-1.

Table 3-1   MyApplication Events

Name	Description
Startup	Raised when the application starts
Shutdown	Raised when the application exits
UnhandledException	Raised when an unhandled exception occurs in the application
StartupNextInstance	Raised when a user attempts to launch a separate instance of the program for applications configured to run as a single instance
NetworkAvailabilityChanged	Raised when the status of the underlying network connection changes

Managing Assembly Information

In previous versions of Visual Studio for the .NET Framework, you typically managed global assembly attributes in the AssemblyInfo.vb code file. As with any other code file in the project, to change the assembly attributes, you needed to open the file in the code editor and update the attributes as necessary. The following are a few common attributes found in AssemblyInfo.vb:

```
<Assembly: AssemblyTitle("IDE Enhancements")>
<Assembly: AssemblyDescription("New Visual Studio 2005 IDE features")>
<Assembly: AssemblyCompany("3 Leaf Solutions")>
<Assembly: AssemblyProduct("Moving to Visual Studio 2005")>
<Assembly: AssemblyCopyright("2005")>
<Assembly: AssemblyVersion("1.0.0.0")>
<Assembly: AssemblyFileVersion("1.0.0.0")>
<Assembly: ComVisible(False)>
```

In Visual Studio 2005, assembly attributes are still stored in AssemblyInfo.vb, but the file is now hidden in Solution Explorer by default. The Application pane provides access to these attributes via the Assembly Information dialog box shown in Figure 3-12. This dialog box is an interface to the underlying assembly attributes; any changes you make to an item listed in this dialog box is automatically written to the underlying AssemblyInfo.vb file. (Of course, you can still access the underlying code file and make changes directly if you prefer.)

Assembly Information

Title

WindowsApplication1

Description

Company

Product

WindowsApplication1

Copyright

Copyright @ 2004

Trademark

Assembly Version

| 1 | 0 | 0 | 0 |

File Version

| 1 | 0 | 0 | 0 |

COM Visible

Guid

3cce026b-5917-4eec-ac56-230c9e8e06c0

Neutral Language

OK   Cancel   Help

Figure 3-12   Assembly Information dialog.

Signing Pane

Every managed assembly that executes on the common language runtime (CLR) is governed by the Code Access Security (CAS) permissions associated with that assembly. During execution, the CLR evaluates the assembly's requested permissions and either grants or denies those permissions, in part by using evidence provided to the CLR about the identity of the code. As a way of establishing the assembly's identity, the Signing pane (shown in Figure 3-13) allows you to add either a key file (.snk) or a key stored in a key container to the project. The compiler uses that key to sign the assembly with a strong name. To accommodate situations where developers need to do a prerelease build but only have access to the public key, the pane also provides a check box to enable delayed signing.

Important   For ClickOnce applications, a signing key is required for publishing. The key is used to strong-name-sign both the application and deployment manifests. This topic is discussed in detail in Chapter 8, "Deploying Applications."

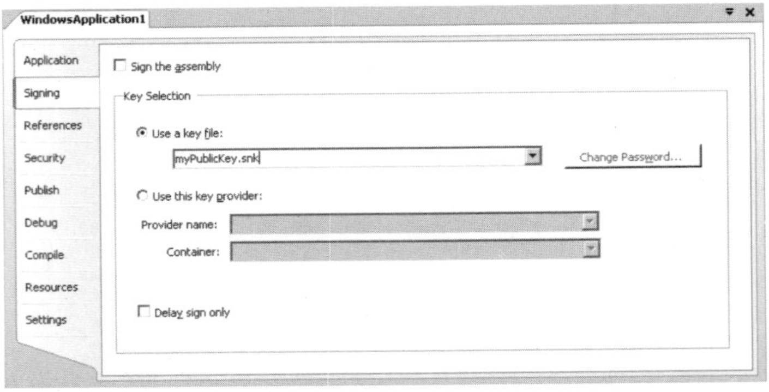

Figure 3-13   Signing pane.

References Pane

You can still access project references and Web references from the project menu as in previous versions of the IDE. However, Visual Studio 2005 adds an additional point of access to these items in the References pane, shown in Figure 3-14. Use the References pane to manage imported namespaces and assembly and Web service references. A significant benefit of this alternative view is that it consolidates project references in a single UI component. The pane contains tools for setting one or more reference paths and for identifying referenced assemblies that are not used in the project and, as a bonus, it also lets you manage namespace import settings.

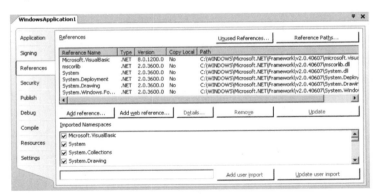

Figure 3-14   References pane.

Compile Pane

In addition to setting default compiler options for each of the various build configurations, the Compile pane (shown in Figure 3-15) also lets you specify individual notification behaviors (such as Warning, Error, or None) for different compilation conditions. Use this pane to set conditional notification options.

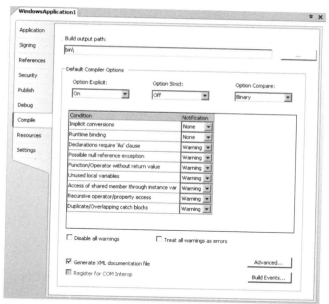

Figure 3-15   Compile pane.

You can also access the Build Events dialog box from this pane. As with earlier versions of the IDE, use this dialog box to specify pre-build and post-build command-line events, as well as to specify the condition under which a post-build event fires. The condition under which the post-build event executes can be Always, On Successful Build, or When The Build Updates The Project Output.

MSBuild Integration

Visual Studio 2005 introduces a new build engine called named MSBuild, which is integrated into the Visual Studio 2005 IDE to dramatically improve the build process. While MSBuild operates under the covers in the Visual Studio 2005 IDE, it has also been specially designed to execute build tasks from a command line.

Resources Pane

The Resources pane of the Project Designer provides a comprehensive resource manager for your project. (See Figure 3-16.) Resource categories include localization strings, images, icons, sound files, and text files. You can access each of the various resource categories from the Categories drop-down list. To add a resource—such as a string, for example—simply type the name of the resource and its associated value in a table displayed in the user interface.

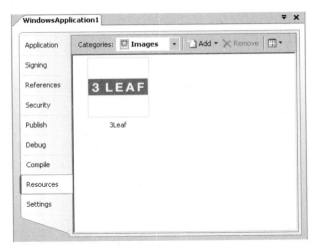

Figure 3-16   Resources pane.

Additionally, for image and icon resources, you can either add an existing image or icon file, or you can create a new image or icon directly inside the development environment (see Figure 3-17).

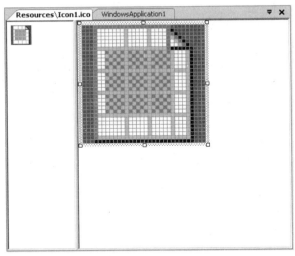

Figure 3-17   Icon designer.

Resources and Framework Integration

The Resources pane is a good example of a place in the IDE that has been closely integrated with the enhanced .NET Framework. Items managed in the Resources page are automatically available in code through the *My* namespace via the MyResources module, which contains a representation of the project resources in code. Synchronization between items managed in the Resources pane and the underlying code file is managed transparently by the Strongly Typed Resource Builder, an integrated Visual Studio 2005 tool. When you make changes to elements in the Resources page, this tool writes those changes to the MyResources module, which in turn is found in the MyResources.vb file. By default, MyResources.vb (and a number of other automatically generated project files) is hidden from view in Solution Explorer. You can display hidden files in Solution Explorer by clicking the Show All Files button.

The code generated by the Strongly Typed Resource Builder is equivalent to the output class produced by the ResGen command-line utility. The key advantage this utility has over ResGen is that you don't need to run it every time you update the resource file; Visual Studio manages the updates for you automatically.

Settings Pane

A common application development task is providing a mechanism for storing application and user settings. This might include state information such as database connection strings, the position and size of forms, preferences for toolbar position and contents, database connection strings, URLs for Web services—the list goes on. Earlier versions of the .NET Framework offered different options for storing settings. For example, you could use dynamic properties or you could add your own section to the application configuration file. The .NET Framework 2.0 represents an evolution of these technologies. The .NET Framework 2.0 introduces new classes for managing application and user settings as strongly typed objects. The classes have been integrated into the Visual Studio 2005 IDE using the Settings pane of the Project Designer.

Levels of Functionality   The Settings pane itself has a number of levels of functionality. First, you can create settings for virtually any CLS-compliant type. It also includes a special type for database connection strings. In fact, when you create a new database connection, Visual Studio automatically adds the connection string to the project settings.

The user interface includes an input table for specifying the name of each setting, its type, and the value for the setting. Another important attribute is whether the setting is applied application-wide or for an individual user. The table includes a column that lets you set the scope to either of these two options.

During most development cycles, applications can be deployed to a number of environments—for example, development, testing, staging, and production. Typically, each environment requires different application settings: a database connection string is an obvious example, as you would not dare to use a production database for testing an application in development. To make it easier to manage different user settings, you can add one or more configuration profiles to your project. The Profiles tool lets you copy settings from an existing profile, saving you the trouble of having to re-create them for each profile instance.

In fact, it's good advice to define settings during the application design phase for the project. Tinker with the settings in the early stages of development. Then, after you have solidified the settings for the application, add profiles for each of the various deployment environments. To adjust a setting for a particular profile, select the current settings profile from the drop-down list to activate the profile and then make changes accordingly.

Tip   If you use multiple settings profiles, keep in mind that there is no direct relationship between the settings profile and the active solution configuration. At compile time, the compiler uses the settings profile that is currently active in the Project Designer. As a best practice, consider creating solution configurations that align with your defined settings profiles.

Settings and Framework Integration   As with items defined in the Resources pane, Visual Studio 2005 automatically provides strongly-typed access to the settings managed in the Settings pane. And also as with project resources, settings are available programmatically via the *My* namespace. Yet while the *My.Resources* object allows only read-only access to project resources at run time (because resource elements are represented in code as read-only properties), the *My.Settings* object exposes user settings as read/write properties, which of course means that you can change them at run time.

The *My.Settings* class derives from the *ApplicationSettingsBase* class. This relationship between the two provides *My.Settings* with two methods for manipulating user settings: a *Save* method, and a *Reset* method. The programming model is very simple for changing user settings. In code, all you need to do is update the user setting exposed as a property of the *My.Settings* object and then call the *Save* method to persist the change. To change all the user settings back to the last saved settings, call the *Reset* method.

Note   The *ApplicationSettingsBase* class is featured in many areas of the .NET Framework. For example, it is inherited by a number of Windows Forms controls to provide run-time access to the properties of the control, such as size, position, and so on. This class also provides the necessary functionality to persist run-time changes to control properties as user settings. For more details on how user settings have been enabled in Windows Forms controls, see Chapter 5, "Constructing User Interfaces."

The *My.Settings* object also exposes the events inherited from the *ApplicationSettingsBase* class. Those events include *PropertyChanged*, *SettingChanging*, and *SettingsSaving*.

New and Improved Tool Windows

The Visual Studio 2005 IDE includes a number of tool windows designed to improve productivity and reduce the amount of code you need to write. This section reviews some of the productivity-enhancing tool windows in Visual Studio 2005 IDE.

Code Editor

If you are familiar with the documentation feature of the C# code editor from past versions of Visual Studio, you'll recognize another new feature of the Visual Basic .NET Code Editor that allows you to automatically insert the tags for generating XmlDoc comments. To use this feature, place your cursor above a member in the code file and type a single quote three times. This generates the following XmlDoc comment tags:

```
''' <summary>
'''
''' </summary>
''' <param name="fireDate"></param>
''' <remarks></remarks>
Public Sub Fire(ByVal fireDate As Date)
    . . .
End Sub
```

While this feature has been available for a number of years in the C# code editor (which uses three forward slash keystrokes instead of single quotes), it is nevertheless a timely addition to the Visual Basic .NET Code Editor.

Data Preview Dialog

The Data Preview dialog box allows you to preview the data returned by any *DataComponent* query in your project. To preview data, open the Data Preview dialog from the Data Designer window (shown in Figure 3-18). You can also access the Data Preview dialog from the Data Sources window.

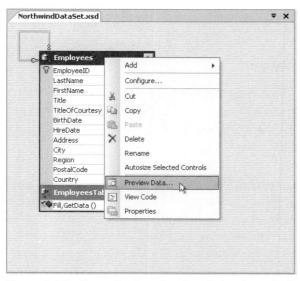

Figure 3-18   Open the Data Preview dialog from the Data Designer.

In the Data Preview dialog, first select the object that you want to preview. If the object is a parameterized query, enter parameter values in a separate control in the dialog box. Then click the Preview button to execute the query; the resulting data is displayed as shown in Figure 3-19.

> **Note**   Queries that change data in the database (such as the INSERT, UPDATE, and DELETE queries) will not affect the database when executed in the Preview Data dialog box.

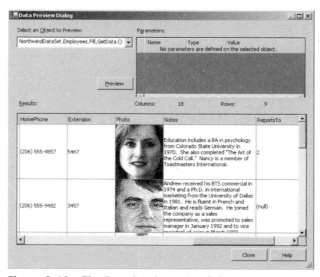

Figure 3-19   The Data Preview Data dialog.

Document Outline

In earlier versions of the Visual Studio 2005 IDE, the Document Outline window allowed you to view the structure of an HTML or ASPX page by providing a visual representation of the markup hierarchy. The window displays the HTML tags, script elements, and controls on the page by using a tree view that you can expand or collapse to focus on specific areas of the page. And by double-clicking any item in the view, you can navigate to it directly on the page. This functionality has been carried forward to Visual Studio 2005 and extended to provide the same visibility into the elements on a Windows Form.

The Document Outline window for a Windows Form layout (shown in Figure 3-20) provides an easy way to manage controls on a form. As with the original incarnation of the Document Outline window, you can expand and collapse containing items as you scroll through the outline. To select a control in the Form Designer, click the item in the tree view. You could reasonably argue that given the complex control layout common in any nontrivial Windows Form application—which might contain a number of deeply nested hidden components, or both—extending document outlining to forms provides a much bigger benefit to developers than it does for simple Web page editing. Additionally, you can also drag and drop controls from one container to another within the container hierarchy.

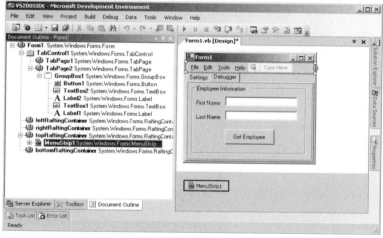

Figure 3-20   The Document Outline window.

> **Note**   Rearranging controls in the Document Outline window is available only for Windows Forms, not Web pages.

Window Docking Enhancements

Another noteworthy enhancement to the development environment is the introduction of docking guides (Figure 3-21). When you rearrange windows within the IDE, changeable icons appear on the design surface to guide you to areas where the window can be placed. If you hover your mouse over the icon, the associated area of the IDE becomes shaded to indicate where the window will appear if you choose to complete the operation.

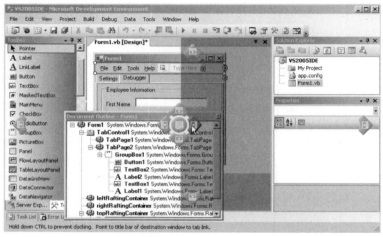

Figure 3-21   Docking guides.

Class Designer

The Class Designer (shown in Figure 3-22) is a visual design tool for examining and manipulating the structure of classes and other types. The tool is fully integrated with the source code underlying the types displayed in the designer; if you make a change to a property name, for example, the code file automatically updates to reflect the change. Conversely, changes made in the source code immediately affect the appearance of its associated object in the designer. This synchronized editing relationship between designer and code makes it easy to create and configure CLR types visually.

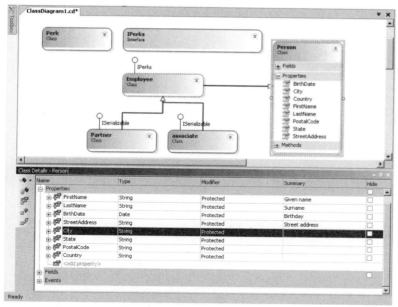

Figure 3-22   The Class Designer.

Writing Correct Code

Visual Studio 2005 includes a number of tools—some are enhancements of old features and some are new features—geared toward the common objective of making it easier for developers to write code correctly at design time. In the following sections, we'll look at some key areas in the IDE that make the coding experience in Visual Studio 2005 less susceptible to error.

IntelliSense Enhancements

The Microsoft IntelliSense technology carries forward key features of prior versions of Visual Studio, such as automatically tracking the most often-used member of a particular type. In addition, IntelliSense has been improved to include a facility for choosing whether to display all the members of a type (as shown in Figure 3-23) or just the most commonly used members.

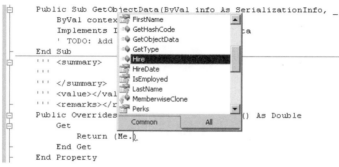

Figure 3-23   The IntelliSense window.

If the All button is selected, every member within the type (including hidden members) is displayed. If you click the Common button, the display changes to show only the most frequently used members of that type. If you work regularly with only a few properties and methods for a given type (particularly those with a large number of members), using IntelliSense in Common mode makes it much easier to locate those items while you're typing in code.

Syntax Error Assistance

Past versions of the Visual Basic development environment have always distinguished themselves in one way or another in the area of providing design-time feedback, particularly when that feedback involved mistaken syntax. The Code Editor displays a squiggly line underneath an item of code containing an error. Placing the cursor over the squiggle displays a ToolTip briefly describing the problem. This form of design-time syntax checking has been an important feature of Visual Studio for many years now and is indeed helpful, but it is still basically hit or miss whether the error description gives you enough information to correct the problem.

With Visual Studio 2005, Microsoft adds to this functionality with the aim of enabling you to correct the error immediately. And it works using the same UI behavior you're familiar with from past versions of Visual Studio. If you write code that the background compiler recognizes as a syntax error, the same squiggly line displays in the Code Editor. If you hover the cursor over the line indicating the error, not only does the same descriptive ToolTip display, but you will also see a small Help icon. Clicking the icon opens a dialog box that not only displays a description of the error, but also lists one or more solutions to the problem (see Figure 3-24). To implement one of the suggested fixes, all you need to do is click the appropriate fix.

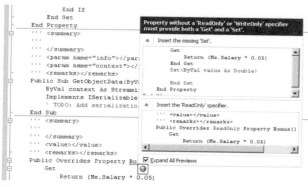

Figure 3-24   Error Correction dialog.

Design-Time Expression Evaluation

The Immediate window in Visual Studio 2005 is enhanced to allow you to test your code without having to execute the application. Assume, for example, that you have built a class in your Visual Basic .NET project and it contains a number of properties and methods. To test this code, you would either add a form or build a console wrapper to instantiate the class. When working in the Immediate window, you can instantiate an instance of the class, set properties on the object, and call its methods. In addition, if you have breakpoints set in your code and call a method or access a property from the Immediate window, execution stops at the breakpoint and allows you to step through the code as if you had explicitly invoked the debugger.

Error List and Task List

Users of earlier versions of Visual Studio will find that the functionality formerly provided entirely in the Task List is now distributed in two separate tool windows. The Error List is a new tool window that displays syntax error messages raised by IntelliSense and build errors reported by the Visual Basic .NET compiler. The scope of the Task List has been reduced in the Visual Studio 2005 IDE to display only reminders of work to be done, such as TODO tasks inserted into your code as comments.

Code Snippets

Code Snippets are another exciting new innovation of the Visual Studio 2005 IDE. This feature lets you insert into the Code Editor templates of code for performing common tasks. For example, imagine you want to add drag-and-drop functionality from a Windows Form control in your application. You might have written this code before on a recent project, but it is unlikely you have committed this to memory. Rather than hunting for the code in an old project file or scouring MSDN or the Web, code snippets let you capture the code in a reusable form that is available to you directly from the Code Editor.

Visual Studio 2005 installs with many useful code snippets categorized by function, as shown in Figure 3-25. These include snippets for reading and writing to files or for validating the format of a date or e-mail strings, just to name a few.

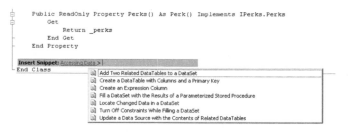

```
     Public ReadOnly Property Perks() As Perk() Implements IPerks.Perks
         Get
             Return _perks
         End Get
     End Property

Insert Snippet: Accessing Data > |
 End Class
```

Add Two Related DataTables to a DataSet
Create a DataTable with Columns and a Primary Key
Create an Expression Column
Fill a DataSet with the Results of a Parameterized Stored Procedure
Locate Changed Data in a DataSet
Turn Off Constraints While Filling a DataSet
Update a Data Source with the Contents of Related DataTables

Figure 3-25   Code snippets.

Code snippets are also validated by scope. This means that only the code snippets that are appropriate for your current position within the code—for example, within a method or function—are available in the menu selections.

Symbolic Renaming

If you're like many developers, when you begin a new Visual Basic .NET project you tend to use the default names for forms and controls and other code elements. Sometime later, when the application has taken shape, you will rename items according to the naming conventions used in your organization. It is a tedious but necessary housekeeping chore if your goal is to write professional code. The symbolic renaming tool helps ease the pain of renaming code elements—and removes the risk of introducing unwanted syntax errors—by providing a simple-to-use method for globally updating names. To use this feature in the Code Editor, right-click an item in the code and select Rename from the context menu, as shown in Figure 3-26.

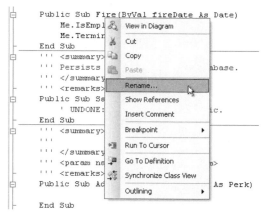

```
     Public Sub Fire(ByVal fireDate As Date)
         Me.IsEmpl        View in Diagram
         Me.Termin
     End Sub            Cut
     ''' <summary>
     ''' Persists        Copy                    base.
     ''' </summary       Paste
     ''' <remarks>
     Public Sub S        Rename...
         ' UNDONE:                                 ic.
     End Sub             Show References
     ''' <summary>       Insert Comment
     '''
     ''' </summary       Breakpoint        ▶
     ''' <param na       Run To Cursor          n>
     ''' <remarks>       Go To Definition
     Public Sub Ad       Synchronize Class View   As Perk)

     End Sub             Outlining         ▶
```

Figure 3-26   Access the symbol Rename tool from the Code Editor.

In the Rename dialog, type the new name of the symbol, as shown in Figure 3-27.

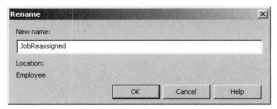

Figure 3-27   The Rename dialog.

Debugger Enhancements

Visual Studio 2005 offers a number of tools for viewing data in the debugging environment. Many of these tools have been around for several versions of Visual Studio (the Watch, Locals, and Autos windows, for example). These tools provide many different views into your application data. Still, you might encounter scenarios where it is still difficult to examine data during debugging. In the sections that follow, we'll explore enhancements to the debugger environment and tools that make it easier for you to diagnose and remedy errors at run time.

DataTips

DataTips have always been an excellent way to quickly view simple data types in the debugger. However, in earlier versions of Visual Studio, for complex data types you saw the name of the type and not the data contained therein, as shown in Figure 3-28. A key improvement to DataTips in Visual Studio 2005 is that they now display the members of complex data types, as shown in Figure 3-29.

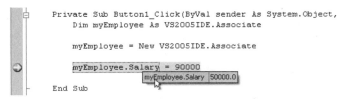

Figure 3-28   Simple data type.

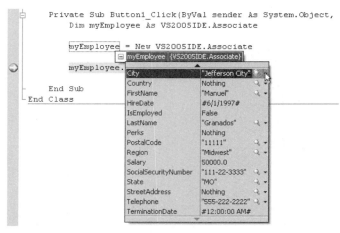

Figure 3-29   Complex data type.

Another enhancement to DataTips is that you get a context menu for both simple types and each member of a complex type. The context menu contains items for adding a watch for the selected type, editing the value for the type, or viewing the hexadecimal value for the type. (See Figure 3-30.)

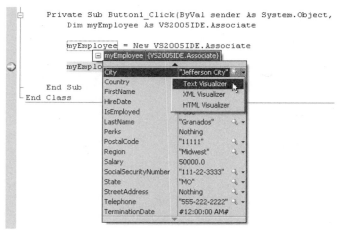

Figure 3-30   DataTip options.

You can also edit member values directly in the DataTip by selecting the value and then typing the new value over it, as shown in Figure 3-31.

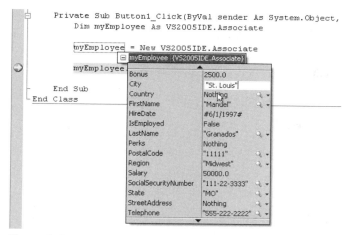

Figure 3-31   Updating a member value.

After you finish changing the member variable, the DataTip automatically displays the updated value, as shown in Figure 3-32.

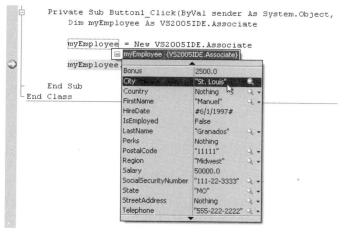

Figure 3-32   The updated member value.

Visualizers

A more sophisticated data inspection tool for the Visual Studio 2005 debugger is the *visualizer*. A visualizer is a dialog box that displays a variable or object in a way that makes sense for a particular data type. String variables, for example, can be visualized as HTML, XML, or plain text by using one of the four default visualizers included with Visual Studio 2005.

All the various debugging tools—DataTips, the Watch window, the Locals window, or the Autos window—display a magnifying glass icon beside a data type that can be viewed using a visualizer. Clicking the magnifying glass allows you to select a visualizer to display the data type of the corresponding object.

In addition to the three text-based visualizers just mentioned, a dataset visualizer is also included by default to let you more easily inspect data contained in a dataset.

Tip   Additional visualizers might be available for download from Microsoft in the future.

Exception Assistant

The Exception Assistant is a new debugging tool introduced with Visual Studio 2005. When a run-time exception occurs, it appears as a dialog box displaying details about the error. Significantly, the Exception Assistant dialog box also includes troubleshooting tips for handling the exception.

The dialog box title bar displays the type of the error, and below that, a description of the error. At the top of the assistant is the troubleshooting tips section, which in most cases will provide links to help content to aid you in diagnosing the problem. In many cases, however, the assistant will offer step-by-step instructions for correcting the error.

Customizing Data Display

Visual Studio 2005 offers several options for customizing the display of data in the debugger. The following section reviews three techniques you can use to manipulate the way data is displayed in the debugger.

Override the ToString Method of Custom Types

The simplest technique for altering the data displayed in the debugger for a custom type is to override the base object *ToString* method, as follows:

```
Overrides Function ToString() As String
    Return Me.FirstName & " " & Me.LastName
End Function
```

Using the Debugger Display Attributes

Other situations call for more control of how the data is displayed. You might want to format the underlying data differently or limit the amount of data presented in the debugger. The .NET Framework provides three attribute classes for controlling how data is displayed in the debugger:

- *DebuggerDisplayAttribute* Apply this attribute to add a summary to a type within the data windows in the debugger. For example, the following code shows how to add a summary to a custom data type:

```
<DebuggerDisplay("Associate ( { FullName } ") >_
Public Class Associate
Private FullName as String
    . . .
End Class
```

The constructor for the *DebuggerDisplayAttribute* accepts a string format specification. The text inside the curly braces can represent a property or method of the containing class. Note that you can use both private and public members of the class.

- *DebuggerBrowsableAttribute*   Apply this attribute to a member in a class to control whether or not it is displayed in the debugger.

```
Public Class Associate
    <DebuggerBrowsable( False ) > _
    Public Property SocialSecurityNumber As String
        . . .
    End Property
End Class
```

In the preceding pseudo code, the *DebuggerBrowsableAttribute* applied to the *SocialSecurityNumber* property of the *Associate* class will prevent that property from displaying in the debugger windows.

- *DebuggerTypeProxyAttribute*   This attribute provides the most flexibility by allowing you to substitute the attributed member with a custom debugger type.

```
<DebuggerTypeProxy( GetType( AssociateProxy ) )> _
Public Class Associate
    . . .
End Class
```

The input parameter for the *DebuggerTypeProxyAttribute* constructor specifies the class used as a proxy for displaying data of that type. As a best practice, you should implement the proxy class as a nested internal class of the data type to which it is applied. By doing this, the nested class can have full access to the private members of the type it is describing.

Walkthrough

This walkthrough demonstrates how you can use the Class Designer to build and visually construct a class hierarchy.

The application is a class library designed to represent data entities for a fictitious professional services company. The class represents two types of employee entities, a partner and an associate. These entities are modeled in the class library using the *Partner* and *Associate* classes, respectively. Because they share a number of common attributes and operations, the *Partner* and *Associate* classes each derive from a base *Employee* class, which, in turn derives from its own base class named *Person*.

In addition, the design calls for the *Partner* and *Associate* classes to be serializable and for the classes themselves to execute custom code during the serialization process. To achieve that goal, both classes implement the *ISerializable* interface, contained in the *System.Runtime.Serialization* namespace.

The abstract *Employee* class also implements a custom interface named *IPerks*, which is included in the project. This interface satisfies a design goal for the project of providing a way to model benefits for different categories of employees, so the implementation of this interface can differ for any type derived from the *Employee* class.

Included in the project file is the file ClassDiagram1.cd, which was generated by the Class Designer tool. If you open this file in the document window of Visual Studio 2005, you will see that it provides a visual representation of the object hierarchy for the class library. Although this particular sample is relatively simple, the diagram allows you to immediately understand the relationship of the various classes in the class library. You can also use the Class Designer to change any of the properties or relationships of the classes. Because the Class Designer is tightly integrated with the Visual Studio 2005 IDE, any changes you make to the objects in the diagram will be reflected immediately in the underlying code files.

Conclusion

The Visual Studio 2005 integrated development environment includes a number of new and improved productivity features. The IDE has also been redesigned with a view toward providing developers with more direct access to the .NET Framework components, such as the new settings and resource architecture.

Chapter 4

Building Datacentric Applications

Chapter 1 introduced you to the basics of ADO.NET and how data access has changed from Visual Basic 6. These next four applications introduce you to the enhancements in Visual Studio 2005 and the .NET Framework 2.0 for building datacentric applications. ADO.NET is a big topic and could easily fill an entire book on its own. These applications are intended as starting points from which you can further research ADO.NET using the MSDN documentation and online resources such as *http://msdn.microsoft.com.*

One of the most common frustrations for developers is having to learn new versions of a product that make older components obsolete or significantly change the way to do common tasks. The inevitable learning curve can often negatively affect productivity in the short term.

Microsoft set a goal for ADO.NET 2.0: enhance and extend it without changing it or breaking what already works. The same functionality from 1.1 is still available in version 2.0, but there are now more productive ways of performing common database tasks. For example, the Data Sources window provides a central place to create and configure the related objects required to access a data source (for example, SQL Server). Smart tags added to controls provide fast access to common development tasks, such as changing the type of a control (for example, changing *TextBox* to *Label*). You can also use smart tags to reconfigure data sources and even create new queries to pull out filtered data based on user input (that is, create parameterized queries).

After exploring the next four applications, you will see how Microsoft Visual Studio 2005 and the .NET Framework 2.0 enhance productivity and make connecting to data sources from your application much easier than with previous development tools.

Application: Table Adapters and the DataConnector Class

In this first application, you are introduced to the new Table Adapter and *DataConnector* classes. These two classes will help to simplify your ADO.NET development tasks by providing powerful features that you can use in your application right away while, at the same time, limiting the amount of code that you have to manually write to perform common tasks.

New Concepts

As mentioned in Chapter 1, a primary design goal for ADO.NET was first-class support for working with disconnected data. ADO.NET provides an intuitive way of dealing with disconnected data through a set of classes that are separated into various namespaces. You do not need to know every class of every namespace to effectively use ADO.NET. Instead, you can concentrate on the namespace containing the classes required to access your particular data source. Table 4-1 lists some of the most common namespaces and classes that make up ADO.NET.

Table 4-1   ADO.NET Namespaces

Namespace	Purpose	Common Classes
System.Data	General classes used throughout ADO.NET	*DataSet, DataTable,* and *DataView*
System.Data.Common	New set of base classes that are used by the different data providers in ADO.NET (such as *SqlClient, OleDb,* and so on)	*DataAdapter, DbCommand,* and *DbConnection*
System.Data.SqlClient	Contains the data provider classes for connecting to Microsoft SQL Server	*SqlConnection, SqlCommand,* and *SqlDataAdapter*
System.Data.SqlTypes	Consists of classes used to represent the native data types used in SQL Server	*SqlString, SqlDateTime,* and *SqlInt32*
System.Data.OleDb	Consists of classes that are used to access OLE DB data sources	*OleDbConnection, OleDbCommand,* and *OleDbDataAdapter*
System.Data.ODBC	Classes used to connect to ODBC data sources	*OdbcConnection, OdbcCommand,* and *OdbcDataAdapter*
System.Data.OracleClient	Classes used to access Oracle data sources	*OracleConnection, OracleCommand,* and *OracleDataAdapter*
System.Xml	Consists of classes that provide standards-based support for accessing and working with XML as data	*XmlAdapter, XmlReader,* and *XmlWriter*

System.Data.DataSet

A *DataSet* object is used to hold data from one or more data sources. It maintains the data as a set of tables with optional relationships defined between those tables. The *DataSet* class is meant to be generic, so it is not tied to any specific type of data source. Data can be loaded into a *DataSet* from many data sources, including Microsoft SQL Server, Oracle databases, Microsoft Access, Microsoft Exchange, Microsoft Active Directory, or any OLE DB or ODBC-compliant data source.

Although not tied to any specific data source, the *DataSet* class is designed to hold relational tabular data as you would find in a relational database such as Microsoft SQL Server. Figure 4-1 is a visual representation of two related tables in a *DataSet*.

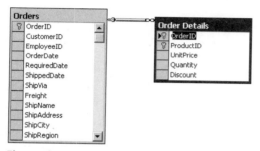

Figure 4-1   Visual representation of two related tables in a DataSet.

Each table shown in Figure 4-1 is realized in the *DataSet* as a *DataTable*. The relationship between the two tables is realized in the *DataSet* as a *DataRelation* object. The *DataRelation* object provides the information that relates a child table to a parent table via a foreign key. Keep in mind that Figure 4-1 is merely a visual representation of the structure of a specific instance of a *DataSet*. A *DataSet* can hold any number of tables with any number of relationships defined between them.

Figure 4-1 is actually a screen capture of the new DataSet Designer in Visual Studio 2005. Figure 4-2 shows the DataSet Designer being used to edit the structure of a data source in the new Data Sources window. The DataSet Designer is discussed further in the "Walkthrough" section for this application that appears later in the chapter.

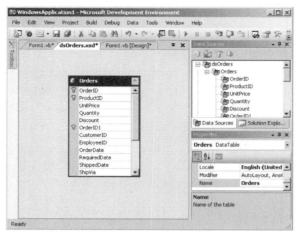

Figure 4-2   Using the DataSet Designer to edit a data source.

Retrieving Data from a Database

Although there are several ways to use a *DataSet*, the most common use is to connect to a database and fill a *DataSet* with data from the database. In ADO.NET, each data provider (*SqlClient*, *OleDb*, and so on) provides a set of specialized classes for interacting with a data source. To retrieve data from a database, you connect to the database, execute a query or stored procedure, and then populate the *DataSet* with the results. To do all this requires a set of objects that work together, including connection and command objects.

Each ADO.NET data provider includes a specialized connection class for connecting to its supported data source types. For example, the *SqlConnection* class allows your applications to connect to SQL Server 7.0 or higher. You could also use an *OleDbConnection* object, but the *SqlConnection* class is optimized for working with SQL Server, making it a better choice. For data sources that do not have a specific ADO.NET data provider, you can use an *OleDbConnection* object as long as there is an OLE DB provider available for the data source. The *OleDbConnection* class is what you would use to connect to nondatabase data sources such as delimited text files.

Once you have established a connection to the data source, additional objects from the data provider have to pull data from the data source and use it to populate a *DataSet*. The way to populate a *DataSet* in Visual Studio .NET 2003 is to use a data adapter object to fill the *DataSet* with data. Each ADO.NET data provider includes its own unique data adapter class. The *SqlClient* provider, for example, includes the *SqlDataAdapter* class. The *SqlDataAdapter* class requires a *SqlCommand* object and a *SqlConnection* object in order to retrieve data. You can provide a SELECT statement or a stored procedure to the data adapter and have it generate its own *SqlCommand* object, or you can explicitly create your own *SqlCommand* object for selecting data and assign it to the *SelectCommand* property of the *SqlDataAdapter*. Calling the *Fill* method of the data adapter tells the data adapter to execute its *SelectCommand* and fill the *DataSet* with the data retrieved by the *SelectCommand*. The following code is an example of filling a *DataSet* with data by using a *SqlDataAdapter*.

```
Dim conn As New SqlConnection
conn.ConnectionString = _
    "server=(local);database=Northwind;Trusted_Connection=True"

Dim adapter As SqlDataAdapter
adapter = New SqlDataAdapter("SELECT * FROM Products", conn)

Dim dsProducts As New DataSet

conn.Open()
adapter.Fill(dsProducts)

conn.Close()
```

Prior to Visual Studio 2005, the data adapter was the only link between the *DataSet* and the actual data source. If you made changes to the data in the *DataSet*, you required a different data adapter for each table in the *DataSet* and had to call the *Update* method of each data adapter.

Although the data adapter approach for reading and updating data is completely supported in Visual Studio 2005, there are also some new ways to read and write data that reduce and simplify the code that you have to write. In this application, you will see how to establish a database connection and retrieve data from the Northwind database by writing only one line of code. This application highlights some new data components and features in Visual Studio 2005 and the .NET Framework 2.0, including table adapters and the *DataConnector* class.

Walkthrough

With Visual Studio 2005, you can create data-driven applications that present your data in a data grid with just one line of code. Of course, more information is required than what is contained in that one line of code. But the tedious work of writing lines and lines of code for setting up the database connection, filling multiple data tables one at a time, and doing the data binding is all handled for you by Visual Studio 2005. Two new IDE features, the Data Sources window and the Data Source Configuration Wizard, assist you in setting up data access by using the new classes, such as *DataConnector*.

This application begins as a new Windows application named NorthwindGrid. Depending on your IDE settings, Visual Studio 2005 might not display the Data Sources window automatically. If the Data Sources window is not displayed, you can select the Data | Show Data Sources menu command. You will then have a new floating window displayed that you can dock in the IDE as shown in Figure 4-3.

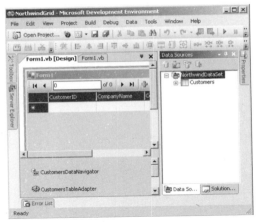

Figure 4-3   The Data Sources window.

Once you have docked the Data Sources window, select the Data Sources tab to make it the active window and either click the Add New Data Source link or the Add New Data Source button on the window's toolbar. This will display the opening page of the Data Source Configuration Wizard. Read the welcome message and then click Next to start the configuration of your data source as shown in Figure 4-4.

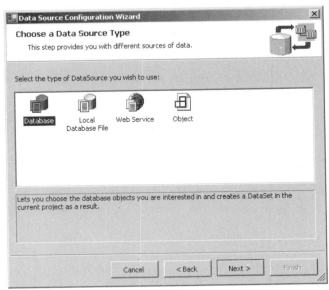

Figure 4-4   The Data Source Configuration Wizard.

The Data Source Configuration Wizard supports four types of data sources. The first option, Database, allows you to create a data source for a database server on your local computer or on a remote server. The second option, Local Database File, allows you to choose either an .MDF SQL Server database file or a Microsoft Access .MDB file. If your data will come from a Web service, you can select the third option to add a new Web Reference to your project. The fourth option is Object. This option allows you to bind your user interface to one of your own classes. Object data sources are covered later in the "Application: Object Data Source" section. This application uses a database data source.

The next step in the Data Source Configuration Wizard is to either select an existing connection or create a new connection for your data source. The first time you run the wizard there are no pre-existing connections available. But on subsequent uses of the wizard you can choose to reuse previously created connections. When you click the New Connection button in the wizard, the Connection Properties dialog is displayed, as shown in Figure 4-5. You can use this dialog to configure all the settings for connecting to your database server.

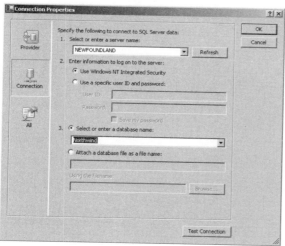

Figure 4-5   The Connection Properties dialog.

The wizard will give you the option to save the resulting connection string to the application configuration file (app.config). If you will use the same connection again in your project, having the connection string saved to app.config automatically is very convenient.

The next configuration step in the wizard, shown in Figure 4-6, asks you to choose the database objects for this data source. You can choose to select any number of tables, views, stored procedures, and functions.

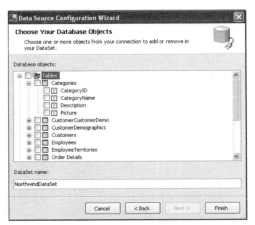

Figure 4-6   Selecting database objects in the wizard.

When you select a database object such as a table, you can expand its node in the tree view (seen in Figure 4-6) and choose to select only specific columns from that table. After you select your database objects, the wizard will build your SELECT statements (or stored procedure and function calls) for you automatically.

After the Data Source Configuration Wizard is finished, a new data source is added to the Data Sources window. (For an example, see Figure 4-3.) The Data Sources window displays the data source as a tree view with a root *DataSet* node containing a node for each database object (table, view, and so on) selected in the Data Source Configuration Wizard. If you expand one of those tables, as shown in Figure 4-7, you see that only the fields selected in the Data Source Configuration Wizard are included in the *DataSet*.

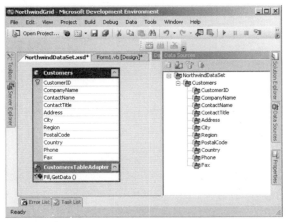

Figure 4-7   DataSet expanded in the Data Sources window.

If you want to display the data from one of the tables in a grid on a form, you simply drag the appropriate node from the Data Sources window to your form. Visual Studio 2005 will automatically create a data-bound *DataGridView* control and an accompanying navigation bar at the top of the form. The resulting form is shown in Figure 4-8.

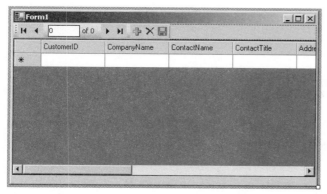

Figure 4-8   A form with a data-bound DataGridView control at design time.

If you have used Visual Studio .NET 2003 to create data-driven applications, you have probably dragged a data adapter onto a form at some point and gone through the Data Adapter
Configuration Wizard. The Data Adapter Configuration Wizard places connection and data
adapter objects in the component tray of your form. Visual Studio 2005 adds four objects to
the component tray: a *DataSet*, a *DataConnector*, a table adapter, and a *DataNavigator*.

> **Note**   The component tray is a special area in the IDE that displays controls hosted on a
> Windows or Web form that do not have a user interface. In Visual Basic 6, controls without a
> user interface (for example, *Timer*) still had to be placed on the form design surface, making
> design-time control placement awkward.

The *DataSet* added to the form in this application is simply an instance of the *DataSet* class
that was created automatically when the data source was created.

DataConnector

The *DataConnector* is a new class in the .NET Framework 2.0. It acts as a data source for other
controls to bind to. The data it exposes is the data that the *DataConnector* consumes from its
own data source. The quintessential use for a *DataConnector* is to connect data-bound controls
with one table in a data source (for example, a *DataTable* in a *DataSet* defined in the Data
Sources window). Without a *DataConnector* component, binding a *DataGridView* control to
only one table in a *DataSet* would require writing code. But by using a *DataConnector* control,
you can configure the data source of the *DataConnector* to be a single table from the *DataSet*.
Then you bind your *DataGridView* to the *DataConnector*. Thus you can see the origin of the
name *DataConnector*—it helps to connect components or controls with a subset of the data in
a *DataSet*. The *DataConnector* can also pass commands from the data consumer through to
the data source.

Table Adapters

Table adapters are new to Visual Studio 2005. They are designer-generated components that connect your *DataSet* objects with their underlying data sources. When you create data components in an application, such as through the Data Source Configuration Wizard, one or more custom table adapters are created automatically. Table adapters are similar to data adapters, but they are strongly typed, which means each table adapter is a unique class that is automatically generated by Visual Studio 2005 to work with only the fields you have selected for a specific database object (for example, a Products table).

When you create a database application using ADO.NET, you generally make extensive use of *DataSet* objects. A *DataSet* holds your data, but it relies on other objects to move data to and from the underlying data source. In the .NET Framework 1.1, data adapter objects were the lifeline to the data source and you had to create a data adapter for every *DataTable* in your *DataSet*. For example, if you were to create a *DataSet* to hold the Orders and Order Details tables from the Northwind database, you would need two data adapters.

The new table adapters in the .NET Framework 2.0 are unlike data adapters in that they can contain multiple queries to support multiple tables from a data source, allowing one table adapter to update multiple tables in your *DataSet*. Using a table adapter for the previous example, you would have one table adapter with two queries: one for the Orders table and one for the Order Details table. In this application, there is only one query in the table adapter (for the Customers table). If you right-click the Customers table in the Data Sources window and select Edit Data Source With Designer, the structure of the data returned for Customers is opened in the DataSet Designer as shown in Figure 4-9.

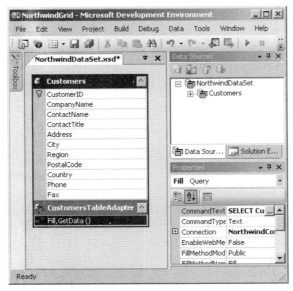

Figure 4-9   The CustomersTableAdapter query.

As you can see in Figure 4-9, there is an item labeled Fill,GetData() at the bottom of the Customers table. This item contains the connection and query information for the Customers table in the table adapter. If you look at the *CommandText* property (in the Properties window), you can see the start of the SELECT statement used to populate the Customers table.

If you require filtered views of the data for a table, you can create additional queries to fill the table in the *DataSet*. For this application, you would right-click the CustomersTableAdapter heading of the Customers table (shown in Figure 4-9) and select the Add Query menu command.

> **Note**   If you create multiple queries in the table adapter, you must ensure that the returned data maps correctly to the table schema; otherwise, the query will fail.

DataNavigator

The new *DataNavigator* component provides services for navigating through data that is bound to user interface controls. The services it provides are somewhat analogous to the Data control from Visual Basic 6 that provided navigation services via a set of navigation buttons. The *DataNavigator* component in ADO.NET is designed to allow navigation among the records in a *DataSet*. It also provides services that allow for adding, editing, and deleting the data.

The functionality of the *DataNavigator* control is exposed through one or more *ToolStrip* controls, shown previously in Figure 4-8. The *ToolStrip* buttons perform tasks such as adding and deleting records.

If you have used the previous versions of ADO.NET, you know that navigation through records in a *DataSet* was not as simple as it could have been. With an ADO *Recordset*, you had *MoveFirst*, *MovePrevious*, *MoveNext*, and *MoveLast* methods that allowed navigation through the *Recordset* data. These navigation features were made possible through the use of a cursor that was used to maintain your current position in the *Recordset* and to navigate through the records. The ADO.NET *DataSet*, which replaced the *Recordset* object as the central record-based data object, has no cursor, nor does it have any knowledge of the data store from which its contents came. Without a cursor or equivalent object to maintain position, navigation was not so easy.

Binding controls on a form to your ADO.NET *DataSet* and providing navigation services that keep all controls in sync is accomplished through the use of two objects known as the *CurrencyManager* and the *BindingContext*. For each data-bound form that you have in your application, you will have at least one *BindingContext* object. This object will be responsible for any *CurrencyManager* objects that exist. You will have one *CurrencyManager* object for each data source on your form. The *CurrencyManager* object is responsible for keeping track of your position in the *DataSet* and for the overall supervision of the bindings to the data source. You call the necessary methods on the *CurrencyManager* object to navigate through the records, and the *BindingContext* ensures that all bound controls are kept in sync. The *DataNavigator* control used in this application provides that functionality in an easier-to-use form.

The components for this application are created and wired together using the visual designer. The navigation bar will function correctly without any code. The only code needed is one line that uses the table adapter to fill a *DataSet* by pulling data from the data source. This is done in the *Load* event handler for the form as follows:

```
Private Sub Form1_Load(ByVal sender As System.Object, _
                  ByVal e As System.EventArgs) Handles MyBase.Load
    Me.CustomersTableAdapter.Fill(Me.NorthwindDataSet.Customers)
End Sub
```

This event handler and the code to fill the dataset and populate the grid are added automatically by Visual Studio 2005. All you have to do is press F5 and see a grid of data loaded from a database. What is accomplished in this application is no small feat, despite the deceptive simplicity of just pointing and clicking. If you look at the *InitializeComponent* method, you will see approximately 300 lines of code that you don't have to write—a substantial productivity enhancement!

Although there is a lot happening, this application is somewhat simple. It shows the basics of connecting to a database and populating a grid control. The remaining data applications will highlight other aspects of ADO.NET in Visual Studio 2005.

The DataSet Designer

It is worth taking some time at this point to look more closely at the DataSet Designer. This utility has been significantly overhauled and is one of the more prominent enhancements to data access in Visual Studio 2005.

In Visual Studio .NET 2003, when you wanted to edit the structure of a *DataSet*, you did so by editing an XML Schema (XSD). Although there was a visual designer, the terminology and user interface were not consistent with a *DataSet* and its constituent objects (for example, a *DataTable*).

With the new Data Sources window, you can right-click it and choose Edit Data Source with Designer. This will open the Dataset Designer and allow you to make changes to the structure of the *DataSet*. With this view of the *DataSet*, you can graphically manipulate the tables and queries in a manner more directly tied to the *DataSet* rather than having to deal with an XML Schema.

To help you understand some of the capabilities of the Dataset Designer, consider a potential issue that can arise in just about any application that will deal with data from a database. There can be times when you have forgotten to add a table that is required for an application to display data. With Visual Studio 2005, you can simply add the missing table in the DataSet Designer window by right-clicking a blank area of the designer surface and choosing Add | Data Component. The designer adds a new table to the DataSet Designer window and opens the Data Component Configuration Wizard.

The Data Component Configuration Wizard is similar to part of the Data Source Configuration Wizard. The Data Component Configuration Wizard prompts you to set up a connection to the data source for the new table and to provide or select queries or stored procedures for data read and write operations. From the wizard, you can launch a QueryBuilder to create a query graphical interface. The tables, views, and functions in the database are available in the QueryBuilder as shown in Figure 4-10.

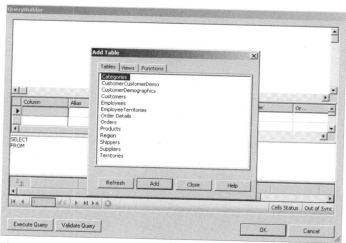

Figure 4-10   The graphical QueryBuilder.

After setting up queries in the wizard, you can choose to have several specialized methods added to your *DataSet*. The *Fill* method, which you can rename as required, is used to populate the table with data. The *GetData* method, which you can also rename as required, returns a reference to a populated instance of the *DataTable*. You can also choose to have methods created for updating the data source with data changes. The wizard page is shown in Figure 4-11.

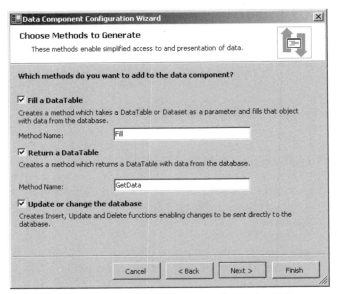

Figure 4-11 The Data Component Configuration Wizard.

When you add a new table to the *DataSet*, the wizard reads the database schema and adds any appropriate relationships to tables that are already in the *DataSet*. These relationships are represented as lines between tables in the DataSet Designer, as shown in Figure 4-12.

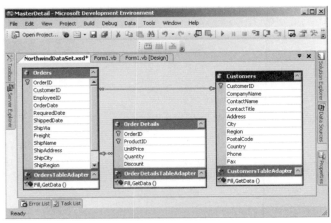

Figure 4-12 Related tables in the DataSet Designer.

One aspect of the designer that can be disconcerting is that the relationship line merely depicts the fact that the two tables are related. But obviously the relationship must be between fields in the table. A visual inspection of the fields in each table can usually make the relationship evident. But if the field list is extremely long, it can be harder to quickly infer the relationship. Fortunately, the designer provides a feature that lets you more clearly indicate the relationship graphically by displaying and editing a label. If you right-click a relationship line and select Show Relation Labels, the relationship name is displayed in the visual designer.

The default name FK_Orders_Customers does not indicate how the Orders and Customers tables are related—it simply tells you that there is a relationship between the two tables. To edit the label so that it indicates a relationship, right-click the relationship line and choose Edit Relationship. This opens the Relation dialog shown in Figure 4-13.

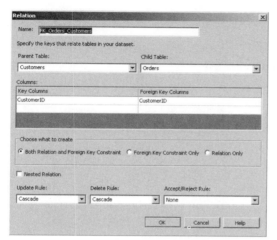

Figure 4-13   The Relation dialog for editing relationships.

The Relation dialog lets you manage the relationship, including the tables and columns that make up the relationship. Changing the name of the relationship will change the label displayed in the DataSet Designer. Changing the name of the relationship to Customers_CustomerID_Orders would make the relationship more self-explanatory, as it expresses that the tables are related on the CustomerID field.

The Relation dialog also allows you to change the type of relationship (foreign key constraint, relation, or both) and what happens to related records when a parent record is updated or deleted (that is, do we use cascading, does it become *SetNull*, *SetDefault*, or does nothing happen). You can also configure the relationship so that changes are automatically accepted or rejected in child records when changes to the parent record are accepted or rejected.

Conclusion

As you can see from this application, Visual Studio 2005 makes data access and display using a grid very easy to configure. The new table adapter model bundles together database connection, command, and data adapter objects, providing a simplified programming model for data-driven applications. With one simple line of code and a few mouse clicks, you have a working database application that will allow database updates, additions, and deletions. And the new DataSet Designer allows you to configure the settings and edit the structure (and subsequent behavior) of your data sources with an easy-to-use visual designer.

The new *DataConnector* class acts as an intermediary between data access objects and data-consuming objects. The new *DataNavigator* component provides navigation services for moving between, adding, and deleting records. A *DataNavigator* component manages *ToolStrip* controls that provide the user interface for moving through records of data. This application uses all these new features to create a useful and practical data-driven user interface with only one line of code entered by hand.

Application: Smart Tags for Data

Smart tags are new features in Visual Studio 2005 that provide easy access to common tasks. This application uses new smart tags for data-bound controls to create and configure the user interface.

New Concepts

Smart tags are generally an entry point into wizards or other tools that let you configure certain aspects of your data sources or data components. Smart tags provide fast access to the most common tasks that developers perform on different types of controls and components. Smart tags are accessible via a small icon that appears when you select or hover your cursor over a control.

Walkthrough

This application consists of a data-bound form that shows data from the Suppliers table in the Northwind database one record at a time (Details view). The purpose of this walkthrough is to explain smart tags. The side effect of completing this walkthrough is that you end up with a working application, but the application itself is not the point of this section. The next application discusses detail and master-details data forms in more detail.

The Data Sources window will be used to add a new data source that points to the Northwind database.

Master-Details Forms

If you select a table in the Data Sources window, a drop-down arrow will appear with a list of view options from which you can select. The default is *DataGridView*, which is used in the Table Adapters and DataConnector application presented earlier. One of the other options in the drop-down list is Details, as shown in Figure 4-14. If you configure a table in the Data Sources window to use the Details view, dragging the table onto a form will prompt Visual Studio 2005 to create individual controls for each field and a *DataNavigator* component for navigating through the records, as shown in Figure 4-15.

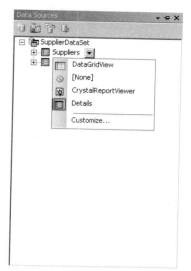

Figure 4-14 Changing the type of user interface created from a Data Source table.

Figure 4-15 A Details view user interface.

In some data-driven applications, users need to see primary key data. In this application, the user sees the *SupplierID* value, which is a primary key field that is auto-generated by the database. Because users should not change this value, the user interface should not enable them to enter a new value. In most cases, you would simply disable the *TextBox* control or change it to a *Label* control. However, with smart tags, you can change a control to another type of control and maintain the data binding with just a few mouse clicks. In this application, the *SupplierID TextBox* control, shown in Figure 4-15, is to be changed to a *Label* control. Instead of deleting the *TextBox* control, adding a *Label* control, and then rebinding the *Label* to the appropriate data source, you can simply select the smart tag arrow for the *TextBox* control and select Label from the Convert To drop-down list, as shown in Figure 4-16. This will change the *TextBox* to a *Label* control, which will prevent data modification in that control but still keep the data source wiring in place.

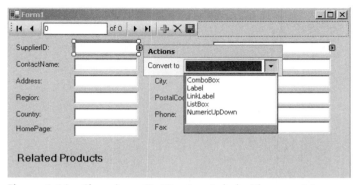

Figure 4-16   Changing a TextBox to a Label with a smart tag.

Smart tags are inherently context-aware. For data-bound controls, even the data type of the underlying data source is used to determine what the smart tag should (or should not) make available. For example, if you select the *Convert To* drop-down list via the smart tag for a control that is bound to an underlying integer field, the list of available controls are appropriate for integer data. If you use the smart tag for the *SupplierID TextBox*, you can convert to a *ComboBox*, *LinkLabel*, *ListBox*, *NumericUpDown*, or *Label*. Because the underlying data type is numeric, *NumericUpDown* is a valid control type that can display that data.

Master-Details Forms

A more powerful smart tag feature in Visual Studio 2005 is the ability to create master-details forms. With this feature, you can transform, with relative ease, a simple Details view form into a more complex master-details data form.

This application uses two related Details views on the same form: a parent section for suppliers and a child section for products supplied by each supplier. The resulting form is shown in Figure 4-17.

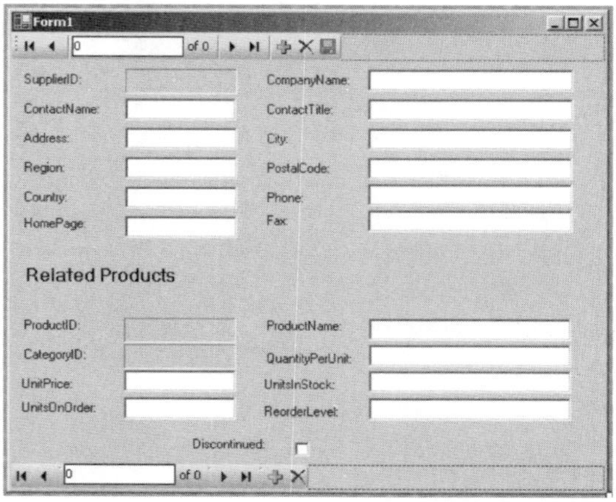

Figure 4-17   Master-details view created with smart tags.

Starting from the original form shown in Figure 4-15, you can use smart tags to create and configure the details section to create a form like that in Figure 4-17. In this application, *SupplierID* is the link between the Suppliers table and the Products table. You will need to use the smart tags for the *DataConnector* to enable the Master Details functionality of this application. When you open the smart tag for the *SuppliersDataConnector* control, you see an option to Configure Master Details as shown in Figure 4-18. Selecting this option opens the Add Related Databound UI dialog box shown in Figure 4-19.

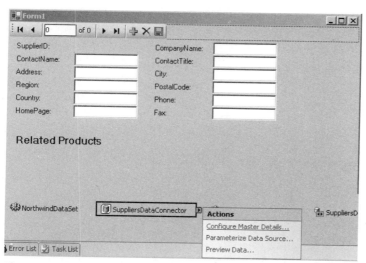

Figure 4-18   Creating a master-details form by using smart tags.

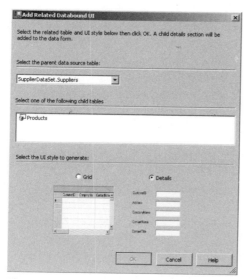

Figure 4-19   The Add Related Databound UI dialog.

When the dialog opens, you will find that there are no values selected in the drop-down list of data sources. Select the appropriate table from the data source drop-down list and Visual Studio 2005 will automatically display related tables in the Child tables section of the dialog. In this case, the Products table is related to the Suppliers table on the *SupplierID* field.

This application uses a Details view to have the products displayed one record at a time (rather than in a grid), so be sure to select the Details view. This means that some method is needed to control the navigation through the products for each supplier. This navigation is handled by a second *DataNavigator* component. Navigation controls are placed on forms in a *RaftingContainer*, which is a flow layout control that holds toolbar-type strip controls such as a *ToolStrip* bar. You can add a new *DataNavigator* to your form by double-clicking *DataNavigator* in the toolbox. You then set the *Raft* property of the *DataNavigator* to one of the pre-existing *RaftContainer* controls (Top, Bottom, Left, or Right). You also have to tie the *DataConnector* property of the new *DataNavigator* to the *DataConnector* that Visual Studio 2005 automatically created for products filtered by *SupplierID* (*FK_Products_SuppliersDataConnector*), which is a part of the relationship created with the Add Related Databound UI dialog (see Figure 4-19).

After adding the details section to the form, you should notice that Visual Studio has added one line of code to the *Load* event handler for the form to populate the Products table in the *DataSet*:

```
Me.ProductsTableAdapter.Fill(Me.NorthwindDataSet.Products)
```

When you run this application, you can navigate through the suppliers and see the first product record change for each supplier. You can then navigate through each product record for each supplier.

Conclusion

Although there are not many smart tags for data controls, you can see that they make development of datacentric applications in Visual Studio 2005 much easier than in Visual Basic 6 or even Visual Studio .NET 2003. This application introduced smart tags and some common tasks you can accomplish with them. The walkthrough of the next application includes the use of smart tags to create parameterized queries to easily filter your result sets.

Application: Master-Details Forms and Parameterized Queries

Most data-driven applications require more than simply binding one table to one grid control. Your data sources are more likely to contain multiple related tables. As a result, you will often find yourself creating applications that need to make use of a master-details view of the data. And a simple one-at-a-time navigation scheme is rarely enough for users to work with real-world quantities of data. Users need to be able to search and filter records. This application shows how you can use new data features to build better data applications faster.

New Concepts

Visual Studio 2005 and the .NET Framework 2.0 contain a number of new features that make it easier to create master-details views of your data. After creating a set of data-bound controls, you can have Visual Studio 2005 automatically create either a grid or Details view of child records in a related table with only one line of code required to fill the *DataSet* with data from the related table.

If you use the default settings when creating your data source and data-bound controls, your applications will show users all the data in your application. An important feature is the ability for users to enter search criteria and see only data that matches the search criteria. With the new Search Criteria Builder in Visual Studio 2005, you can add a parameterized query to your application and a user interface for searching and filtering data without writing any code!

Walkthrough

In this application, order data from the Northwind database is displayed for each customer by using a master-details view. This setup requires data from two tables from the database to be displayed on a form. The two tables are related in the database already, so Visual Studio 2005 will detect the relationship. However, you have to provide some additional information to ensure that the appropriate orders are displayed when you navigate from one customer to the next.

Application User Interface

The application is a standard Windows application that contains a master-details form with customer information (master data) at the top of the form bound to individual controls. The customer orders (detail data) are displayed in a grid. Figure 4-20 shows the application user interface.

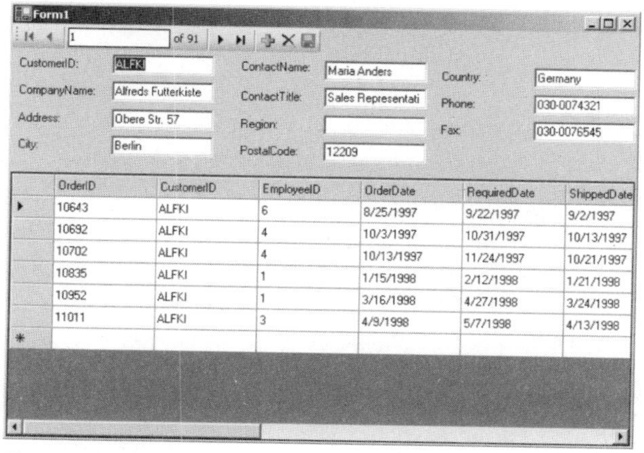

Figure 4-20   The application user interface.

Using a grid control for the orders allows the user to see more orders for a customer simultaneously. A Details view section can also display one record at a time, but the approach used for this application is standard in many line-of-business applications.

The first step in creating a master-details form is to configure a data source. One nice feature of Visual Studio 2005 is its ability to remember previously created connection strings, which you can select from rather than redoing the same configuration setup. This feature is one of many small but useful productivity enhancements that you will find in Visual Studio 2005.

The data for this application comes from the Orders and Customers tables from the Northwind database. After the data source has been created in the Data Sources window (as described in the previous application), controls can be added to a form. Some controls will be bound to the master data, and some controls will be bound to the detail data. And then the crucial link has to be established between the master data and the detail data so that only the orders for the currently selected customer are displayed.

In the Table Adapters and DataConnector application, a *DataTable* was dragged onto a form from the Data Sources window and a grid control was created automatically. A grid view is the default view in Visual Studio 2005, but it is not the only option when using the Data Sources window to automatically generate controls. If you select a table in the Data Sources window, a drop-down arrow will appear that provides a list from which you select different view options. The default view is *DataGridView*, which is used in the Table Adapters and DataConnector application and which will be used for the details section of this application. One option in the drop-down list is Details. If you configure a table in the Data Sources window to use Details view, dragging the table onto a form will prompt Visual Studio 2005 to create individual controls for each field and a *DataNavigator* component for navigating through the records.

Once the master section is on the form, you can provide the linking information between the master data (customer information) and the detail data (customer orders). Visual Studio 2005 makes this extremely easy, especially compared to the process of linking data together manually using Visual Studio .NET 2003. First you select the *DataConnector* that exposes the parent data that will be related to the child data. In this application, it is the *CustomerDataConnector* that will be used. Setting up the related data here can be done either from the Data menu or via one of the new smart tag operations. When you open the smart tag, one of the options is Configure Master Details. Selecting that smart tag operation opens the dialog window shown in Figure 4-21.

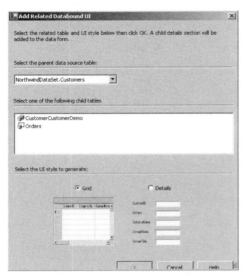

Figure 4-21 Adding relationships to data-bound items on the form by using the Configure Master Details option.

From this dialog window, you first select the parent table from the drop-down list, and then select the child table. Next, you decide whether to display the child rows as a grid or in Details view. In this application, Customers is the parent table and Orders is the related child table. The child data is displayed using a grid.

After closing the dialog window, the Orders grid is added to the form automatically. Table adapter and *DataConnector* components are also added to the form. The table adapter, named *OrdersTableAdapter* in this application, provides the logic for filling a *DataSet* with order data. The *DataConnector* serves as the data source for the *DataGridView* control that displays the order data.

To display any data in this application, the tables in the *DataSet* must be filled with data. There are two table adapters in this application: one for customer data, and one for order data. When the *Fill* method is called on a table adapter, the table adapter fills its corresponding table in the *DataSet* with data from the database. To fill both tables in this application, you have to call the *Fill* method for each table adapter. The following code in the *Form1_Load* event handler calls both *Fill* methods:

```
Me.CustomersTableAdapter.Fill(Me.NorthwindDataSet.Customers)
Me.OrdersTableAdapter.Fill(Me.NorthwindDataSet.Orders)
```

If you were to run the application at this point, you could navigate through the various customers with the navigation controls. The order information in the grid would change according to the currently selected customer.

For a trivial demonstration, simply browsing through records one at a time is fine. But in the real world your users will need to be able to locate a specific customer quickly. Visual Studio 2005 helps solve this problem by allowing you to create a parameterized query for your forms.

In this application, users will be able to type a customer name and navigate directly to the customer's record. To enable this type of lookup, you first select the *CustomersDataConnector's* smart tag, and then select the Parameterize Data Source operation. (You can also access this feature through the Data menu.) Following these steps will open the Search Criteria Builder dialog shown in Figure 4-22.

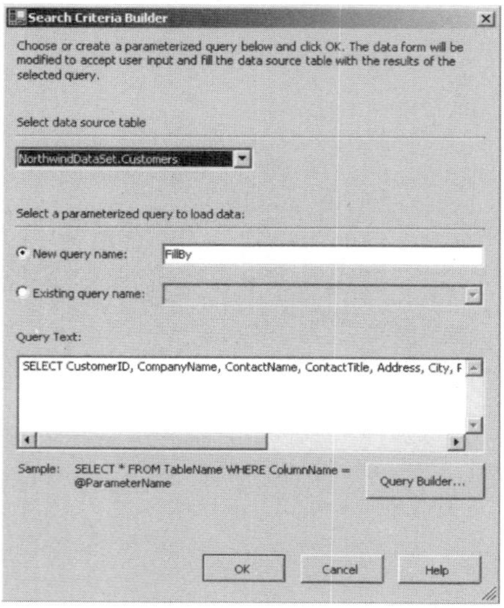

Figure 4-22   The Search Criteria Builder dialog used to build a parameter query.

The Search Criteria Builder assists you in creating a parameterized query that will return a filtered result set based on the user's input. There are essentially two ways to build this query: you can write the SQL yourself, or you can use the visual QueryBuilder. Visual Studio 2005 attempts to provide most of the query for you by examining the fields you have already selected and bound to the controls on your form. In most cases, you simply have to complete the WHERE clause. Just scroll to the end of the SELECT statement already provided in the query text box and add a filter such as the following:

```
WHERE CompanyName LIKE @Company
```

This addition tells the query to select all the chosen fields where the value in the CompanyName field matches the pattern that the user will enter (for example, *B%*). The *@Company* parameter is an input parameter and will be replaced with the value that the user enters in the user interface. The parameter name can be whatever you want. It is called *@Company* in this application to reflect its purpose in the query—to filter the results by company name.

The name of the query, which you also configure in the Search Criteria Builder, also becomes the name of the method used to fill the appropriate *DataTable* in your *DataSet* with the results of your query. The Search Criteria Builder encourages the use of the *FillBy* prefix when naming queries. You do not have to use this in your query name, but it is a good idea to leave it as a prefix. In this application, the query is named FillByName.

As mentioned, you can also build your query graphically by using the QueryBuilder as shown in Figure 4-23. One of the greatest benefits of creating your query this way is the ability to validate the query prior to having it execute in your code.

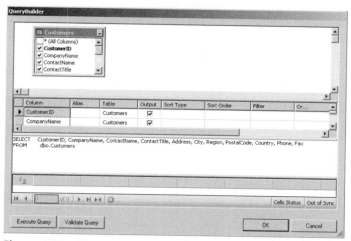

Figure 4-23   The QueryBuilder dialog used to graphically build a query.

> **Important**   If you decide to generate your query by using the QueryBuilder, ensure that you have selected the same fields that are present on your form. If you fail to select the appropriate fields, some of your controls on the form might not contain any data.

After you configure a new parameterized query, a new *ToolStrip* bar is placed on your form for the user to enter criteria for your new query. In this application, the user will enter the company name as a parameter to the query in the *FillByCompanyName ToolStrip*.

When you first start the application, the default *Fill* method that was created when the data source was created is executed in the *Form1_Load* event handler. If you then type a value (for example, B's Beverages) into the *FillByCompanyName ToolStrip* bar and press Enter (or click FillByCompanyName), the master records are filtered. As you then navigate through the filtered records (if there is more than one matching record), the details grid is updated to show the orders for the current customer. Figure 4-24 shows the application with a filtered set of master records.

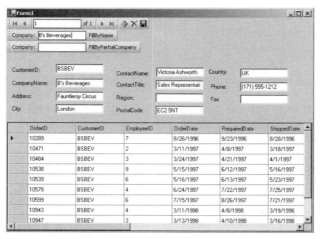

Figure 4-24   Filtered set of Customer records.

DataNavigator

The previous application introduced the *DataNavigator*, but it did not drill down into the amount of coding effort that it actually saves you when writing data-driven applications. You will no doubt have noticed that the *DataNavigator* not only contains controls for moving through records but also includes controls for adding, deleting, and saving records.

By default, the Save button in the navigator *ToolStrip* is disabled. Obviously, many database applications have limited value without the ability to add, edit, and delete data and then save the changes. In this application, the Save button is enabled and some code is added to its click event handler to propagate changes to the database. The code retrieves the changed rows in the *DataSet* and then passes only the changed rows to the *Update* method of the table adapter as shown here:

```
Private Sub dataNavigatorSaveItem_Click(ByVal sender As System.Object, _
                           ByVal e As System.EventArgs) _
                           Handles dataNavigatorSaveItem.Click

    OrdersTableAdapter.Update(NorthwindDataSet.Orders.GetChanges())

End Sub
```

Notice the various objects and methods that are involved in doing the updating. The changed data is in the *Orders* table in the *NorthwindDataSet*. The changed data is pulled out by calling *GetChanges* and then passed to the *Update* method of the *OrdersTableAdapter*, which sends the changes to the database. The *Update* method passes insert, update, and delete changes to the database.

You might be wondering how the *Update* method can find the deleted rows in the *Orders* table since they were deleted. What in fact happens is that deleted rows are simply marked as deleted and left in the *DataTable*. This behavior allows you to later access the rows that have been marked for deletion and choose whether to submit the deletions to the database. The *RowState* of a *DataRow* object in the *DataTable* indicates whether a row is deleted, added, modified, unmodified, and so on.

When you call the *OrdersTableAdapter.Update* method, you are actually causing SQL statements to be sent to the database for execution. The *RowState* of a row determines whether the SQL statement to use is an INSERT, UPDATE, or DELETE statement. When you create a Data Source and use the Data Source Configuration Wizard to automatically generate INSERT, UPDATE, and DELETE queries for you, Visual Studio 2005 actually creates the queries and all the code for using them.

The location where this code can be found has changed in Visual Studio 2005. You have to navigate to the NorthwindDataSet.Designer.vb code module to see this code. Where previous versions of Visual Studio .NET placed this code directly in the Windows Forms Designer Generated code section, you now have to choose View All Files on the Solution Explorer window and then expand your NorthwindDataset.xsd view to see the code module.

If you view this application with Visual Studio 2005, you will wonder where this code came from because Visual Studio 2005 does a good job of hiding it. In Visual Studio 2005, Microsoft has created what they refer to as "sandboxes" for the designer and for the developer. Code generated by the developer is stored in a regular .vb file, as with Visual Studio .NET 2003. But code generated by the designer is stored in a separate .vb file. The reason for this design is quite simple. In Visual Studio .NET 2003, designer-generated code was wrapped in the same .vb file as the developer's code, but it was wrapped in a *#Region*. Some programmers had to (or chose to) edit some of the code created by the Visual Studio .NET 2003 tools and wizards, despite recommendations not to do so. Because the designer generated the code, the designer was also entitled to rewrite the generated code, thus overwriting any changes made by a developer.

To resolve this issue, Visual Studio 2005 places the code that you write in your .vb file as before, but it is completely separate from the designer-generated code that you will find in a .Designer.vb file. Each item in your project (for example, a form) can have both a .Designer.vb file and a regular .vb file. By default, you do not see the designer files in the Solution Explorer. You can force Visual Studio 2005 to show them by turning on the Show All Files feature in the Solution Explorer. The code just listed came from the NorthwindDataSet.Designer.vb file for this application. At the same time, you might also notice that this is now possible through the use of partial classes in the same way the Partial keyword is used in the designer.vb definition of Form1.

The few lines of code written here plus the plethora of designer-generated code creates a fully functional database application—including the ability to update the data and save it to the database.

Conclusion

This application demonstrates the ease with which you can build a data application that displays values from multiple related tables. The ability to easily create and configure a master-details style user interface in Visual Studio 2005 allows you to display related records simultaneously by writing only a trivial amount of code.

This application also introduced you to the new smart tags for data that allow you to quickly accomplish common tasks such as creating a parameterized query. Smart tags for data are discussed more in the next application, where you will see how to use them to your benefit to reduce the amount of work you have to do and the amount of code that you have to write.

Application: Object Data Source

This application shows you how to use an object as a data source in Visual Studio 2005.

New Concepts

One of the powerful new ADO.NET features in Visual Studio 2005 is a much more natural way to use an object as a data source. This object can be a pre-existing object or one that you create as a part of the project or as a separate class library. Although you could create your own objects in Visual Studio .NET 2003 and use them as data sources for things like data binding, it was cumbersome and code-intensive at best.

In the .NET Framework 2.0, any object that exposes public properties can serve as a data source. In this application, a simple class that represents a computer is used. The *Computer* class will contain properties for Model #, Serial #, CPU, amount of RAM, and hard-drive space. A data source based on this object is used to populate *TextBox* controls to display the various properties in the user interface.

To show an alternative way to do data binding, this application creates an array of *Computer* objects and uses the *BindingContext* to navigate through the array of objects in much the same way as you would navigate through records in a *DataSet*.

Walkthrough

The user interface for this application is a simple form with a few labels, *TextBox* controls for the properties of the *Computer* class, and navigation buttons for viewing *Computer* objects one at a time. The form is shown in Figure 4-25.

Figure 4-25   The Object Data Source form.

The *Computer* class is defined in a separate class library that the main Windows application references. The *Computer* class is a simple class that has five private member variables (*m_Model*, *m_Serial*, *m_CPU*, *m_RAM*, and *m_HDSpace*) exposed via public properties (*Model*, *Serial*, *CPU*, *RAM*, *HDSpace*). The following code defines the *Computer* class.

```
Public Class Computer
    Private m_Model As String
    Private m_Serial As Integer
    Private m_CPU As String
    Private m_RAM As String
    Private m_HDSpace As String

    Public Property Model() As String
        Get
            Return m_Model
        End Get
        Set(ByVal value As String)
            m_Model = value
        End Set
    End Property

    Public Property Serial() As Integer
        Get
            Return m_Serial
        End Get
        Set(ByVal value As Integer)
            m_Serial = value
        End Set
    End Property
```

```
    Public Property CPU() As String
        Get
            Return m_CPU
        End Get
        Set(ByVal value As String)
            m_CPU = value
        End Set
    End Property

    Public Property RAM() As String
        Get
            Return m_RAM
        End Get
        Set(ByVal value As String)
            m_RAM = value
        End Set
    End Property

    Public Property HDSpace() As String
        Get
            Return m_HDSpace
        End Get
        Set(ByVal value As String)
            m_HDSpace = value
        End Set
    End Property
End Class
```

To create a data source based on an object, you start by adding a new data source in the Data Sources window, much like you would do if you were creating a data source for a database. But in the Data Source Configuration Wizard you select Object instead of Database when choosing the type of data source. (See Figure 4-26.) You then select the class you want to use as a data source by using the wizard. If your application does not already contain a reference to the assembly that defines the class you want to use, you can add a new reference right from the Data Source Configuration Wizard. (See Figure 4-27.)

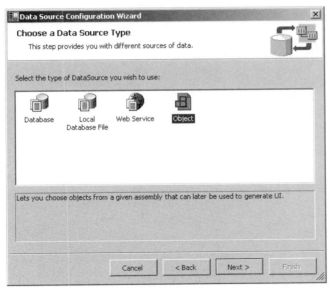

Figure 4-26   Selecting an Object type data source in the Data Source Configuration Wizard.

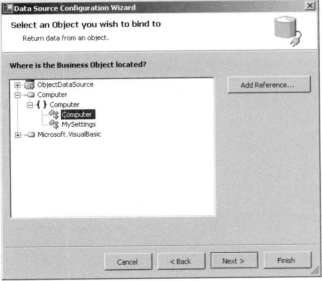

Figure 4-27   Selecting the object (class) to bind to in the Data Source Configuration Wizard.

Binding Objects the Hard Way

The following code shows the hard way to tie the user interface to the array of *Computer* objects:

```vb
Private Computers(5) As Computer.Computer
Private myBindingManager As BindingManagerBase

Private Sub Form1_Load(ByVal sender As Object, _
                       ByVal e As System.EventArgs) Handles Me.Load

  CreateComputers()
  txtModel.DataBindings.Add("Text", Computers, "Model")
  txtSerial.DataBindings.Add("Text", Computers, "Serial")
  txtCPU.DataBindings.Add("Text", Computers, "CPU")
  txtHDSpace.DataBindings.Add("Text", Computers, "HDSpace")
  txtRAM.DataBindings.Add("Text", Computers, "RAM")
  myBindingManager = BindingContext.Item(Computers)
End Sub

Private Sub cmdPrevious_Click(ByVal sender As System.Object, _
                             ByVal e As System.EventArgs) _
                             Handles cmdPrevious.Click

  myBindingManager.Position -= 1
End Sub

Private Sub cmdNext_Click(ByVal sender As Object, _
                          ByVal e As System.EventArgs) Handles cmdNext.Click

  myBindingManager.Position += 1
End Sub


Private Sub CreateComputers()

  Computers(0) = New Computer.Computer
  Computers(0).CPU = "Pentium 2.4GHz"
  Computers(0).Model = "GK2400"
  Computers(0).Serial = 123456
  Computers(0).HDSpace = "200GB"
  Computers(0).RAM = "1GB"

  Computers(1) = New Computer.Computer
  Computers(1).CPU = "Pentium 2.8GHz"
  Computers(1).Model = "GK2800"
  Computers(1).Serial = 65123
  Computers(1).HDSpace = "120GB"
  Computers(1).RAM = "512MB"
```

```
    Computers(2) = New Computer.Computer
    Computers(2).CPU = "Pentium 2.0GHz"
    Computers(2).Model = "GK2000"
    Computers(2).Serial = 12216
    Computers(2).HDSpace = "80GB"
    Computers(2).RAM = "256MB"

    Computers(3) = New Computer.Computer
    Computers(3).CPU = "Pentium 3.0GHz"
    Computers(3).Model = "GK3000"
    Computers(3).Serial = 123124
    Computers(3).HDSpace = "200GB"
    Computers(3).RAM = "2GB"

    Computers(4) = New Computer.Computer
    Computers(4).CPU = "Pentium 2.5GHz"
    Computers(4).Model = "GK2500"
    Computers(4).Serial = 154156
    Computers(4).HDSpace = "120GB"
    Computers(4).RAM = "1GB"
End Sub
```

The form includes a global array to hold five computer objects and a *BindingManagerBase*, which keeps track of the current position in the array of objects.

The *Load* event handler for the form calls the *CreateComputers* procedure to populate the array with values for five computers. This provides the values for the user to navigate through using the Next and Previous buttons. Then the *TextBox* controls are bound to the *Computers* array by using the *DataBindings* collection of each *TextBox* control.

The *cmdNext_Click* and *cmdPrevious_Click* click event handlers both use the *BindingManager-Base* to change the current position of the binding context, thus causing a different record to be displayed in the form.

An Easier Way to Bind Objects

Now that you have seen how to bind objects the hard way, it is time to look at doing this the easy way. Doing this will add the now familiar navigator bar at the top of our form. The only coding task you have to handle is a single line of code to provide the data. In this case, you have to set the *DataSource* property of a *DataConnector* rather than filling a *DataSet*.

Earlier in this walkthrough, you saw how to create a data source based on an object. The resulting view in the Data Sources window is set to *DataGridView* as shown in Figure 4-28.

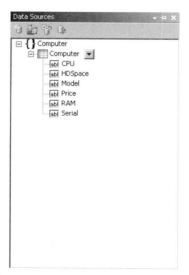

Figure 4-28   The Data Sources window showing an Object data source Gridview.

As with other types of data sources, you can simply drag an object from the Data Sources window onto your form. Figure 4-29 shows a *DataGridView* created by dragging the *Computer* object data source onto the form for this application.

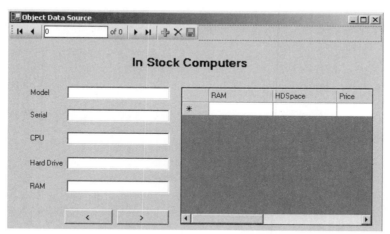

Figure 4-29   Bound form with a DataGridView for displaying object data.

You can see that dragging the grid onto the form prompts Visual Studio 2005 to also create a navigator bar at the top of the form. At this point, the component tray contains *ComputerData-Connector* and *ComputerDataNavigator* objects as shown in Figure 4-30. These two items are similar to the *DataConnector* and *DataNavigator* components used in the previous data applications. You will also notice that there are no table adapters or *DataSet* objects in the component tray. That is because they have no purpose when dealing with an object as a data source.

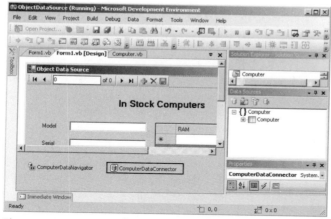

Figure 4-30   Component tray with Object data source components.

Now that the grid is positioned on the form and the navigator is in place to allow navigation, one line of code is needed in the *Load* event handler of the form to set the array of *Computer* objects as the *DataSource* for the *DataConnector* that the *DataGridView* is bound to:

```
Me.ComputerDataConnector.DataSource = Computers
```

With that one line of code, the grid is bound to the *Computers* array. The final application with the bound *DataGridView* is shown in Figure 4-31.

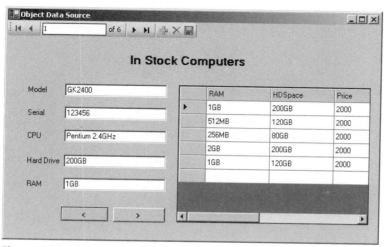

Figure 4-31   A bound DataGridView using the DataConnector and DataNavigator components.

Conclusion

Binding to an object as shown in this application allows you to take advantage of the convenience of data binding while using business objects to represent your data instead of database-centric classes such as *DataSet* and *DataTable*. Using object data sources does put some extra responsibility on you as the developer because you have to provide the logic for saving changes made to the in-memory collection of objects. But the ability to work with your own business entity classes instead of *DataTables* can be beneficial in many situations, such as in n-tier systems that require the user interface to be completely ignorant of the type and structure of the underlying data stores for a given system. In such a situation, the presentation layer can retrieve a set of objects from a middle tier and bind those objects directly to the user interface. Certainly object data sources are not appropriate for all applications, but in many situations they are an extremely powerful and useful option. And Visual Studio 2005 makes data binding with objects amazingly easy.

Chapter 5

Constructing User Interfaces

This chapter explores the controls and improvements to existing controls that are provided by version 2.0 of the Microsoft .NET Framework. These features allow you to create professional-looking applications that provide a better end-user experience and reduce your coding effort.

Application: New Windows Forms Controls

This application demonstrates many of the new controls available in Microsoft Visual Studio 2005 for creating compelling Windows Forms user interfaces.

New Concepts

Visual Studio has a long history of providing a large library of prebuilt controls that allow developers to quickly create user interfaces for Microsoft Windows applications. However, the capabilities and visual style of these components often resulted in applications that had a look and feel significantly different from other Microsoft products such as Microsoft Office and Internet Explorer. Visual Studio 2005 introduces many new controls to address this issue. These controls provide the same advanced look and feel and customization support as Microsoft Office, which allows you to provide your users with a familiar experience and increased personalization options.

ToolStrip Control

Today's professional applications provide many features that allow users to fully customize the positioning, formatting, and content of their menus and toolbars. Users expect to be able to perform such tasks as moving toolbars around, selecting which buttons to display, and controlling how much information is presented with each item. In addition, they expect the rendering of these controls to be clean and consistent across applications. The *ToolStrip* is a new toolbar control that supports all these features and provides the base functionality for the

MenuStrip and *StatusStrip* controls. You are no longer limited to just adding buttons to your toolbars. The *ToolStrip* allows you to add seven different types of items, such as the *ToolStrip-Button*, *ToolStripComboBox*, *ToolStripTextBox*, and *ToolStripSplitButton*.

The first thing you will notice when you add a *ToolStrip* to a form is that it looks like an Office toolbar by default. Many controls support a new pluggable rendering framework that allows you to select how you want the control to look. There are currently two main "looks" for the *ToolStrip*, and you select which one you want with the *RenderMode* property. Providing a value of *System* indicates that you want the control to follow the current Windows system display settings. Providing a value of *Professional* indicates that you want the control to look like its counterpart in Microsoft Office.

There are many new types of behavior—including rafting, merging, and item overflow—supported by the *ToolStrip*. Rafting is the behavior that allows a user to drag and drop a toolbar to various locations on the form and have the toolbar automatically "snap" into position. The integrated development environment (IDE) automatically provides support for rafting by adding multiple *RaftContainer* controls to the form when you add your *ToolStrip*. You specify the initial location for the *ToolStrip* by setting its *Raft* property. At run time, the user will be able to move the *ToolStrip* to any of the other *RaftContainers*.

Merging is the behavior you see when the items from two *ToolStrips* are combined into a single *ToolStrip*. You can specify whether or not a particular strip supports merging with the *Allow-Merge* property. You can then govern each item's merge behavior with the *MergeAction* and *MergeIndex* properties.

Item reordering is the behavior that allows a user to rearrange toolbar and menu items. You can enable item reordering by setting the *AllowItemReorder* property to *True*. At run time, users will be able to move items by dragging and dropping them while pressing the Alt key.

FlowLayoutPanel and TableLayoutPanel Controls

Visual Studio 2005 provides two new layout controls that address some common control positioning scenarios. The normal *Panel* control uses absolute positioning to determine the location of each of its child controls. The *FlowLayoutPanel*, on the other hand, positions each control relative to the one just prior to it as you add them to the panel. By default, it flows controls from left to right and top to bottom, but you can control the flow direction by using the *FlowDirection* property. The *FlowLayoutPanel* is useful in situations where you want controls to automatically reposition themselves as the contents of one of the children changes or as the size of the panel changes.

The *TableLayoutPanel* is a panel that contains an invisible table structure that allows you to place a single control in each table cell. You can specify how many rows and columns the internal table should have as well as the sizing rules for each row and column. The *TableLayout-Panel* is useful when you need to define major, fixed-size sections of a form. You can also use it to quickly create tabular data-entry interfaces. However, keep in mind that you can add only a single control to each cell. So, if you want a cell to contain more that one child control, you need to first add a *Panel* to the cell and then add your two child controls to the *Panel*.

WebBrowser Control

Visual Studio 2005 now provides an optimized, managed wrapper for the well-known ActiveX Web browser control. This control provides access to the full DHTML rendering capabilities of Internet Explorer. You can use this control to add many kinds of Web browsing capabilities to your applications. For example, you could allow users to read HTML documentation files from within your application. Or you could allow a user to link to content on the Internet. Using the *WebBrowser* control is straightforward, and it provides some powerful options that enable deep integration between your DHTML and WinForm assets.

You can download and display a document by simply calling the *Navigate* method and providing a URL to the resource. Once it's loaded, you can programmatically access the DHTML DOM through the *Document* property. Through this property, you can directly read and modify the structure of the document. You can perform standard navigation tasks through methods such as *GoForward*, *GoHome*, *GoSearch*, and *GoBack*. You can even expose a managed object to script code to allow script in the page to call into your managed application. All you have to do is supply an object to the *ObjectForScripting* property. Monitoring the progress of a download is accomplished by handling the *WebBrowser*'s events, such as *Navigating*, *Navigated*, *ProgressChanged*, and *DocumentCompleted*.

ActiveDocumentHost Control

The *ActiveDocumentHost* control provides a bridge between your Windows Forms application and OLE resources. You can load and display a resource by calling the *LoadFrom* method and providing the path to the resource. The *ActiveDocumentHost* will launch an instance of the application that is registered for that particular type of resource. For example, if you load a Microsoft Word document, the *ActiveDocumentHost* will automatically launch Microsoft Word and display the document in a read-only state. By default, double-clicking the control will cause it to switch to an editable mode and display the editing application's toolbars and menus. You can control most aspects of this through properties such as *ShowMenus* and *ShowToolbars*.

Walkthrough

This walkthrough demonstrates how you can use these new controls to create Windows Forms interfaces that look more professional and are easier to use.

Creating Office Interfaces

The *DocumentBrowser* form presents an interface that draws many of its design elements from various Microsoft products, including Office and Internet Explorer. Notice that the two *Tool-Strips* are rendered as Office-type toolbars, with a vertical gradient background and "grips" at their left edge. One of the *ToolStrips* includes a text box. There is also a third *ToolStrip* control in the bottom-left corner of the form with two items, *Documents* and *Web Pages*. This *ToolStrip* has been modified by setting its *LayoutStyle* to *Vertical* to give it a bit of a Microsoft Outlook style. The status bar at the bottom of the form is a *StatusStrip* control with two children, a *StatusStripPanel* and a *ToolStripProgressBar*. The progress bar has been configured to display progress as a continuous strip by setting its *Style* property to *Continuous*.

When you run the application, click and drag the tool strips to any edge of the form and you will see that they will automatically dock to that side. This action is possible because there is a *RaftingContainer* control at each edge of the form. These containers are automatically added by Visual Studio when you add the *ToolStrips* to the form. You can also reorder items and even move an item from one *ToolStrip* to another by holding down the Alt key and dragging an item.

Interacting with Web Content

The application uses the *WebBrowser* control to load and display Web content. At run time, click the Web Pages button in the bottom-left corner of the form. Next, enter a URL into the Address text box in the tool strip. Click the Go button to navigate to the document.

> **Note**   If you do not have access to the Internet, an HTML page named "MSDN Home Page.htm" is available in the application directory.

As the application loads, you should notice the progress bar and status text updating at the bottom of the form. When the document finishes loading, you will see an entry appear in the History List to the left of the browser pane. This progress monitoring is accomplished by handling numerous *WebBrowser* events.

The process starts with the *btnGo_Click* event handler. In this procedure, you tell the *WebBrowser* to load a document by calling the *Navigate* method:

```
wbrBrowser.Navigate(txtAddress.Text)
```

When the *WebBrowser* starts navigating to the resource, it raises the *Navigating* event. The *wbrBrowser_Navigating* event handler retrieves the URL from the event arguments and posts a message to the *StatusStripPanel* indicating that the download is in progress:

```
SetStatus("Navigating to '" + e.Url + "'")
```

While the *WebBrowser* is loading the document, it periodically raises its *ProgressChanged* event. The *wbrBrowser_ProgressChanged* event handler updates the progress bar in the *StatusStrip* first, resetting it if it is already showing 100 percent, and then increments it by a value of 5:

```
If pbrProgress.Value >= pbrProgress.Maximum Then
    ClearProgress()
End If
pbrProgress.Increment(5)
```

When the *WebBrowser* is finished loading the document, it raises the *DocumentCompleted* event. You can use this event to notify your user that the content is available or perhaps to log the results of the download. The *wbrBrowser_DocumentCompleted* event handler retrieves the title of the document from the URL of the document from the event arguments. This information is used to populate a new *ListViewItem* and added to the history list view. The procedure ends by resetting the status text and the progress bar:

```
Dim title As String = e.Url
Dim visited As String = DateTime.Now.ToString()
Dim docInfo As New ListViewItem(New String(1) {title, visited})

lvwHistory.Items.Add(docInfo)

SetStatus(String.Empty)
ClearProgress()
```

Interacting with Document Content

The application also allows you to load and display files that have been registered to allow OLE hosting. Office documents, sound files, and .avi movie files are all examples of "active" data. You can load a file by first selecting the Documents button in the bottom-left corner of the form. Then, enter a local path to the desired file in the Address text box and click the Go button. The document will display inside the *ActiveDocumentHost*. If the document is editable, you can double-click the *ActiveDocumentHost* to launch the document in its associated host application. The menu and toolbars of the host application will display in the *DocumentBrowser* form.

The *ActiveDocumentHost* has fewer progress-related events than the *WebBrowser* control. However, it does raise a *Loaded* event when it has finished loading and displaying the document. The *ahdDocument_Loaded* event handler starts by retrieving information about the loaded document. It then creates a *ListViewItem* and adds it to the history list view:

```
Dim url As String = adhDocument.SourceDocument
Dim visited As String = DateTime.Now.ToString()

Dim docInfo As New ListViewItem(New String(1) {url, visited})

lvwHistory.Items.Add(docInfo)

SetStatus(String.Empty)
ClearProgress()
```

Conclusion

The new Windows Forms controls provided by the .NET Framework 2.0 allow you to create applications that are more professional looking and more powerful than ever before without having to rely on third-party components. The *ToolStrip* provides you with a powerful mechanism for creating menu, tool, and status bars that look and behave like their counterparts in other applications your users are familiar with. This can translate directly into quicker user adoption and higher user satisfaction. The *WebBrowser* and *ActiveDocumentHost* allow you to integrate external data into your applications. The *WebBrowser* is designed for the reliable and versatile downloading and rendering of DHTML content, while the *ActiveDocumentHost* provides a mechanism for hosting and editing OLE data types.

Application: Changes to Existing Windows Forms Controls

This application examines some changes and additions to the Windows Forms framework that affect a broad set of existing and new Windows Forms controls.

New Concepts

The .NET Framework 2.0 and Visual Studio 2005 introduce many new features to Windows Forms development that will have a broad impact on how you work with Windows Forms controls at both design time and run time. These features affect a wide range of behaviors, including control layout and positioning, run-time data entry, and application configuration and personalization.

Margins and Padding

Ensuring that your controls are positioned and spaced consistently is important for creating applications that are easy to learn and navigate. Unfortunately, the process of positioning controls is at best laborious and time consuming. One aspect of proper positioning involves making sure that there is a consistent amount of space between controls. For example, you might have a series of buttons at the bottom of a form that need to have exactly ten pixels of space between each of them. This generally involves placing one button, recording its *Left* property and modifying the *Left* property of the next button to the desired amount. Another example is when you have a container control and you want to make sure that constituent controls are no closer than eight pixels from the edge of the container. At a minimum, this setup involves placing the first control to serve as an anchor point and then aligning the other controls to it as appropriate.

The .NET Framework 2.0 introduces two new concepts, margins and padding, to controls that greatly simplify the work involved in scenarios like those just mentioned. *Margin* is the external space between two controls, while *padding* is the internal space between a control's edge and its contents. So, the right edge of one button and the left edge of another button is the margin between them. On the other hand, the space between a panel's edge and its constituent controls is the panel's padding. The *Control* class now has *Padding* and *Margin* properties so that a control can declare and enforce its spacing requirements.

The *Margin* and *Padding* properties are used by the Visual Studio IDE at design time to provide margin and padding indicators and to autosnap controls according to their *Margin* and *Padding* properties. Both of these properties are of the *Padding* type, which is a simple structure that allows you to provide unique values for each edge of the control: *Top*, *Bottom*, *Left*, and *Right*. So, if you have a *Panel* whose *Padding.Left* is set to 5, and you are placing a child control on the *Panel*, the IDE will automatically provide you with feedback when the left side of the child control is five pixels from the left side of the *Panel*. This allows you to quickly place controls exactly where they need to be without having to manually set location properties. These properties are also honored at run time as controls are resized or relocated.

Auto-Completion

If you have used Internet Explorer, you have seen auto-completion in action. Auto-completion is the behavior you see when you enter data in a text control and the system automatically suggests what it thinks you might be entering. This feature is generally most beneficial when the user has to enter strings that are either long or complex. A prerequisite necessary for an auto-completion solution to work is the existence of some set of data that the system can use to look up possible matches.

You can now easily add auto-completion support to text boxes and combo boxes in your Windows Forms applications. Both controls have three new properties: *AutoCompleteMode*, *AutoCompleteSource*, and *AutoCompleteCustomSource*. You enable auto-completion by setting the *AutoCompleteMode* to *Append*, *Suggest*, or *SuggestAppend*. Setting *AutoCompleteMode* to *Append* results in the most likely match being automatically appended to the current data. Using *Suggest* results in a drop-down list populated with one or more suggested completion strings. *SuggestAppend* performs both tasks. The control also needs a source list from which it can search for suggestions as the user enters data. The *AutoCompleteSource* property allows you to select from some system sources such as *FileSystem*, *HistoryList*, *RecentlyUsedList*, *AllUrl*, and *CustomSource*.

If you select *CustomSource*, you must provide a list of strings to the *AutoCompleteCustomSource* property. This can be done at either design time or run time. Custom sources are very powerful, as they allow you to provide auto-complete behavior for business data. For example, you could query a list of product categories from a database when the form loads and supply a list of category names to serve as both the display source and auto-complete source for a combo box. This approach would allow your users to quickly select a category without having to enter the full category name or manually navigate through a long list of items.

Configuration

The .NET Framework 1.1 provides a basic application configuration mechanism that allows you to define read-only application settings in the application configuration file. You access these settings through the *System.Configuration.AppSettings* class, which retrieves settings by key and returns a weakly typed object that you must cast to an appropriate type. This mechanism is useful for simple scenarios focused on relatively static data that is generally modified only by an administrator. However, many other application configuration scenarios require a more robust and flexible solution. The .NET Framework 2.0 and Visual Studio 2005 provide a new configuration system for Windows Forms applications. This system addresses the limitations of the previous solution and introduces many new concepts that result in a more integrated and efficient design-time experience and a more personalized end-user experience.

Note   Presented here is a description of what will be available in the release-to-market (RTM) version. At the time of this writing, the configuration system is only partially implemented.

Important   From this point forward, "configuration system" refers to the new configuration system provided by the .NET Framework 2.0 and Visual Studio 2005.

Configuration Settings   The configuration system provides much more robust support for the definition, reading, and writing of configuration settings. Each setting is defined by its name, data type, scope, default value, and accessibility. All settings are strongly typed, and you can specify any serializable type. The configuration system supports many mechanisms for persisting a setting's value, including string representation, XML serialization, and binary serialization.

You can also define a setting to have one of two scopes, User or Application. Application settings are read-only, and their value is shared across all users of an application on a machine. By default, these values are stored in the application configuration file. User settings are stored and managed on a per-user basis and stored in user.config files. You can configure user settings to be read/write or read-only. A major feature of user settings is the configuration system's support for roaming Windows profiles. If you specify that user settings should roam with the user's Windows profile, those settings will automatically follow them when they run the application from another machine. The following is an example of some configuration settings:

```
<userSettings>
  <WindowsApplication1.MySettings>
    <setting name="DefaultView" serializeAs="String">
      <value>AllEmployees</value>
    </setting>
    <setting name="Credentials" serializeAs="System.Net.NetworkCredentials">
      <value>some binary representation...</value>
```

```
        </setting>
      </WindowsApplication1.MySettings>
    </userSettings>
    <applicationSettings>
      <WindowsApplication1.MySettings>
        <setting name="Employee_CS" serializeAs="String">
          <value>server=localhost;initial catalog=northwind</value>
        </setting>
      </WindowsApplication1.MySettings>
    </applicationSettings>
```

Wrapper Classes   The configuration system requires that you use wrapper classes to access the settings stored in the configuration store. These wrapper classes provide the strongly typed interface to the configuration system and provide metadata that fully describes each setting. This allows a user of the wrapper class to understand how each setting is configured without having to directly access the configuration files.

> **Note**   You should be aware that the configuration system connects to the settings store through a pluggable architecture. Initially, the system will only support storing settings in configuration files, but there will eventually be many potential settings stores.

The following is the wrapper class for the settings shown previously:

```
Imports System.Configuration
Imports System.Net
Public Class SettingsWrapper
    Inherits System.Configuration.ApplicationSettingsBase

    <ApplicationScopedSettingAttribute(), _
        DefaultSettingValueAttribute("server=local;initial catalog=northwind")> _
    Public Overridable ReadOnly Property Employee_CS() As String
        Get
            Return CType(Me("Employee_CS"),String)
        End Get
    End Property


    <UserScopedSettingAttribute(), _
    DefaultSettingValueAttribute("AllEmployees")> _
    Public Overridable Property DefaultView() As String
        Get
            Return CType(Me("DefaultView"),String)
        End Get
        Set
            Me("DefaultView") = value
        End Set
    End Property


    <UserScopedSettingAttribute()> _
    Public Overridable Property Credentials() As NetworkCredential
        Get
            Return CType(Me("Credentials"), NetworkCredential)
```

```
        End Get
        Set
            Me("Credentials") = value
        End Set
    End Property
End Class
```

You use the wrapper class in your application code to access and modify your configuration settings. For example, the following code retrieves the *NetworkCredential* stored in the user setting named *Credentials*.

```
Dim wrapper as New SettingsWrapper()
Dim cred as NetworkCredential = wrapper.Credentials
```

IDE Support You can manually create both the configuration files and the wrapper classes, but Visual Studio 2005 provides full IDE support for both tasks. In Visual Basic .NET, you can access the Settings Designer by right-clicking a project in Solution Explorer and selecting Properties. In the property pages list, select Settings. You will be presented with a designer that allows you to define all aspects of your application and user settings. When you save your changes in the designer, Visual Basic will automatically create and populate the appropriate configuration files. It will also create a wrapper class and make it accessible through the *My* Object as *My.Settings*.

Visual Studio also fully integrates your settings into the Windows Forms design experience to provide a convenient mechanism for binding control properties to application and user settings. The design experience is similar to what exists today for data binding. There is a new section in the Properties window named *(ApplicationSettings)*. When you select this property, you are presented with a dialog that lets you bind individual control properties to configuration settings. Because settings are strongly typed, the IDE can even filter the list of available settings to only show those that are compatible with the type of the currently selected property. The code generated by this process handles populating a control's properties from setting values, but the process does not add code to update those setting values when the property changes or when the application ends.

Currently, you need to manually implement the persistence of any changed values to the settings store. This is not a difficult task, but it can be time consuming when you consider that it is common to have many control properties pointed to configuration settings. To ease this burden, some controls will provide built-in support for auto-loading and persisting their property values. This support will mainly apply to layout and formatting-oriented properties such as *Location* and *Size* on container controls such as *Form* and *SplitContainer*. Other controls, such as the *ToolStrip*, might support other properties such as the order of its items and its current rafting location. Controls that support automatic configuration persistence have two new properties, *SaveSettings* and *SettingsKey*.

Walkthrough

This walkthrough demonstrates how you can use padding, auto-completion, and the new configuration system to create more powerful user interfaces.

Using Padding

A design goal of this application was to examine easy ways to replicate the look and feel of Microsoft Office applications. For example, Microsoft Outlook organizes functional areas of the interface into panels separated by movable splitters. Each visual panel has a single pixel and a dark blue border, and there is consistent spacing around the outside of and between the panels. You can use many combinations of controls to achieve this look, and this application examines one of them.

The main container control is the *SplitContainer*, which displays the history list and some buttons on the left and displays the Web and document content on the right. The *SplitContainer* consists of two *Panels* separated by a *Splitter*. Although the *Panel* control does not allow you to specify a border color directly, you can still easily achieve the look described previously. First, set the *Panel* control's *BorderStyle* property to None. Next, set the *BackColor* property to your desired border color. Finally, set the *Padding.All* property to define the width of your border. Now, when you place a control on the *Panel* and set its *Dock* property to Fill, the *Panel* will provide a colored border around your control.

Using Auto-Completion

The Address text box in the tool strip uses auto-completion to suggest URLs to resources as you type them in. If you select the text box, you will see that its *AutoCompleteMode* property is set to Suggest. This setting is consistent with Internet Explorer's auto-completion behavior. The *AutoCompleteSource* property changes based on what type of resource you are searching for. When you click either the Documents or Web Pages buttons in the bottom-left corner of the form, the *DocTypeButton_Click* event handler runs. This event handler performs some basic state maintenance tasks on the interface. One of these tasks is to change the *AutoCompleteSource* of the text box. If the user clicked the Web Pages button, the *AutoCompleteSource* is set to provide suggestions from all resolvable URLs. If the user clicked the Documents button, the *AutoCompleteSource* is set to just use the file system:

```
txtAddress.AutoCompleteSource = AutoCompleteSource.AllUrl
.
.
.
txtAddress.AutoCompleteSource = AutoCompleteSource.FileSystem
```

You can test this behavior by running the application, clicking the Web Pages button, and entering a URL starting with **http://**. You should see a list of suggestions automatically appear in a drop-down list under the text box. If you enter a file path staring with a drive letter, such as **C://**, you should not get any suggestions. Next, click the Documents button and again enter a URL starting with **http://**. This time you should not get any suggestions because the *Auto-CompleteSource* is using only the file system.

Using the New Configuration System

At the time of this writing, the new configuration system is not fully functional in Visual Studio .NET. However, it is still worth looking at what is available and how it is implemented. This application uses the configuration system to provide personalization services to users by automatically saving some interface state when the form closes. This information is reloaded when the application starts so that the user is presented with the interface just the way she left it. In particular, the application stores the position of the splitter in the *SplitPanel* and *Window-State* of the form between user sessions. Additionally, the application allows the user to turn this feature on and off through an options dialog.

You can view the setting configuration by going to the project properties and selecting the Settings tab. You will see three settings defined: *WindowsStartupState*, *RememberFormState*, and *SplitterDistance*. These settings are typed as *FormWindowState*, *Boolean*, and *Int32*, respectively. Default values are also specified. Notice that although all three of these settings are User settings, you can easily define them as application settings as well. If you want to see where the configuration files and wrapper classes reside, click the Show All Files button in Solution Explorer and expand My Application. Under My Application, you will see MySettings.settings and MySettings.vb. MySettings.settings is the XML configuration file containing the settings definitions. MySettings.vb is the wrapper class that provides access to these settings.

The application uses the *WindowsStartupState* and *SplitterDistance* settings on startup if the *RememberFormState* setting is set to True. This decision happens in the *DocumentBrowserForm_Load* event handler. The application also writes these property values back to the configuration settings when the application is closing. The *DocumentBrowserForm_FormClosing* event handler starts by checking a *Boolean* setting to determine whether or not the user wants interface changes to be persisted. If so, it simply reads the data from the relevant properties and assigns them to the appropriate configuration setting. Once all the settings have been set, you call the wrapper's *Save* method to push the changes to the configuration files:

```
If My.Settings.RememberFormState Then
    My.Settings.WindowStartupState = Me.WindowState
    My.Settings.SplitterDistance = SplitContainer1.SplitterDistance

    My.Settings.Save()
End If
```

The user can change the *RememberFormState* setting by selecting the Tools | Options menu command from the main form. This opens the *OptionsForm*, which provides a check box through which the user can modify the value of the *RememberFormState* setting.

Conclusion

Margins and padding, auto-completion, and the new configuration system represent some of the major advances in Windows Forms technology that will be available with the release of the next version of the .NET Framework and Visual Studio. These features have a broad impact on the Windows Forms experience for both developers and end users. Developer productivity enhancements such as margins and padding allow you to lay out interfaces more efficiently and with greater consistency. End-user productivity enhancements such as auto-completion allow users to complete tasks faster and with less opportunity for error. Finally, the improved configuration system offers new levels of flexibility, management, customization, and personalization to all Windows Forms applications.

Chapter 6
Building Web Applications

The majority of Visual Basic programmers do at least some Web development. Two common reasons for developing solutions as Web applications are to work with a simple deployment model and to have the broadest potential user base (that is, anyone with a browser).

Although each successive version of the Microsoft .NET Framework has made the deployment of Microsoft Windows applications easier, Web applications continue to have deployment and reach advantages in many situations. The familiar event-driven drag-and-drop development paradigm in Visual Studio 2005 allows you to decide to build a Web application based on target users and the desired deployment model rather than the Web programming experience of the development team.

In the early years of Web programming, programmers built applications that parsed incoming HTTP requests and generated HTML output using string manipulation. Libraries such as the CGI library for Perl were used to handle common tasks, but ultimately the responsibility for properly parsing and handling requests fell to the programmer. Over time, the development paradigm evolved and new Web development technologies emerged, such as Java servlets or the combination of ASP and COM components to generate HTML output. These newer technologies often required programmers to work in multiple development environments, they still required a lot of code to generate basic HTML output, and the resulting applications were difficult to debug, maintain, and deploy. Then the release of the .NET Framework (including ASP.NET 1.0) and Microsoft Visual Studio .NET introduced developers to a better way of building Web applications using server controls, event handlers, code-behind classes written in any .NET language, and efficient one-way data binding.

Visual Studio 2005 builds on the innovation introduced in Visual Studio .NET and makes Web development easier than ever before for both experienced and novice Web developers.

ASP.NET was a huge leap forward for Web developers. ASP.NET 2.0 is another big leap forward. One of the key areas of improvement is the drastically reduced number of lines of code required for common tasks such as data access.

Application: Zero-Code Web Sites

This application demonstrates the improvements in ASP.NET 2.0 that give you the ability to create powerful, interactive Web applications without writing any Microsoft Visual Basic code.

New Concepts

Most nontrivial Web applications require some sort of data store, whether it is a Microsoft SQL Server database, a Microsoft Access data file, an XML file, or some other type of data source. Depending on the complexity of the application, the UI displays data either retrieved directly from the data store or obtained from a set of business objects. In ASP.NET 1.1, even a simple Web page used to display a list of products directly from a database requires numerous lines of code for connecting to the database and binding the data to a server control. In ASP.NET 2.0, many common data access scenarios can be implemented using only declarative ASPX markup—no programming required.

The new "zero code" features in ASP.NET 2.0 cover the most common data access scenarios. The simplest scenario is one-way data binding using a server control to display data from a data source. A common example of this is displaying a list of states or provinces in a drop-down list. A more complex scenario is one-way data binding using multiple controls where the value selected in one control influences the values displayed in a dependent control—for example, displaying a list of countries in a drop-down list and then displaying a country-specific list of states or provinces in another drop-down list when a country is selected. For certain server controls, ASP.NET 2.0 even includes built-in sorting and paging.

The most impressive "zero code" feature in ASP.NET 2.0 is the ability to easily provide the user interface and data access logic for adding, updating, and deleting data without writing the type of plumbing code required for these basic operations in ASP.NET 1.1.

Declarative Languages

The phrase *zero code Web site* is perhaps a bit of a misnomer because the ASP.NET markup language (that is, the ASPX language) is increasingly being recognized as a declarative programming language. Referring to ASPX as a programming language might seem a bit confusing if you come from a strictly imperative programming background using languages such as C, C++, Java, and Visual Basic because declarative programming is quite a different programming model. For many programmers, an XML-based language just does not "feel" like a programming language. Imperative programming tends to map quite directly to the way a computer operates at a very low level. At any given point in time, your program is in a specific state reached by executing the instructions you provided. By executing additional instructions, your program will end up in a new state. When you program with an imperative language, you reach a desired goal by providing the specific operations required to reach the goal (that is, you tell the computer how to reach your goal). When you program with a declarative language, you specify your goal and a compiler or interpreter uses its predefined algorithms to determine the appropriate operations to reach that goal.

If you are not used to thinking about declarative programming, these concepts might seem a bit foreign, but you are probably already a more experienced declarative programmer than you realize. Consider the following declarative code:

```
SELECT * FROM Products WHERE ProductID = 55
```

You probably recognize this as SQL code. SQL is an example of a popular declarative language. The SELECT query expresses an end result: select all the columns from each row of the Products table that has a value of 55 in the *ProductID* column. The burden of expressing this query as a set of executable operations is taken care of by the query processing engine of whatever database this query is sent to.

Now consider a block of ASP.NET markup:

```
<form runat="server">
    <asp:TextBox id="txtCountry" Text="Canada" runat="server"/>
    <asp:Button id="btnSave" Text="Save" runat="server" />
</form>
```

This "code" does not contain a set of instructions but rather defines an end result: a form containing a text box prefilled with "Canada" and a button labeled "Save." ASP.NET has a predetermined algorithm for turning these declarations into output appropriate for various types of browsers (for example, HTML for Internet Explorer). You do not have to provide any of the specific operations required to get the correct output because ASP.NET takes care of that for you.

As the applications in this section demonstrate, ASP.NET markup provides a lot of power with very little programming effort required. The ASPX language can be used to control much more than just layout or simple mappings to HTML. ASPX allows you to define behavior including a rich user interface and database communication. When you work with ASPX, you are working with a lot more than just a data format for encoding a user interface—you are programming with one of the latest and most popular declarative languages.

Data Binding

Prior to the release of the .NET Framework, data binding had garnered a bad reputation because it was awkward to use in Visual Basic 6 for applications that required any moderately complex behavior. Version 1.0 of the .NET Framework introduced new data-binding functionality that mimics what most developers would code themselves to get data-binding behavior.

One of the greatest things that the .NET Framework brought with it was the ability for Web developers to use one-way data binding on Web forms that is both efficient and easy. You simply provide a bindable server control such as a *DropDownList* with a data source and the server control takes care of iterating through the data and generating the appropriate HTML for each data item. Although it's quite easy to do, data binding in ASP.NET 1.1 still requires code to create the data source, assign it to the appropriate data control, and then call the *DataBind* method of the data control to actually induce the control to iterate through the data source. In ASP.NET 2.0, you only have to encapsulate the settings for the data source and bindings in the ASPX and let the server controls take care of the rest of the work.

Walkthrough

The simplest data binding in ASP.NET 2.0 is a read-only tabular display of data from a data source. Using the Visual Studio 2005 IDE, you first create a new Web form and drag a data source control onto the form. This application uses the *SqlDataSource* control, although controls are also available for alternate data sources such as a Microsoft Access data file or an XML document. The *SqlDataSource* control takes care of connecting to your Microsoft SQL Server database and retrieving the requested data.

When you add a new *SqlDataSource* control to your form, the Data Source Configuration Wizard guides you through the setup for the control. The first step is to establish the connection settings for the control to communicate with the database. Figure 6-1 shows that first step with a connection to the Northwind database already configured.

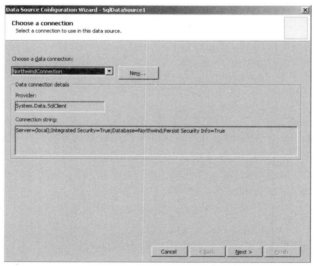

Figure 6-1   Data Source Configuration Wizard.

Next you specify the data you want the data source control to select from the data source. This application uses a straightforward query to select all rows from the Products table of the Northwind database:

```
SELECT * FROM [Products]
```

With a connection and a SELECT query, the *SqlDataSource* control has all the information it needs to retrieve data from the database. The resultant ASPX markup generated by the wizard is:

```
<asp:SqlDataSource ID="ProductsDS" Runat="server"
    SelectCommand="SELECT * FROM [Products]"
    ConnectionString="<%$ ConnectionStrings:NorthwindConnection %>">
</asp:SqlDataSource>
```

You will notice that the new syntax for declaratively reading connection strings from the web.config configuration file is used. The corresponding entry from web.config is as follows (with line breaks added for readability):

```
<connectionStrings>
    <add name="NorthwindConnection"
        connectionString="Server=(local);
                          Integrated Security=True;
                          Database=Northwind;
                          Persist Security Info=True"
        providerName="System.Data.SqlClient" />
</connectionStrings>
```

Now that the Web form has a data source control, you can add other controls that support data binding and bind them to the data source control. For a simple tabular display, the new *GridView* control needs no special configuration–just give it the ID of the data source control and it generates a complete table of data. You can use the Common Tasks smart tag for the *GridView* to assign the data source or simply use the following ASPX markup to set the *DataSourceID* attribute of the *GridView*:

```
<asp:GridView ID="ProductsGrid" Runat="server" DataSourceID="ProductsDS">
</asp:GridView>
```

The end result in the visual Web designer is shown in Figure 6-2. The *SqlDataSource* control is visible in design view, but when it is viewed in Internet Explorer, as shown in Figure 6-3, only the data table generated by the *GridView* is visible.

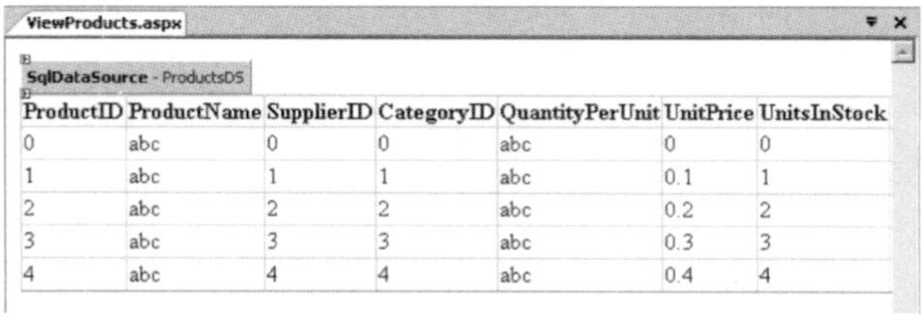

ProductID	ProductName	SupplierID	CategoryID	QuantityPerUnit	UnitPrice	UnitsInStock
0	abc	0	0	abc	0	0
1	abc	1	1	abc	0.1	1
2	abc	2	2	abc	0.2	2
3	abc	3	3	abc	0.3	3
4	abc	4	4	abc	0.4	4

Figure 6-2   GridView bound to a SqlDataSource with zero code.

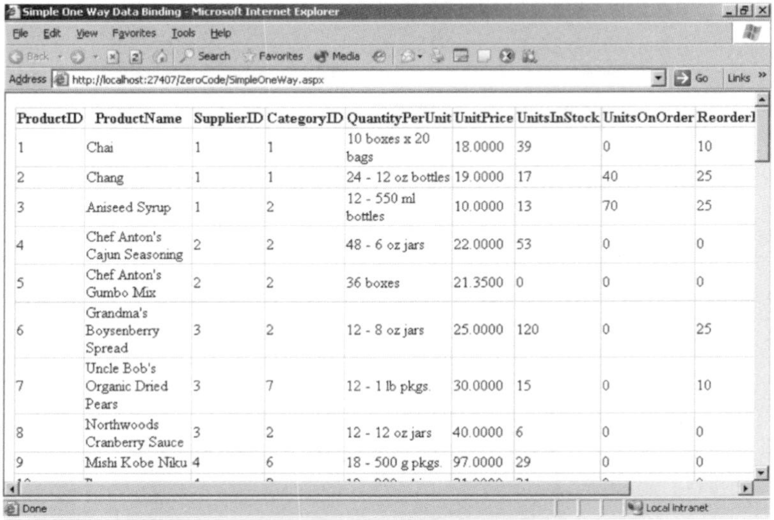

ProductID	ProductName	SupplierID	CategoryID	QuantityPerUnit	UnitPrice	UnitsInStock	UnitsOnOrder	Reorderl
1	Chai	1	1	10 boxes x 20 bags	18.0000	39	0	10
2	Chang	1	1	24 - 12 oz bottles	19.0000	17	40	25
3	Aniseed Syrup	1	2	12 - 550 ml bottles	10.0000	13	70	25
4	Chef Anton's Cajun Seasoning	2	2	48 - 6 oz jars	22.0000	53	0	0
5	Chef Anton's Gumbo Mix	2	2	36 boxes	21.3500	0	0	0
6	Grandma's Boysenberry Spread	3	2	12 - 8 oz jars	25.0000	120	0	25
7	Uncle Bob's Organic Dried Pears	3	7	12 - 1 lb pkgs.	30.0000	15	0	10
8	Northwoods Cranberry Sauce	3	2	12 - 12 oz jars	40.0000	6	0	0
9	Mishi Kobe Niku	4	6	18 - 500 g pkgs.	97.0000	29	0	0

Figure 6-3 Final output viewed in Internet Explorer.

Two-Way Data Binding

Although one-way data binding with zero code is convenient, the overall productivity benefit for creating a quick read-only display is not all that significant. The more daunting tasks in ASP.NET 1.1 are doing two-way data binding for CRUD (create, read, update, and delete) operations and presenting a usable interface, including features such as sorting and paging (for example, presenting 10 records per page with Next and Previous buttons). ASP.NET 2.0 makes short work of two-way data binding and requires, once again, zero code. The secrets lie in the abilities of the data source and *GridView* controls.

In the first page of this application, you saw how to create a *SqlDataSource* control configured to only select data. But the *SqlDataSource* control can also be used to update, insert, and delete data. The *SqlDataSource* control just requires the appropriate SQL commands and parameters for the different types of queries. You can type the many lines of ASPX markup yourself, or you can use the advanced features of the Data Source Configuration Wizard to create the markup for you.

When setting up the data selection for the Data Source Configuration Wizard, an Advanced Options button is available that opens the dialog window shown in Figure 6-4. Selecting the first check box will prompt the wizard to probe the database for the structure of the data using the select information you provide. After querying the database for the structure, the wizard will automatically create all the ASPX markup required for the *SqlDataSource* control to perform CRUD operations against your database.

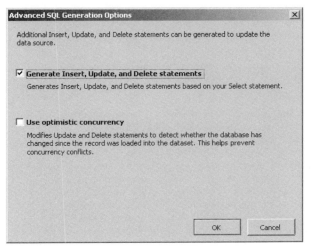

Figure 6-4   Advanced SQL generation options for the Data Source Configuration Wizard.

In Visual Studio .NET 2003, there are wizards to help you create the code for doing CRUD operations (for example, the Data Adapter Wizard), but the result is Visual Basic (or C#) code that you must then bind to data controls programmatically. Plus the generated code is placed in the "designer generated" region of the code file, where you make changes at your own peril because those changes will be lost if you invoke the wizard again. And moving the generated code out of the "designer generated" region means you cannot use the wizard to alter the adapter settings. By contrast, the Data Source Configuration Wizard in Visual Studio 2005 generates ASPX markup that declaratively expresses the update, insert, and delete commands with corresponding parameters. The following ASPX listing shows the markup generated by the wizard for the Northwind Products table.

```
<asp:SqlDataSource ID="SqlDataSource1" Runat="server"
    SelectCommand="SELECT [Products].* FROM [Products]"
    ConnectionString="<%$ ConnectionStrings:NorthwindConnection %>"
    DeleteCommand="DELETE FROM [Products]
                  WHERE [Products].[ProductID] = @ProductID"
    InsertCommand="INSERT INTO [Products] ([Products].[ProductName],
                  [Products].[SupplierID], [Products].[CategoryID],
                  [Products].[QuantityPerUnit], [Products].[UnitPrice],
                  [Products].[UnitsInStock], [Products].[UnitsOnOrder],
                  [Products].[ReorderLevel], [Products].[Discontinued])
                  VALUES (@ProductName, @SupplierID, @CategoryID,
                  @QuantityPerUnit, @UnitPrice, @UnitsInStock,
                  @UnitsOnOrder, @ReorderLevel, @Discontinued)"
    UpdateCommand="UPDATE [Products] SET
                  [Products].[ProductName] = @ProductName,
                  [Products].[SupplierID] = @SupplierID,
                  [Products].[CategoryID] = @CategoryID,
                  [Products].[QuantityPerUnit] = @QuantityPerUnit,
                  [Products].[UnitPrice] = @UnitPrice,
                  [Products].[UnitsInStock] = @UnitsInStock,
```

```
                              [Products].[UnitsOnOrder] = @UnitsOnOrder,
                              [Products].[ReorderLevel] = @ReorderLevel,
                              [Products].[Discontinued] = @Discontinued
                         WHERE [Products].[ProductID] = @ProductID">
    <DeleteParameters>
        <asp:Parameter Type="Int32" Name="ProductID"></asp:Parameter>
    </DeleteParameters>
    <UpdateParameters>
        <asp:Parameter Type="String" Name="ProductName"></asp:Parameter>
        <asp:Parameter Type="Int32" Name="SupplierID"></asp:Parameter>
        <asp:Parameter Type="Int32" Name="CategoryID"></asp:Parameter>
        <asp:Parameter Type="String" Name="QuantityPerUnit" />
        <asp:Parameter Type="Decimal" Name="UnitPrice"></asp:Parameter>
        <asp:Parameter Type="Int16" Name="UnitsInStock"></asp:Parameter>
        <asp:Parameter Type="Int16" Name="UnitsOnOrder"></asp:Parameter>
        <asp:Parameter Type="Int16" Name="ReorderLevel"></asp:Parameter>
        <asp:Parameter Type="Boolean" Name="Discontinued"></asp:Parameter>
        <asp:Parameter Type="Int32" Name="ProductID"></asp:Parameter>
    </UpdateParameters>
    <InsertParameters>
        <asp:Parameter Type="String" Name="ProductName"></asp:Parameter>
        <asp:Parameter Type="Int32" Name="SupplierID"></asp:Parameter>
        <asp:Parameter Type="Int32" Name="CategoryID"></asp:Parameter>
        <asp:Parameter Type="String" Name="QuantityPerUnit" />
        <asp:Parameter Type="Decimal" Name="UnitPrice"></asp:Parameter>
        <asp:Parameter Type="Int16" Name="UnitsInStock"></asp:Parameter>
        <asp:Parameter Type="Int16" Name="UnitsOnOrder"></asp:Parameter>
        <asp:Parameter Type="Int16" Name="ReorderLevel"></asp:Parameter>
        <asp:Parameter Type="Boolean" Name="Discontinued"></asp:Parameter>
    </InsertParameters>
</asp:SqlDataSource>
```

Other data controls such as the *GridView* can now be used to modify data in the database via the *SqlDataSource* control. To enable data modification for a *GridView* control, set the *AutoGenerateDeleteButton* and *AutoGenerateEditButton* properties to *True* in the Properties window as shown in Figure 6-5.

Figure 6-5   GridView properties for enabling data modification.

The resulting markup is not much different from the one-way data binding example. All that has been added is a *CommandField* element with two attributes that tell ASP.NET to generate edit and delete link buttons:

```
<asp:GridView ID="GridView1" Runat="server"
    DataSourceID="SqlDataSource1" DataKeyNames="ProductID">
    <Columns>
        <asp:CommandField ShowDeleteButton="True"
                          ShowEditButton="True">
        </asp:CommandField>
    </Columns>
</asp:GridView>
```

When you view this *GridView* in your browser, you see Edit and Delete links for each row of data. If you click an Edit link, the row changes to a set of editable controls (normally text boxes) as shown in Figure 6-6. Clicking Update saves the changes to the underlying data source (which is Microsoft SQL Server in this case). That's two-way data binding without writing a single line of code!

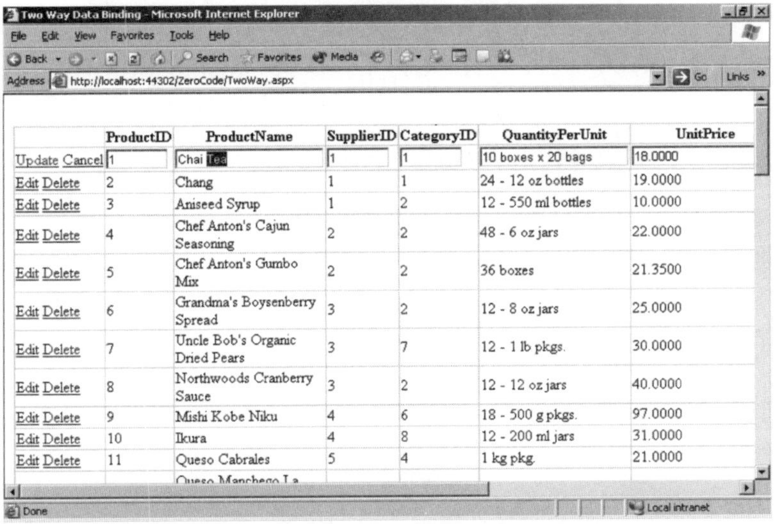

Figure 6-6   Editing products in Internet Explorer with zero code.

Prettifying a Zero-Code Site

These zero-code features are certainly compelling, but so far they're not very visually appealing or user friendly. As home and business users become more accustomed to the Web for work and pleasure, they demand more visually appealing Web pages—even for editing inventory data. Fortunately, ASP.NET 2.0 has plenty of support for formatting and otherwise enhancing the appearance of zero-code Web sites. For example, the *GridView* control allows you to control color, font, and layout information to create an attractive yet practical data table.

The fastest way to select a professional prepackaged look for your data control is to use the Auto Format feature, which is accessible via the Common Tasks smart tag window as shown in Figure 6-7. You can also use the Common Tasks window to enable sorting and paging for a *GridView* control. If you ever tried to work with paging in ASP.NET 1.1, with the *DataGrid* for example, you will appreciate how simple it is with the *GridView* control—just select one check box. The *GridView* and *SqlDataSource* take care of the rest of the details to control paging.

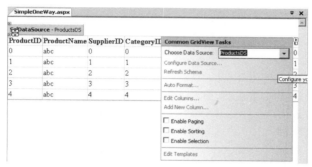

Figure 6-7   GridView Common Tasks smart tag dialog window.

The Auto Format dialog lets you choose from a number of prebuilt formats that include colors, fonts, row style, alternating row style, selected row style, header row style, and more. Figure 6-8 shows the Auto Format dialog being used to select a format for a *GridView* that will support paging (with up to 10 records per page) but not sorting.

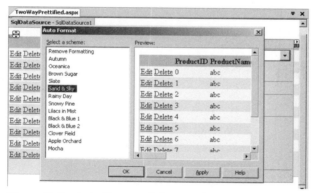

Figure 6-8   Auto Format dialog window.

The Auto Format feature in Visual Studio 2005 generates a number of elements and attributes for the selected control. The following markup was generated using the Sand & Sky format:

```
<asp:GridView ID="GridView1" Runat="server"
    AutoGenerateColumns="False" DataKeyNames="ProductID"
    DataSourceID="SqlDataSource1" BorderWidth="1px"
    BackColor="LightGoldenrodYellow"
    GridLines="None" CellPadding="2"
    BorderColor="Tan" ForeColor="Black">
```

```
        <FooterStyle BackColor="Tan"></FooterStyle>
        <PagerStyle ForeColor="DarkSlateBlue" HorizontalAlign="Center"
                BackColor="PaleGoldenrod">
        </PagerStyle>
        <HeaderStyle Font-Bold="True" BackColor="Tan"></HeaderStyle>
        <AlternatingRowStyle BackColor="PaleGoldenrod"></AlternatingRowStyle>
    ...
</asp:GridView>
```

Maintaining the same format for grids of data throughout your Web site by duplicating all this formatting for each grid would be an arduous task. Fortunately, this format could be applied universally in a Web site by creating a new Theme, as described in an upcoming application.

Note   When paging is enabled, you can use the *PageSize* attribute of the *GridView* control to change the number of rows of data displayed on each page.

Conclusion

Every Web application is unique, but there are always some similarities. One similarity is basic data access for either a read-only display or an interface for viewing and modifying data. The new zero-code features in ASP.NET 2.0 make it possible to write useful Web application building blocks without writing any code! Using wizards and other design-time features, Visual Studio 2005 can generate for you all the ASPX markup for defining a nontrivial Web application. Data access is just one of the common tasks available with zero code. As you will see in the next two applications, you can also create a Web site with authentication features, including new user registration and user login, without writing any code.

Application: Membership, Profiles, and Roles

This application highlights the new membership, profile, and role-based security features in ASP.NET 2.0 that make it easier to secure your Web applications.

New Concepts

Most real-world Web applications have some restricted sections that require users to be authenticated so that access can be granted or denied based on whether a user is authorized to use a protected resource. A common example is an administration section for updating content or viewing site statistics. ASP.NET supports several authentication schemes, including integrated Windows authentication and Passport authentication. Windows and Passport authentication are appropriate for some types of applications, but for many applications neither is practical. Windows authentication requires a user account for every user. Passport authentication is cost-prohibitive for small and medium-size sites. Therefore, the choice for many sites is custom authentication logic and a custom data store for storing credentials and other user-related data, such as first name, last name, address, and so on. ASP.NET 1.1 sites can take advantage of Forms Authentication for things like setting an authentication cookie, and they can use a general-purpose API for determining whether a user is logged in and what authorization roles that user belongs to. But creating the plumbing for managing user accounts is the responsibility of the Web developer.

The result has been countless ASP.NET Web applications put into production with almost identical authentication models implemented in each one. This common authentication model is so pervasive that it should be embedded right into the Web application platform. And that is exactly what ASP.NET 2.0 provides with its new membership and user profile features.

Membership

The new membership features in ASP.NET 2.0 simplify user management in three key ways:

1. They automatically create a data store. (ASP.NET 2.0 ships with built-in providers for Access and Microsoft SQL Server.) When you attempt to use membership features, ASP.NET 2.0 checks whether the specified data store is configured. If it is not, ASP.NET creates it. A template for an Access membership data file and scripts for creating a Microsoft SQL Server membership database are both included with ASP.NET 2.0.

2. They include server controls for creating and validating users and displaying user-specific information and login status. New controls such as the *Login*, *LoginStatus*, *CreateUserWizard*, and *ChangePassword* controls provide prebuilt user-interface building blocks, including functionality for the most common membership-related tasks. These controls are highlighted in the New Web Controls application.

3. They provide an application programming interface (API) for programmatically managing users. The Membership API is accessed via the *Membership* class and includes helpful methods such as *CreateUser*, *DeleteUser*, and *ValidateUser*.

With ASP.NET 2.0 Membership, you can actually create a Web site with protected pages, automatic redirects to a login page, user creation (registration), and user login without writing any code! As you will see in the "Walkthrough" section for this application, a few XML elements in web.config and a few server controls are all you need to create an authentication-enabled Web application with ASP.NET 2.0.

User Profiles

The membership features in ASP.NET 2.0 let you collect basic user information that is important for authentication, such as username, password, e-mail address, and a secret question/ answer pair for password retrieval. But often you will need to collect and store additional information, such as first name, last name, Web site or Weblog URL, job title, and possibly much more. The new user profile features in ASP.NET 2.0 give you the ability to define additional pieces of information about a user that your application must store. You simply specify in web.config the pieces of information you require and then populate the corresponding fields in a special *Profile* object at runtime.

The *Profile* object that ASP.NET 2.0 generates is specific to your application and contains strongly typed properties that map to the entries in your application's web.config file. The Visual Studio IDE reads these entries at design time and builds a specialized class (inherited from *HttpProfileBase*) automatically so that your application-specific properties are available in the Intellisense menu and can be verified by the compiler. The "Walkthrough" section for this application shows you how to set up user profiles in web.config and then how to access user-specific profile data at run time.

Role-Based Security

Authenticating users on your Web site allows you to identify users, but without additional role-based authorization you cannot restrict access to Web resources based on the user's identity. ASP.NET has always included built-in support for determining whether a user is in a role via the user's security principal object. When using Windows authentication, roles come from the Windows security groups. But when using Forms authentication in ASP.NET 1.1, you have to build your own security principal object and populate its roles collection as each Web request is authenticated. As a developer, you are also responsible for writing the code to maintain a data store for user roles and to load that data at run time.

ASP.NET 2.0 expands the role-based security story with the introduction of ASP.NET role management, including the new *Roles* class and the *<roleManager>* configuration section for web.config. ASP.NET role management provides the most common role-based security features that you would have previously had to build yourself. The *Roles* class provides an API for creating and deleting roles, adding and removing users from roles, enumerating roles, enumerating the users in a role, enumerating the roles a user is in, and more. ASP.NET role management takes care of persisting the role membership data, loading it at run time, and adding the appropriate roles to a user's security principal.

Walkthrough

This application demonstrates the use of the new membership, profile, and role-based security features in ASP.NET 2.0. This walkthrough includes details about configuring these new features and working with them programmatically.

Membership

ASP.NET Membership is easy to configure in Visual Studio 2005. When you create a new Web site in Visual Studio 2005, the Solution Explorer looks similar to the example shown in Figure 6-9.

Figure 6-9   Solution Explorer before accessing the Membership API.

When you access the Membership API at run time, the membership database specified in the ASP.NET configuration is created automatically if it does not exist. ASP.NET 2.0 ships with a template for a Microsoft Access data file for membership, as well as with a set of SQL scripts for creating a Microsoft SQL Server membership database. The type of data store used to persist membership data is controlled using ASP.NET configuration. If a data provider is not explicitly stated in web.config, the default from the machine.config file is used. In this application, the default from machine.config is the provider for Microsoft Access, so an Access data file is automatically created in the Data subfolder of the Web site when the Membership API is accessed.

Figure 6-10   Solution Explorer showing an auto-generated membership data file.

This first Web form in this application accesses three of the most useful methods in the Membership API: *CreateUser*, *ValidateUser*, and *GetAllUsers*. The Membership API also contains the other types of maintenance features you would expect for authentication management, such as looking up users by e-mail address, modifying users, deleting users, and setting passwords. The methods in this API are easy to use and quite self-explanatory. For example, the simplest version of the *CreateUser* method takes two obvious parameters: username and password. An overloaded version of *CreateUser* also takes an e-mail address. The following line of code is all that you have to write to create a new user in your membership database:

```
Membership.CreateUser(txtUserName.Text, txtPassword.Text)
```

The *CreateUser* method call creates the user in the database, but at some point you will need to retrieve that data from the database so that you can validate the user's credentials. All of this happens automatically by simply calling the *ValidateUser* method:

```
If Membership.ValidateUser(txtUserName.Text, txtPassword.Text) Then
    FormsAuthentication.SetAuthCookie(txtUserName.Text, False)
    Response.Redirect(Request.Path)
End If
```

The Membership API makes it almost trivial to do the types of common user management tasks that you would otherwise have to write all the data access and business logic for. For example, to retrieve a list of all users in the membership database, simply enumerate through the collection of users returned by the *GetAllUsers* method:

```
Dim users As MembershipUserCollection = Membership.GetAllUsers()
```

The full source for Default.aspx in this application includes *TextBox* controls for username and password and *Button* controls to create a user or log in as a user. The Web form also contains a *ListBox* to hold a list of all users in the membership database. A *Label* is used to display login status. The following ASPX markup and Visual Basic code is the subset of Default.aspx that deals with membership (that is, the code without user profile and role-based security features added):

```
<%@ page language="VB" %>

<script runat="server">

    Sub Page_Load(ByVal sender As Object, ByVal e As System.EventArgs)
        Dim users As MembershipUserCollection = Membership.GetAllUsers()
        Dim userArray As New ArrayList(users.Count)
        For Each mu As MembershipUser In users
            userArray.Add(mu.Username)
        Next
        UserList.DataSource = userArray
        UserList.DataBind()

        If User.Identity.IsAuthenticated Then
            lblLoginStatus.Text = "You are currently authenticated as " + _
                            User.Identity.Name
        End If

    End Sub

    Sub btnCreate_Click(ByVal sender As Object, _
                    ByVal e As System.EventArgs)
        Membership.CreateUser(txtUserName.Text, txtPassword.Text)
    End Sub

    Sub btnLogin_Click(ByVal sender As Object, ByVal e As System.EventArgs)
        If Membership.ValidateUser(txtUserName.Text, txtPassword.Text) Then
            FormsAuthentication.SetAuthCookie(txtUserName.Text, False)
            Response.Redirect(Request.Path)
        End If
    End Sub
</script>

<html>
<head runat="server">
    <title>Untitled Page</title>
</head>
<body>
    <form id="form1" runat="server">
    <div>
        Username: <asp:TextBox ID="txtUserName"
                    Runat="server"></asp:TextBox>
```

```
        <br />
        Password: <asp:TextBox ID="txtPassword"
                   Runat="server"></asp:TextBox>
        <br />
        <asp:Button ID="btnCreate" Runat="server" Text="Create User"
                   OnClick="btnCreate_Click" />
        <asp:Button ID="btnLogin" Runat="server" Text="Login"
                   OnClick="btnLogin_Click" />
        <asp:Label ID="lblLoginStatus" Runat="server"></asp:Label>
    </div>
    <p>
        Users in Membership database:
        <br />
        <asp:ListBox ID="UserList" runat="server"></asp:ListBox>
    </p>
    </form>
</body>
</html>
```

Figure 6-11 shows Default.aspx at run time with only the membership features added. As you will see in the New Web Controls application, ASP.NET 2.0 even makes the user interface aspect of authentication easier by providing new security controls such as the *Login* and *LoginStatus* controls.

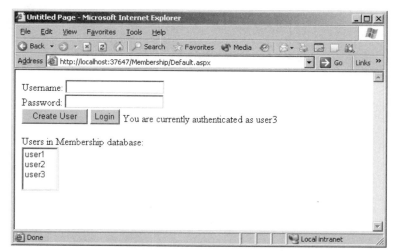

Figure 6-11   Web form in Internet Explorer showing all users in the membership database.

> **Note**   The default authentication mode in ASP.NET is Windows. To use Forms Authentication, which is what this application uses, you must set the *Mode* attribute of the *<authentication>* element in web.config to *"Forms"*.

User Profiles

User profiles in ASP.NET 2.0, sometimes referred to as *user personalization* or *profile personalization*, are configured in the web.config file for a Web site. You state declaratively in the configuration file the data you want to store for each user and then populate the corresponding properties in a special *Profile* object. The following subset of a web.config file configures a Web site to store *FirstName* and *LastName* string values for each user:

```xml
<?xml version="1.0"?>
<configuration>
   <system.web>
        <authentication mode="Forms" />
        <profile inherits="System.Web.Profile.HttpProfileBase, System.Web,
              Version=2.0.3600.0, Culture=neutral,
              PublicKeyToken=b03f5f7f11d50a3a">
         <properties>
            <add name="FirstName" type="System.String" />
            <add name="LastName" type="System.String" />
         </properties>
        </profile>
   </system.web>
</configuration>
```

Visual Studio 2005 reads this configuration information from the web.config file and dynamically creates a specialized class that inherits from *HttpProfileBase*. The specialized class contains all the properties defined in the web.config file with the proper data types. Figure 6-12 shows an example of a custom profile property being made available in Intellisense.

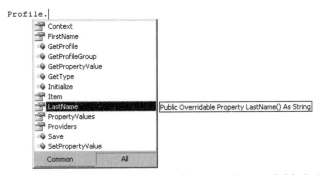

Figure 6-12   Strongly typed profile properties available in Intellisense.

At run time, ASP.NET 2.0 takes care of managing the persistence of the profile data. As a programmer, your only tasks are to read and write that data. The following code shows how you set the *FirstName* and *LastName* properties and save them to the profile data store:

```
Profile.FirstName = txtFirstName.Text
Profile.LastName = txtLastName.Text
Profile.Save()
```

To read the data back from the *Profile* object, simply invert the assignment statements:

```
txtFirstName.Text = Profile.FirstName
txtLastName.Text = Profile.LastName
```

By default, these profile properties can be set only for (and therefore are stored only for) authenticated users. But in some situations you will want to capture information when a user is browsing anonymously and maintain that data when the user logs in to your site. ASP.NET user profiles support this type of scenario natively. You must explicitly enable anonymous profiling using the *<anonymousIdentification>* element in web.config. Then any properties that you want to support for anonymous users must have the *allowAnonymous* attribute set to true. The following XML from web.config shows these settings for this application:

```
<anonymousIdentification enabled="true" />
<profile inherits="System.Web.Profile.HttpProfileBase, System.Web,
        Version=2.0.3600.0, Culture=neutral,
        PublicKeyToken=b03f5f7f11d50a3a" >
  <properties>
    <add name="FirstName" type="System.String" />
    <add name="LastName" type="System.String" />
    <add name="FirstVisit" type="System.String" allowAnonymous="true" />
  </properties>
</profile>
```

Role-Based Security

ASP.NET 2.0 role management provides a number of related features for creating and maintaining roles and role membership. To enable role management for a Web site, add the *<roleManager>* element to your web.config file. When you are configuring role management, you can choose to have the roles for a user encrypted and cached in a cookie. Although the caching is useful for reducing the number of trips to the data store to obtain user role information, it can also introduce a problem in which the roles in the cookie do not match a recently updated set of roles in the server-side data store. This difference can be especially problematic when you are changing role membership a lot. For this application, cookie caching is disabled by setting the *cacheRolesInCookie* attribute of the *<roleManager>* element to false:

```
<roleManager enabled="true"
             cacheRolesInCookie="false" />
```

Now every time an authenticated request is processed, the roles will be re-read from the data store and loaded into the user's security principal object.

Before you can assign users to roles, you must create the roles. This is done using the *CreateRole* method of the *Roles* class. Roles are stored on a per-application basis, so the roles created for this application are completely independent from the roles for other applications.

```
Roles.CreateRole("Admin")
Roles.CreateRole("Editor")
Roles.CreateRole("Reviewer")
```

Chapter 6:   Building Web Applications   **163**

Once you have created roles, you can do the expected maintenance tasks, such as obtaining a list of all roles in your application. The *GetAllRoles* method returns an array of *String* objects containing the names of the roles previously created:

```
Dim allRoles() As String = Roles.GetAllRoles
```

Now that the roles actually exist, users can be assigned to roles. For assigning one user to one role at a time, use the *AddUserToRole* method:

```
Roles.AddUserToRole(UserList.SelectedValue, RolesList.SelectedValue)
```

If you want to add multiple users to a role simultaneously, you can use the *AddUsersToRole* method. If you want to add one user to multiple roles, you can use the *AddUserToRoles* method. And to add multiple users to multiple roles simultaneously, you can use the *AddUsersToRoles* method.

ASP.NET 2.0 role management also adds one new feature that solves a small but frustrating limitation from ASP.NET 1.1—the ability to get a list of all the roles for a user without having to write data-access code to read from the underlying data source:

```
Roles.GetRolesForUser(User.Identity.Name)
```

Figure 6-13 shows the culmination of these features into a simple user interface that lets you create a user, create roles, assign users to roles, and then log in as a user and see all the roles in the application plus all the roles that the individual user belongs to.

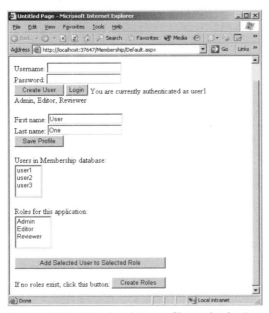

Figure 6-13   Membership, profile, and roles in use.

Conclusion

User management is an almost ubiquitous Web development task for which there are some very well-established patterns, including authentication using a username and password; storing user profile information such as first name, last name, and address; and role-based authorization. ASP.NET 1.1 provides some support for user management—such as a generic authentication model and built-in differentiation between authenticated and anonymous users—and it provides some support for role-based authorization. But with ASP.NET 1.1, the bulk of the burden for creating and maintaining the logic and data stores to do commonplace user management tasks fell to the developer. Similar code including data access for credentials, profiles, and roles has been written over and over again by countless developers. Finally, with ASP.NET 2.0 there is support for common user management chores built right into the ASP.NET Web platform.

Application: New Web Controls

This application demonstrates some of the new Web controls in ASP.NET 2.0, such as the new security controls that provide prebuilt user interface elements for the new ASP.NET 2.0 membership system.

New Concepts

There are a lot of new controls in ASP.NET 2.0—too many to introduce in one sample application. There are new data-source controls, new data-bound controls, new security controls, new Web part controls, new navigation controls, and new mobile-aware features in the controls from ASP.NET 1.1. This application highlights the new controls that are most applicable to general Web development—hopefully, they are the ones that will fulfill some of your most immediate needs as a Web developer.

Security Controls

Any Web site that uses authentication to verify a user's identity or restrict access to protected resources requires some sort of user interface for all the different authentication tasks, such as logging in, registering (creating a new account), displaying login status, displaying a personalized logout link, and resetting passwords. In ASP.NET 1.1, you were on your own for all these user interface components. In ASP.NET 2.0, there is a set of new security controls with which you can add basic security features to your site without even writing a single line of code.

The security controls included in the preview version of Visual Studio 2005 are as follows:

- *Login*: This is a composite control that ties into the ASP.NET membership features. It contains *TextBox* controls for entering a username and password, as well as a Submit button. This control also includes a number of customizable features, including formatting and all the various pieces of text that can appear, such as instructional text, login failed text, and title text for the control. You can also choose to have the control display hyperlinks to registration and password recovery pages. The *Login* control even includes built-in required field validation for both username and password. (Validation can be disabled.) You can write code to support a *Login* control—in the *Authenticate* event handler, for example—but it is entirely unnecessary. Even the simplest use of the *Login* control with absolutely zero code provides a complete working authentication interface.

■ *CreateUserWizard*: This control provides a wizard-style interface for creating a new user in the membership system. The *CreateUserWizard* is a lot more than a simple form for entering a username and password. It includes field validation for all of its fields, including optional regular expression validation for e-mail addresses. It prompts the user to enter a proposed password twice and confirms that the passwords match. The *Create-UserWizard* control can also gather a security question and answer from the user if the underlying membership provider supports security questions. The "Walkthrough" section for this application also shows how you can add custom steps to the wizard to collect additional information from the user during registration.

■ *LoginName*: This control is a placeholder that displays the username of the user. If the current user is anonymous (that is, not authenticated), this control does not render any output. The *LoginName* exposes a *FormatString* property that you can use to display more than just the username. For example, the *FormatString* could be set to `"Welcome, {0}"`, which would produce the output `"Welcome, UserTwo"` when UserTwo is logged in.

■ *LoginView*: This control provides templates in which you can create different content for anonymous and authenticated users. The *LoginView* control is also role-aware, so you can actually create different templates for authenticated users in different roles.

■ *PasswordRecovery*: This control provides the user interface and corresponding functionality to help users retrieve or reset their passwords. The control has three views: Username, Question, and Success. The Username view allows the user to enter the username for which a password has to be retrieved or reset. The Question view prompts the user for the answer to a question that was entered during registration. The Success view displays a success message after the password has been delivered via e-mail. The options available for password retrieval are determined in part by the Membership provider used to provide membership services. ASP.NET 2.0 includes providers for Microsoft Access and Microsoft SQL Server. Both of these providers support password retrieval and security questions. Other providers, such as a third-party offering or one you create yourself, might not support all those features. Also, the default for both of the built-in providers is to store password hashes. (Clear text and encrypted text are the other options.) Password hashes cannot be used to determine the original password, so by default the only recovery scheme available is to reset the password and e-mail the new password to the user.

■   *LoginStatus*: This control produces a Login or Logout hyperlink based on the login status of the current user: an anonymous user sees a Login link, and an authenticated user sees a Logout link. The actual text for the hyperlink as well as the target of the link is, of course, customizable. The Logout link can be configured to do one of three things after the user has logged out: refresh the current page, redirect the user to the login page, or redirect the user to some other page.

■   *ChangePassword*: This composite control provides users with an interface for changing their passwords. The default is to require the user to type the current password once and the new password twice. Like the other security controls, *ChangePassword* is completely customizable.

Site Map Controls

The new *SiteMapPath* control provides part of a new site map solution built into ASP.NET 2.0. The *SiteMapPath* control provides a "breadcrumb" navigation interface that is popular on many Web sites. In ASP.NET 1.1, you had to create all the logic for breadcrumb navigation or buy a third-party solution. The *SiteMapPath* control only requires your Web site to have an XML file called web.sitemap that defines the hierarchy of pages in your site. The *SiteMapPath* control determines where the current page sits within the site map hierarchy and automatically creates the breadcrumb navigation. If the *SiteMapPath* control is placed on a Web form not included in the site map file, the *SiteMapPath* simply does not render a breadcrumb trail.

ASP.NET 2.0 also includes a new *SiteMapDataSource* control that reads the web.sitemap file and acts as a data source for other controls such as a *TreeView*. The "Walkthrough" section for this application shows how to create a web.sitemap file, how to use the *SiteMapPath* control, and how to create a site map tree by using the *SiteMapDataSource* control.

Substitution Control (Post-Cache Substitution)

Output caching is a technique for saving the output from an ASP.NET Web form and reusing the same output to fulfill multiple requests for the same page. Output caching is a huge boon for Web site performance when it can be used. In ASP.NET 1.1, there was no way to alter the contents of a cached page for individual users, so many Web pages could not benefit from output caching because of some small portion of the page content that had to be customized for each user (for example, a personalized greeting or the number of items in the user's shopping cart).

Page-fragment caching is a way of caching the output from user controls on a Web form. If you can design your Web forms as a set of user controls, you can get some of the performance benefit of output caching while having control over page elements that have to be personalized. But page-fragment caching can be awkward to use because you have to break your pages into user controls to allow for even the simplest per-request customization. ASP.NET 2.0 introduces a new way to benefit from output caching *and* do per-user customization. This new approach is called *post-cache substitution*.

Post-cache substitution is accomplished by placing *Substitution* controls on a Web form and then providing the name of a shared (static) callback method that ASP.NET can call to obtain content to inject into the cached output. Although post-cache substitution is obviously not going to provide as much of a performance boost as pure output caching, the extra cost of calling the callback method is directly tied to the performance characteristics of the callback method.

Walkthrough

This walkthrough shows you how to use the new security Web controls in ASP.NET 2.0. This walkthrough also demonstrates how to use the new site map controls and how to do post-cache substitution using the new *Substitution* control.

Security Controls

ASP.NET 2.0 introduces seven new security controls to cover the most common authentication and user management needs in Web applications. A small time investment (to discover the capabilities of these seven controls) can yield much larger time savings as you build new Web applications or migrate existing applications to ASP.NET.

Login Control   Although it is not the most complex of the security controls, the *Login* control can be considered the core security control because it provides the interface that actually collects credentials and validates them against the membership database. The *Login* control contains a considerable number of properties that let you configure the display and behavior of the control. Figure 6-14 shows some of the *Login* control properties you can edit in the Properties window.

Figure 6-14   Properties window for the Login control.

You can configure the *Login* control to redirect the user to a specific page after successfully validating the user's credentials. You can also configure the *Login* control to either refresh the current page or redirect the user to your site's login page after an unsuccessful login attempt. You can also modify all the text displayed by the control, including the labels, instructions, help text, the failure message, and the control title.

This application uses most of the default settings for the *Login* control. The ASPX markup for the *Login* control on the login.aspx page of this application is as follows:

```
<asp:Login ID="Login1" Runat="server"
    CreateUserText="Register for a new account"
    CreateUserUrl="Register.aspx"
    PasswordRecoveryText="Forgot your password?"
    PasswordRecoveryUrl="PasswordRecovery.aspx" >
</asp:Login>
```

The *CreateUserUrl* attribute tells the *Login* control to provide a hyperlink to the user registration page. The *CreateUserText* attribute specifies the text displayed for that hyperlink. Similarly, the *PasswordRecoveryUrl* attribute tells the *Login* control to provide a hyperlink to a page where users can have their passwords reset. The *PasswordRecoveryText* attribute specifies the text displayed for that hyperlink. Figure 6-15 shows the *Login* control in Internet Explorer after a failed login attempt.

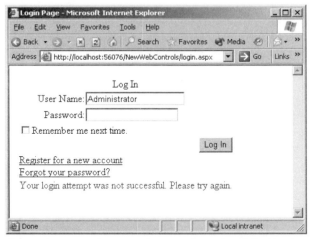

Figure 6-15   Login control at run time after failed login attempt.

CreateUserWizard Control   To log in, you will first have to create an account. As you saw in the previous application, you can do this via the *Membership.CreateUser* method, but that would require you to build your own user interface and write at least one line of code. With the *CreateUserWizard*, you simply add one control to a Web form and set a few properties. The control takes care of the rest of the details.

The *CreateUserWizard* is actually a very powerful control because it lets you add your own custom steps to the wizard. In this application, a new step has been added to the wizard that asks new users for their favorite color, which is then stored using the built-in ASP.NET user profile features.

The *CreateUserWizard* lets you configure almost everything about its appearance and behavior—everything from labels and prompts to the regular expression used to validate e-mail addresses. One attribute you will want to set for this control is the *ContinueDestination-PageUrl*, which determines where the *CreateUserWizard* control redirects the user after successfully creating a new account. The following ASPX listing is the markup that defines the *CreateUserWizard* control for the Register.aspx page in this application. Note the *<asp:WizardStep>* element used to define a custom step in the wizard.

```
<asp:CreateUserWizard ID="CreateUserWizard1" Runat="server"
                      ContinueDestinationPageUrl="default.aspx"
                      OnContinueClick="CreateUserWizard1_ContinueClick">
  <WizardSteps>
    <asp:WizardStep Runat="server" ID="SignStep"
                    Title="What is your favorite color?"
                    StepType="Step">
      What is your favorite color?<br />
      <asp:TextBox Runat="server" ID="txtColor"></asp:TextBox>
    </asp:WizardStep>
  </WizardSteps>
</asp:CreateUserWizard>
```

Figures 6-16, 6-17, and 6-18 show the steps that the user goes through to create a new account. Notice the custom step (Figure 6-17) in the wizard that asks for the user's favorite color.

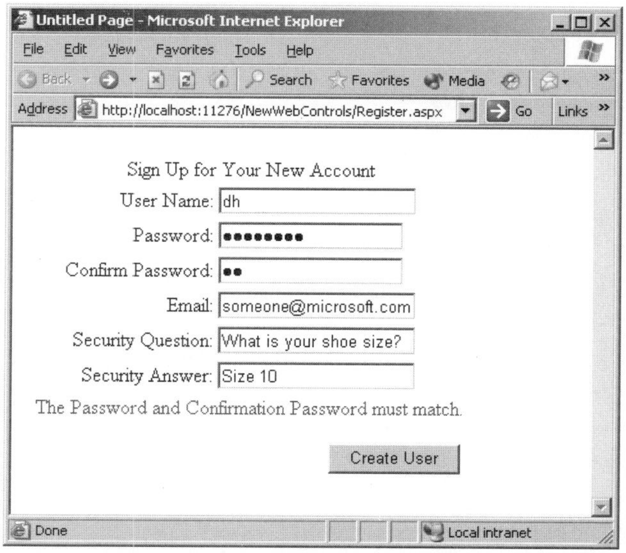

Figure 6-16   CreateUserWizard control showing the ConfirmPasswordCompareErrorMessage.

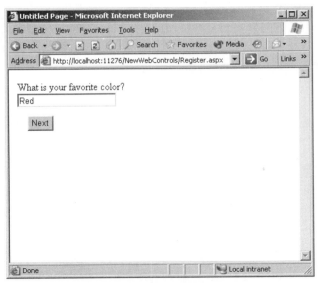

Figure 6-17   CreateUserWizard custom wizard step.

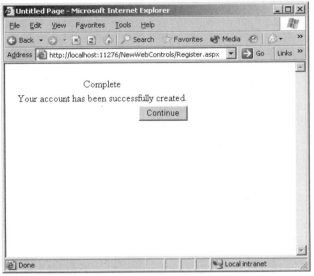

Figure 6-18   CreateUserWizard final success step.

When the user clicks the Continue button on the final success step, the *CreateUserWizard* control raises a *ContinueClick* event for which you can write an event handler. At that point, the user will be logged in automatically (unless you change the *LoginCreatedUser* attribute to false). In the event handler, you can access the controls in custom wizard steps and retrieve the values entered by the user during the account-creation process. The following code shows how to obtain a reference to the *txtColor* control and save the user's favorite color in the user's profile:

```
Sub CreateUserwizard1_ContinueClick(ByVal sender As Object, _
                                ByVal e As System.EventArgs)
  Dim txtColor As Control
  txtColor = CreateUserwizard1.FindControl("txtColor")
  If Not txtColor Is Nothing Then
    Profile.FavoriteColor = DirectCast(txtColor, TextBox).Text
    Profile.Save()
  End If
End Sub
```

LoginName Control   The *LoginName* control is the simplest of the new security controls. If the current user is authenticated, the *LoginName* control displays the username. If the current user is not authenticated, the *LoginName* does not display any output. The following ASPX markup shows how the *LoginName* control is used in this application:

```
Thank you for using our site,
<asp:LoginName ID="Loginname1" Font-Bold="true" Runat="server" />
```

In this example, the username is in bold but the greeting preceding the username is not. If both the greeting and the username were going to have the same font weight, the greeting could be placed in the *FormatString* attribute as shown here:

```
<asp:LoginName ID="Loginname1"
            FormatString=" Thank you for using our site, {0}"
            Runat="server" />
```

LoginView Control   If you have ever created a Web page that had to render different content for different types of users, you know that the code is reasonably simple but tedious to create and maintain. Even in ASP.NET 1.1 you have to do a lot of work placing the content within server controls that can act as containers (for example, *<div runat="server">*) and then writing the logic to show and hide the server controls based on the type of user viewing the page.

The *LoginView* control has built-in support for user roles, so you can create different views for authenticated users based on role. The *LoginView* control handles the task of selecting the appropriate view based on the current user's roles. The following code is from the Default.aspx page in this application. The *LoginView* control in this example has four views: one for anonymous users, one for authenticated users, one for authenticated users in the Admin role, and one for authenticated users in the NormalUser role.

```
<asp:LoginView ID="Loginview1" Runat="server">
    <RoleGroups>
        <asp:RoleGroup Roles="Admin">
            <ContentTemplate>
                Hello, Admin.
            </ContentTemplate>
        </asp:RoleGroup>
        <asp:RoleGroup Roles="NormalUser">
            <ContentTemplate>
                Ah, a normal user
            </ContentTemplate>
```

```
        </asp:RoleGroup>
    </RoleGroups>
    <LoggedInTemplate>
        <div align="center">
            Thank you for using our site,
            <asp:LoginName ID="Loginname1" Font-Bold="true"
                           Runat="server" />
        </div>
    </LoggedInTemplate>
    <AnonymousTemplate>
        Welcome to our Web site. You are not
        currently logged in.
        <a href="login.aspx">Click here</a> to sign up
        for a free account.
    </AnonymousTemplate>
</asp:LoginView>
```

One of the great features of the *LoginView* control is that all the templates you create do not clutter your visual design surface in Visual Studio 2005, so your design-time representation of the Web form is not skewed in the same way it can be when working with multiple *<div runat="server">* or *<asp:Panel>* controls. Figure 6-19 shows the *LoginView* control from Default.aspx in Visual Studio 2005 at design time.

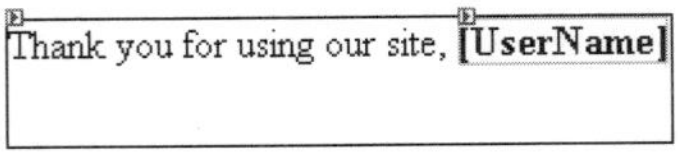

Thank you for using our site, **[UserName]**

Figure 6-19   LoginView control at design time.

The Default.aspx page in this application also contains the code below. The code contains two *Click* event handlers that both call the *SetRole* method but pass in different role names. The *SetRole* method creates the Admin and NormalUser roles if they do not already exist. Then the *SetRole* method removes the current user from all roles. Finally, the *SetRole* method adds the current user to the role specified in the *roleName* parameter. When Default.aspx is then rendered, the *LoginView* on the page displays the appropriate view based on the user's current role membership.

```
Sub bntMakeAdmin_Click(ByVal sender As Object, _
                       ByVal e As System.EventArgs)
    SetRole("Admin")
End Sub

Sub btnMakeNormalUser_Click(ByVal sender As Object, _
                            ByVal e As System.EventArgs)
    SetRole("NormalUser")
End Sub

Sub SetRole(ByVal roleName As String)
    If Roles.GetAllRoles().Length = 0 Then
        Roles.CreateRole("Admin")
        Roles.CreateRole("NormalUser")
    End If
    For Each r As String In Roles.GetRolesForUser(User.Identity.Name)
```

```
        Roles.RemoveUserFromRole(User.Identity.Name, r)
    Next
    Roles.AddUserToRole(User.Identity.Name, roleName)
End Sub
```

PasswordRecovery Control   The *PasswordRecovery* control is deceptively simple at first glance. The ASPX markup required for a fully functional e-mail-enabled password recovery solution is a mere one line:

```
<asp:PasswordRecovery ID="Passwordrecovery1" Runat="server" />
```

With this one line of markup, ASP.NET 2.0 empowers your Web site with the ability for users to enter their username, answer their security question, and have a new password sent to them by e-mail. And as with the other security controls, the *PasswordRecovery* control is highly configurable.

Figures 6-20 and 6-21 show the steps that users go through when resetting a password.

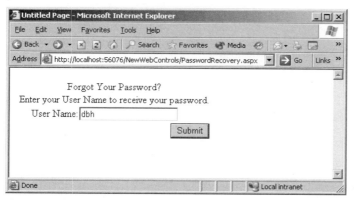

Figure 6-20   First step in password recovery.

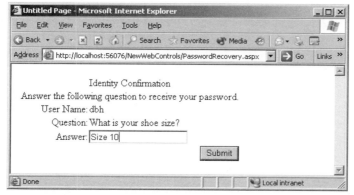

Figure 6-21   Second step in password recovery.

LoginStatus Control   The *LoginStatus* control is not a very complex control like some of the other security controls, but it is very convenient. Web sites commonly have a login link somewhere that takes users to a login page. After a user logs in, that link becomes a logout link. In many Web development environments, you would have to write the logic to check the user's login status and render the appropriate HTML (for example, by enabling the appropriate *HyperLink* or *LinkButton* control in ASP.NET 1.1). In ASP.NET 2.0, all you need is a *LoginStatus* control:

```
<asp:LoginStatus ID="Loginstatus1" Runat="server"  />
```

The *LoginStatus* control can be configured in several ways. For example, you can state what the control should do after a user logs out: refresh the page, redirect to another page, or redirect to the login page. Figure 6-22 shows the Login link seen by an anonymous user. Figure 6-23 shows the Logout link seen by an authenticated user.

Figure 6-22   LoginStatus control rendered for an anonymous user.

Figure 6-23   LoginStatus control rendered for an authenticated user.

ChangePassword Control   The *ChangePassword* control provides an interface for users to change their passwords. As with the other security controls, *ChangePassword* can be used with a single line of ASPX markup or it can also be completely customized. The following markup is from the Default.aspx page of this application. It changes only the type of navigation that the control presents to the user: instead of buttons the control will use hyperlinks.

```
<asp:ChangePassword ID="ChangePassword1" Runat="server"
                    CancelButtonType="Link"
                    ChangePasswordButtonType="Link"
                    ContinueButtonType="Link">
```

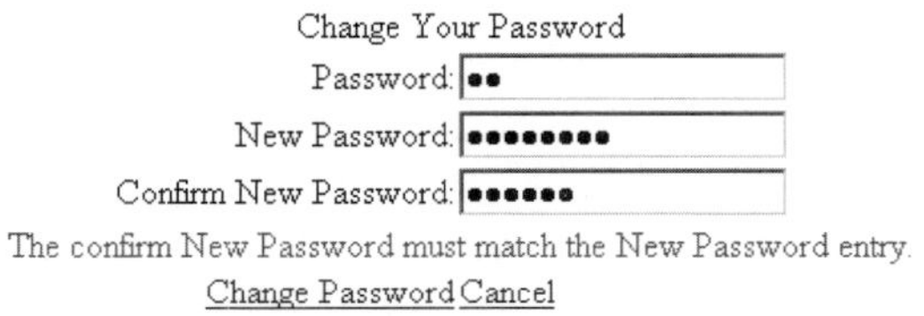

Figure 6-24   ChangePassword control with links instead of buttons for navigation.

Site Maps

Site maps are an essential part of many Web sites. They can act as a launching point into any part of your site and help improve search engine rankings. Site maps are commonly maintained as HTML documents, but there are many drawbacks to maintaining a site map as HTML. One of the biggest problems is that site maps contain hierarchical data that can change regularly. Maintaining that data in HTML requires you to think about formatting and placement issues every time you add, move, or delete a page. In ASP.NET 2.0, you can maintain your site map in a special file called web.sitemap. The web.sitemap file for this application looks like this:

```
<siteMap>
    <siteMapNode title="Home" description="Home" url="default.aspx" >
        <siteMapNode title="Login"
                     description="Home"
                     url="login.aspx" />
        <siteMapNode title="Register"
                     description="Home"
                     url="register.aspx" />
        <siteMapNode title="Forgot Password"
                     description="Home"
                     url="PasswordRecovery.aspx" />
        <siteMapNode title="Articles"
                     description="Articles"
                     url="Articles/default.aspx" >
            <siteMapNode title="Article One"
                         description=""
                         url="Articles/Article1.aspx" />
        </siteMapNode>
    </siteMapNode>
</siteMap>
```

Every page in your site can be entered in the site map as a *<siteMapNode>* element. Because every page is a *<siteMapNode>* element and every *<siteMapNode>* element can contain other *<siteMapNode>* elements, you can easily change the structure of your Web site without worrying about indentation and other formatting issues that Webmasters have to struggle with when they maintain site maps as HTML.

Because the site map is stored as XML, it is easy to work with in a number of ways. One of the new data source controls introduced in ASP.NET 2.0 is the *SiteMapDataSource*. The *SiteMapDataSource* automatically reads web.sitemap and exposes that data for other controls to use. The following markup is from SiteMap.aspx. It binds a *TreeView* control to a *SiteMapDataSource*. The result can be seen in Figure 6-25.

```
<asp:SiteMapDataSource ID="SiteMapDataSource1" Runat="server" />
<asp:TreeView ID="TreeView1" Runat="server"
              DataSourceID="SiteMapDataSource1">
</asp:TreeView>
```

Figure 6-25   TreeView control bound to a SiteMapDataSource.

Another important part of many Web sites is the breadcrumb navigation trail that shows you where you are within the hierarchy of pages in that Web site. The hierarchical information displayed in breadcrumb navigation is generally the same hierarchical data in a site map, so it makes perfect sense to have a control that can create the breadcrumb navigation based on the site map. The *SiteMapPath* control in ASP.NET 2.0 reads the site map and renders appropriate breadcrumb navigation based on where the current page fits in the site hierarchy. The following ASPX markup is from Articles/Article1.aspx:

```
<asp:SiteMapPath ID="SiteMapPath1" Runat="server">
</asp:SiteMapPath>
```

When viewed in Internet Explorer, the *SiteMapPath* produces the navigation path shown in Figure 6-26.

Figure 6-26   SiteMapPath control rendered in Article1.aspx.

Post-Cache Substitution

The *Substitution* control, which allows you to inject data into cached pages, is really little more than a placeholder for data to be substituted at run time. The only interesting attribute of the *Substitution* control is *MethodName*. The *MethodName* attribute specifies a method to be called at run time to obtain the data to be substituted for the placeholder in the cached output. The name of the method does not matter, but it has to be shared (static) and must accept an *Http-Context* object as a parameter.

The ASPX markup that follows is from PostCacheSubstitution/default.aspx. The page contains some static text and a *Label* control named *cacheTime*. The current time is put into the *Text* property of *cacheTime* when the *Page_Load* event handler fires. This page uses the *@Output-Cache* directive to cache page output for 60 seconds. That means that the content of the page, including the text in the *cacheTime Label* control, is generated once and then retrieved from the cache for any subsequent requests during those 60 seconds. The *Page_Load* event handler will execute on the first request for this page, but it will not execute again until the first request after the content in the output cache expires (after 60 seconds).

The *Substitution* control is an exception to the output caching model. The callback method specified in the *MethodName* attribute is called on every request. ASP.NET passes the current *HttpContext* to the callback method, so it has complete access to the assortment of objects normally available during request fulfillment, such as *Request*, *Server*, and *User*. In this example, the callback method is named *Substitute*. *Substitute* returns a string that replaces the *Substitution* control in the output before it is sent to the user's browser:

```
<%@ page language="VB"%>
<%@ OutputCache Duration="60" VaryByParam="none" %>

<script runat="server">
    Public Shared Function _
                Substitute(ByVal context As HttpContext) As String
        Return "The time this page was requested was: " + _
            Now.ToString("hh:mm:ss")
    End Function
```

```
Sub Page_Load(ByVal sender As Object, ByVal e As System.EventArgs)
    cacheTime.Text = Now.ToString("hh:mm:ss")
End Sub
</script>

<html>
<head runat="server">
    <title>Untitled Page</title>
</head>
<body>
    <form id="form1" runat="server">
    <div>
        This is cached output</div>
        <div>
            The time when the page was cached was:
            <asp:Label ID="cacheTime" Runat="server"></asp:Label>
        </div>
        <div> </div>
        <div>
            <asp:Substitution ID="Substitution1" Runat="server"
                MethodName="Substitute" />
        </div>
        <div> </div>
        <div>This is cached output</div>

    </form>
</body>
</html>
```

Figure 6-27 shows the output from this Web page after refreshing the browser 10 seconds after the first request. Notice that the time in the *Label* is different from the time returned by the *Substitute* method. Most of the page content came from the output cache, but the part that says, "The time this page was requested was: 11:17:08" came from the callback method of the *Substitution* control.

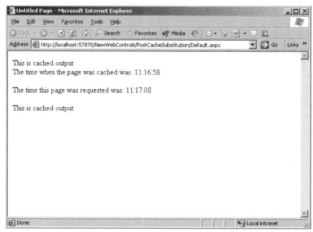

Figure 6-27   Post-cache substitution using the Substitution control.

Conclusion

This application has only scratched the surface of some of the new controls available in ASP.NET 2.0. As a Web developer, you will recognize the potential time savings that these new controls offer as well as the opportunity to have a common implementation for things like user management, security-related UI, and site maps that you can use in all your Web sites.

Application: Master Pages and Themes

This application introduces Master Pages and Themes, two new features in ASP.NET 2.0 that provide the built-in skinning and template functionality that was noticeably absent from ASP.NET 1.1.

New Concepts

Almost every real-world Web site composed of more than one page requires a consistent look across pages. Maintaining the same graphic design and layout on every page is cumbersome without some sort of template-based solution. Web developers using various Web technologies have tried many different ways to create template-based Web applications that are easy to create and update. Unfortunately, this is an area where ASP.NET 1.1 was weak.

Many ASP.NET 1.1 developers resorted to the awkward approach of using header and footer user controls that had to be placed on every page. Although tolerable in many situations, this approach provides a poor design-time experience, makes interactions with graphic designers difficult, and can be surprisingly constricting and inflexible when trying to create "skinnable" sites. In fact, header and footer controls are used only to emulate a template-based Web site. Content from individual pages is not injected into a template—individual pages simply contain common elements, the user controls, that produce a consistent look on each page.

> **Note**   A "skinnable" site is a Web site that has more than one presentation option for the same content by changing fonts, colors, images, layout, and so on.

ASP.NET developers who were discontented with the "header and footer" approach have chosen alternatives such as custom template-based solutions. Several common techniques for implementing custom solutions can be easily found on the Web. Most approaches make it much easier for graphic designers to create templates that can be selected at run time. Although more flexible than header and footer controls, custom solutions still provide a poor design-time experience and add more complexity for you to manage.

An ideal solution is one that lets your graphic designer create a template with one or more content areas specified. Then as you build individual Web pages, you simply point to the template and indicate which content goes into which content area in the template. As you build these individual pages, the design environment should provide visual feedback so that you know how the final page will look with the content injected into the template.

Master Pages

Master pages in ASP.NET 2.0 provide the design-time and run-time support for true template-based development that Web developers have been longing for. Here are the basic steps to use master pages:

1. **Create a master template.**   This can be easily done by an HTML graphic designer. Placeholders for page-specific content simply have to be designated using the *<asp:ContentPlaceholder>* server control.

2. **Make the template a master page.**   Turning a template into an ASP.NET 2.0 master page is as easy as adding the *@Master* directive to the ASPX markup.

3. **Create individual content pages.**   Individual Web forms can be created as usual except that the content must be placed inside of *<asp:Content>* tags that reference the content placeholders in the template. When working in Visual Studio 2005, you can specify the master page when creating a content page and have the visual designer create the *<asp:Content>* tags for you.

4. **Reference the master page.**   Any ASP.NET 2.0 Web form can be a content page by referencing a master page in the *@Page* directive. You can either edit the ASPX markup directly or use the Properties window for the Web form.

The visual Web designer in Visual Studio 2005 offers complete support for creating and editing both master and content pages. You will normally create a master page first and then reference the master page when you add new Web forms to your application. The "Walkthrough" section for this application shows you how to do that.

Themes

Master pages make it easy to control the layout of a Web site and define common visual elements, such as a corporate logo in the top-left corner or a navigation bar along the left-hand side of every page. But there are other visual elements you will need to control across a Web site, such as the font and color used for text boxes or formatting for grids of data. Cascading style sheets (CSS) are commonly used to centralize control of many aspects of a Web user interface. Every page in a Web site can reference the same cascading style sheet, giving you the ability to change one file and affect the entire Web site. But cascading style sheets are not a complete solution for ASP.NET developers. For example, a complex control such as the *Grid-View* has a number of visual elements that are not easily controlled using CSS. If you want every *GridView* to use the same fonts and colors, you have to explicitly format each and every *GridView*.

Themes in ASP.NET 2.0 provide a new way to control the presentation of server controls without abandoning your existing investment in cascading style sheets. A theme in ASP.NET 2.0 is a folder containing style sheets and .skin files. The .skin files define the desired formatting attributes for server controls in your Web application. When the theme is applied to a Web form, the attributes defined in the .skin files are applied to the appropriate server controls. For example, the SmokeAndGlass theme that ships with ASP.NET 2.0 contains the following attributes for *Label*, *TextBox*, *Button*, and *LinkButton* in a .skin file:

```
<asp:Label runat="server" ForeColor="#585880"
           Font-Size="0.9em" Font-Names="Verdana" />

<asp:TextBox runat="server" BackColor="#FFFFFF" BorderStyle="Solid"
             Font-Size="0.9em" Font-Names="Verdana"  ForeColor="#585880"
             BorderColor="#585880" BorderWidth="1pt"
             CssClass="theme_textbox" />

<asp:Button runat="server" BorderColor="#585880" Font-Bold="true"
            BorderWidth="1pt" ForeColor="#585880" BackColor="#F8F7F4" />

<asp:LinkButton runat="server" Font-Size=".9em" Font-Names="Verdana"/>
```

When a *Label* is placed on a Web form, it will have a *ForeColor* value of #585880 and use the Verdana font. A *Button* or *TextBox* will have the same *ForeColor*. You should note that these entries in the .skin file do not have *ID* attributes because they do not represent actual instances of server controls. When an instance of a *Label* control is created on a Web form, it will have its own *ID* attribute but be assigned the other attribute values from the skin regardless of any attribute values specified for the control in the Web form. The only way to override the visual appearance of a themed control is to disable "theming" on that control by using the *EnableTheming* attribute:

```
<asp:Label EnableTheming="False" ID="lblText" runat="server" Text="A" />
```

With ASP.NET 2.0 Themes, you can continue to use your existing cascading style sheet classes and inline style attributes. Style sheet files (.css) in a theme folder are automatically referenced by any themed pages using the *<link>* tag. However, be forewarned that settings in .skin files usually take precedence over CSS settings because most server controls render attributes such as *BackColor* as inline styles that will override settings from CSS classes or previous inline styles.

Walkthrough

This walkthrough shows you how to easily provide a consistent user interface across a Web site using master pages and themes.

Creating a Master Page

Master pages are as easy to create as any other ASP.NET Web form. There are only two differences: the *@Master* directive instead of *@Page*, and *ContentPlaceHolder* controls to indicate the places where content pages will inject page-specific content. To create a new master page using Visual Studio 2005, right-click the root node in the Solution Explorer and select Add New Item. In the Add New Item dialog, select Master Page. Figure 6-28 shows the Add New Item dialog with Master Page selected. Notice that the file extension for a master page is .master instead of the usual .aspx extension.

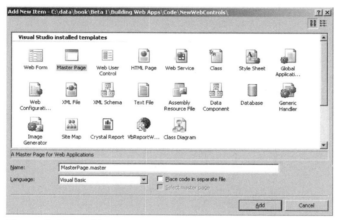

Figure 6-28   Add New Item dialog.

The design-time experience in the visual Web designer is exactly like working with any Web form. The only difference is the use of *ContentPlaceHolder* controls. Figure 6-29 shows a master page in design view with a *ContentPlaceHolder* control in a table.

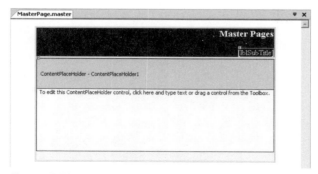

Figure 6-29   Master page in design view in Visual Studio 2005.

The ASPX markup behind the master page in Figure 6-29 is very straightforward. Most of the markup is regular HTML for defining an HTML document with a table in the body. The lines specific to master pages are in bold:

```
<%@ Master Language="VB"%>
<html>
  <head runat="server">
    <title>Untitled Page</title>
  </head>
  <body>
    <form id="form1" runat="server">
      <div align="center">
        <table width="500" border="0">
          <tr style="background-color: DarkBlue"
              valign="middle">
            <!-- Header title row-->
            <td>
              <h2 align="right"
                  style="color: white; font-size: 14pt">
                Master Pages
              </h2>
            </td>
          </tr>
          <tr>
            <td style="background-color: Beige;">
              <asp:ContentPlaceHolder
                ID="ContentPlaceHolder1" Runat="server">
              </asp:ContentPlaceHolder>
            </td>
          </tr>
        </table>
      </div>
    </form>
  </body>
</html>
```

The *@Master* directive identifies this Web form as a master page. This particular master page has only one content area identified as *ContentPlaceHolder1*. The name of the *ContentPlaceHolder* control is actually very important. Content controls in content pages are associated with placeholders in the master page by using the *ID* of the *ContentPlaceHolder*.

Using a Master Page

With Visual Studio 2005, creating a content page that uses a master page is almost effortless. When adding a new Web form to your Web site, select the Select Master Page check box in the Add New Item dialog as shown in Figure 6-30.

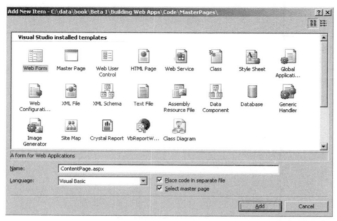

Figure 6-30   Add New Item dialog for adding a content page.

Visual Studio 2005 will next prompt you to select an existing master page from your Web site as shown in Figure 6-31.

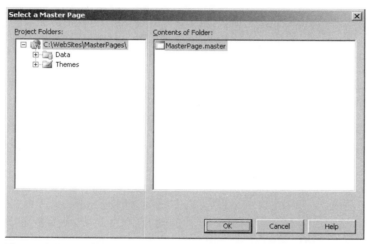

Figure 6-31   Select a master page for the new Web form.

When you open the new content page in the visual Web designer, the layout from the master page is displayed but is dimmed and grayed out, providing a quick visual reference as to how the page will ultimately look and where the page-specific content will be displayed. Visual Studio 2005 creates the *Content* controls for you, one for each *ContentPlaceHolder* control in the master page. Figure 6-32 shows a content page using the master page created earlier for this application.

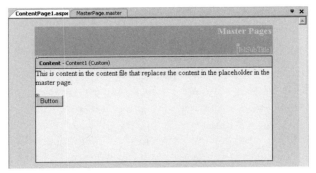

Figure 6-32   Content page in design view.

The ASPX markup generated for a content page is quite simple because much of the markup that provides the structure for the resulting HTML document is defined in the master page. There are just two key pieces of information required in the content page: the master page file to use, and the mappings between *Content* controls and *ContentPlaceHolder* controls. The following ASPX markup shows the source behind the page shown in Figure 6-32:

```
<%@ page language="VB" masterpagefile="~/MasterPage.master"  %>

<asp:Content ID="Content1"
    ContentPlaceHolderID="ContentPlaceHolder1"
    Runat="server">

    This is content in the content file that replaces
    the content in the placeholder in the master page.

</asp:Content>
```

In the preceding markup, the *MasterPageFile* attribute is used in the *@Page* directive to specify the master page. In the *Content* control, the *ContentPlaceHolderID* attribute is used to map *Content1* in the content page to *ContentPlaceHolder1* in the master page.

You can choose a new master page at run time by setting the *MasterPageFile* property of a Web form. A new master page can be used only if it contains *ContentPlaceHolder* controls corresponding to all the placeholders referenced by the *Content* controls in the content page. The *MasterPageFile* has to be changed before the page is initialized. For example, the following code could be used in the *Page_PreInit* event handler to select an alternate master page on every fifth load of the page (on average):

```
Sub Page_PreInit(ByVal sender As Object, ByVal e As System.EventArgs)
    Dim rnd As New System.Random
    If rnd.Next(1, 5) = 1 Then
        Me.MasterPageFile = "~/MasterPage2.master"
    End If
End Sub
```

This code will fail, however, if MasterPage2.master does not define the same *ContentPlace-Holder* controls as the original master page file.

Instead of dynamically choosing a master page at run time, you might find it more practical to manipulate the master page programmatically. Master pages in ASP.NET 2.0 are not static templates. Master pages are classes from which objects are instantiated on the server, and they expose a complete set of events. In fact, the *MasterPage* class inherits from *System.Web.UI.User-Control* and exposes the same events as a *UserControl*, including *Init*, *Load*, and *PreRender* events. Furthermore, you can add your own custom properties and methods to a master page that content pages can use to interact with your master page. Consider the following *Property* added to the master page for this application:

```
Public Property SubTitle() As String
    Get
        Return lblSubTitle.Text
    End Get
    Set(ByVal value As String)
        lblSubTitle.Text = value
    End Set
End Property
```

The *SubTitle* property is a wrapper around the *Text* property of a *Label* control added to the master page. From the content page, the following code can be used to set the *SubTitle* property of the master page:

```
Dim m As MasterPage_master
m = DirectCast(Master, MasterPage_master)
m.SubTitle = "Now Showing:  Content page at " + Now.ToString()
```

The *Master* property of the content page is a property exposed by the *System.Web.UI.Page* class. The *Master* property returns a *MasterPage* object that has to be cast to the actual type of your derived master page class. A master page file saved as FileName.master is given the class name *FileName_master*, so the derived type in this example is *MasterPage_master*. Once cast properly, the custom properties and methods of the master page can be accessed in a type-safe way.

If you are interested in accessing controls in the master page directly, you can use the *Find-Control* method to obtain a reference to the target control (if it exists). The following code uses *Master.FindControl* to access the subtitle *Label* directly:

```
Dim lblSubTitle As Control
lblSubTitle = Master.FindControl("lblSubTitle")
If Not lblSubTitle Is Nothing Then
    If TypeOf lblSubTitle Is Label Then
        DirectCast(lblSubTitle, Label).Text = "Hello world"
    End If
End If
```

> **Note**   The documentation for Visual Studio 2005 states that you can access custom public properties of a master page directly from the *Master* property of a content page. For example, *Master.UserLoginName = "ethan"* where *UserLoginName* is a custom property of your master page. In the preview version of Visual Studio 2005 used for this book, the *Master* property always returns a *System.Web.UI.MasterPage* object, so accessing *Master.UserLoginName* will cause a compile error. You must cast *Master* to the type of your master page and then access the custom properties as shown in the previous example. A streamlined way to do the cast is: *DirectCast(Master, MasterPage_master).UserLoginName*.

Using Themes

Themes are controlled using the *theme* attribute of the *@Page* directive, or a theme can be specified for an entire Web site in web.config using the *<pages>* element. Selecting a theme in the *@Page* directive is very straightforward:

```
<%@ page language="VB" Theme="BasicBlue"  %>
```

Specifying a theme for an entire site is just as easy except that the settings go in the web.config file rather than in the *@Page* directive:

```
<?xml version="1.0" encoding="UTF-8" ?>
<configuration>
    <system.web>
        <pages theme="BlackAndWhite" />           <compilation debug="false" />
        <globalization requestEncoding="utf-8" responseEncoding="utf-8" />
    </system.web>
</configuration>
```

In this application, the BlackAndWhite theme is a custom theme that uses a black back color with a white fore color for a few common controls. Figure 6-33 shows the end result when viewed in a browser:

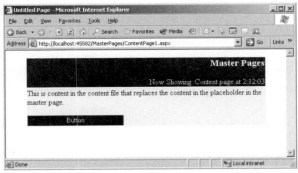

Figure 6-33   Content page in Internet Explorer using the BlackAndWhite theme.

Creating a Custom Theme

Using the prebuilt themes in ASP.NET 2.0 is fine for testing out the new technology, but it's not very practical for real-world development because every site requires its own visual tweaks to stay aligned with corporate branding strategies or to realize the vision of a graphic design artist. Fortunately, ASP.NET Themes are easy to create. First you create a Themes folder in your Web site folder. Then within that Themes folder, you create a folder with the name for your Theme, such as BlackAndWhite. Then you create .css and .skin files in which you can define almost any of the visual characteristics of server controls and other HTML. Figure 6-34 shows the .skin file for a Web site project and the BlackAndWhite theme folder visible in the Solution Explorer.

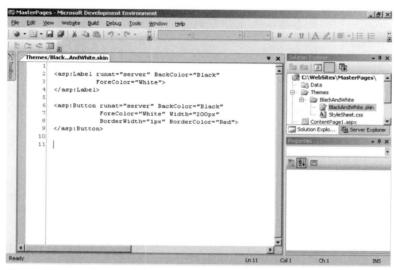

Figure 6-34   Editing a .skin file in Visual Studio 2005.

Conclusion

Prior to ASP.NET 2.0, Microsoft Web developers were at a disadvantage because of the limited support for robust Web site templates and skins. Many developers relied on the "header and footer user controls" approach for maintaining a consistent look for a Web site, but they were disappointed by the poor design-time experience and the difficulty in integrating the work done by Web graphic designers into the user controls to create visually appealing Web sites. The introduction of master pages and themes in ASP.NET 2.0 makes the creation of template-based Web sites simple and flexible. And the design-time experience in Visual Studio 2005 is exceptional. Combining master pages with themes makes it easy to create professional and consistent-looking Web pages without sacrificing developer productivity or the long-term maintainability of a site.

Chapter 7
Microsoft .NET Framework Enhancements

The .Net Framework 2.0 contains many improvements and additions that cover a broad range of functionality. This chapter examines some of these features and demonstrates how you can use them to reduce your coding effort while increasing your application's usability, security, and maintainability.

Application: Base Class Library Enhancements

This application demonstrates many enhancements made to the Base Class Library, such as type improvements, expanded application tracing, typed resources, and generic collections.

New Concepts

The .NET Framework 2.0 includes some powerful additions that can be implemented in any .NET application. You can use these new features to improve application tasks such as converting and validating data, monitoring execution speed, and capturing and logging application events.

Type Enhancements

The .NET Framework basic types, such as *System.String* and *System.DateTime*, have always provided many methods for working with data of that particular type. However, some data-manipulation and type-conversion scenarios were not addressed well. For example, the *String* type's *Split* method allows you to parse a delimited string into an array. An item is added to the array for every element in the string. If the string has empty elements (that is, two delimiters adjacent to one another), an empty item is added to the array. This is sufficient most of the time, but in some cases you might want to ignore empty elements instead of having them added to the array. A new *Split* overload has been added to the *String* type to handle these situations. You can now split a string and provide a second parameter indicating whether or not you want to ignore empty elements. The following code splits a string containing four elements, one of which is empty. A value of true for the second parameter instructs the method to ignore empty elements, so the resulting array contains only three items.

```
Dim colorArray() as String
Dim colors as String = "Red,Blue,,Green"
colorArray = colors.Split(separators, True)
```

Another common task is to parse string data into another data type—for example, when a user enters a date and you need to parse that value into a *DateTime* variable. Previously, the *Parse* method was the only mechanism available for this. Unfortunately, the *Parse* method throws an exception if the string cannot be parsed into the appropriate type. This behavior requires that you wrap any call to the *Parse* method inside of a *Try...Catch* block to handle the exception, which can be a performance issue if the application often encounters invalid data. A new method named *TryParse* has been added that accepts two parameters. The first is the string you want to parse, and the second is the variable the parsed value will be assigned to if the parse is successful. The method returns a *Boolean* indicating whether or not the parse was successful. This allows you to check the return value to determine whether the assignment variable contains the parsed value. The following code will attempt to parse the specified string. If the parse is successful, it will display a message box with the parsed value. Otherwise, it displays a failure message.

```
Dim inputString as String
Dim parsedValue as DateTime
Dim tryResult as Boolean

tryResult = DateTime.TryParse(inputString, parsedValue)
If tryResult Then
    MessageBox.Show("The parsed date is " & parsedValue.ToString() & ".")
Else
    MessageBox.Show("The parse failed. ")
End If
```

One of the first operations you commonly need to perform on string data is to determine whether the variable contains a value or is null or empty. This need is so common that a new method named *IsNullOrEmpty* has been added to the *String* class. This is a shared member that simply returns a *Boolean* indicating whether or not the provided string is equal to *Nothing* or an empty string. Calling *IsNullOrEmpty* is equivalent to using the *IsNothing* function and comparing the variable to *String.Empty*. The following code uses *IsNullOrEmpty* to verify that a string variable contains data before attempting to parse it:

```
If Not String.IsNullOrEmpty(inputString) Then
    DateTime.TryParse(inputString, parsedValue)
End If
```

Generic Collections

The .NET Framework has always provided many powerful collection classes through the *System.Collections* and *System.Collections.Specialized* namespaces. These classes, such as *Array-List* and *Hashtable*, allow you to store objects of any type and easily add, remove, and search for items. However, this flexibility comes at the expense of type safety. The built-in collections are not considered type safe because there is no way to implicitly guarantee that all members of the collection are of a particular type. You have to explicitly implement type safety by writing code that enforces your type constraints anytime an item is added to the collection. In addition, anytime you retrieve an item from the collection, you must manually cast the returned object to your desired type. These type-checking and type-conversion routines are typically implemented in custom collection classes that you write as wrappers around one of the framework provided collections. The following code shows a basic custom collection class that performs these tasks for storing *Product* objects in an *ArrayList*:

```
Public Class ProductCollection
    Private myProducts As New ArrayList
    Public Sub Add(ByVal prod As Product)
        myProducts.Add(prod)
    End Sub
    Public Function Item(ByVal index As Integer) As Product
        Return CType(myProducts(index), Product)
    End Function
End Class
```

The addition of Generic Collections to the .NET Framework allows you to create type-safe collections with very little code. In fact, you can create a fully implemented version of the product collection class just described with one line of code, as will be shown a little later. The .NET Framework provides generic collections through the *System.Collections.Generics* namespace and includes generic implementations such as *List*, *KeyValuePair*, *Stack*, *Queue*, and others. They are called *generics* because they contain a generic collection implementation. You tell the generic what type you want it to store when you instantiate it. The compiler is then able to create a specific collection class that is optimized for storing the type you specify and has strong-typed members. The following code creates an instance of the *System.Collections.Generics.List* class that is typed for storing *Product* objects. The *List* class is essentially a generic version of the *ArrayList*.

```
Dim products As New System.Collections.Generic.List(Of Product)
```

Notice that the syntax for instantiating a generic is a little different than instantiating a nongeneric class. You use the *Of* clause to provide the data type that the collection will store. Some generics, such as the *KeyValuePair*, allow you to specify more than one data type parameter. The *KeyValuePair* generic collection needs two data type parameters, one to specify what type to accept for keys and another to specify what type to accept for values. The resulting instance has members that are strong-typed, so you do not need to write any type-checking or conversion code. The following code shows the use of some methods of the generic *List* created earlier for storing *Product* objects:

```
Dim prod as new Product("Chai Tea")
Dim products As New System.Collections.Generic.List(Of Product)

Products.Add(prod)
Products.Item(0).Description = "A great tasting tea. "
```

Typed Resources

Resource files have always provided a convenient mechanism for packaging application resources such as interface strings and images. However, in previous versions of the .NET Framework, retrieving a resource from a resource file always returned an object that then had to be manually converted to your desired type. Visual Studio .NET 2005 now solves this problem by automatically creating strongly typed resource wrappers whenever you edit a resource file. These wrappers allow you to easily access resources without having to perform casting operations or know the details of how to use the *System.Resources.ResourceManager* class.

Exceptions and Tracing

The .NET Framework provides the *System.Exception* class for encapsulating error information and classes in the *System.Diagnostics* namespace for tracing application event information. The *Exception* class has always provided properties that expose error state, such as *Message*, *StackTrace*, and *HelpLink*. A new member named *Data* has been added to the exception class, allowing you to attach any other information you feel is relevant to the exception. For example, you might want to attach some values representing application state at the time of the exception.

The *System.Diagnostics* namespace provides classes for outputting application event information to an external store such as a file or the Event Log. The .NET Framework 2.0 adds the *TraceSource* class to provide you with more flexibility over how event data is traced. Each *TraceSource* instance has its own name and collection of *TraceListeners*. A trace listener is responsible for sending a trace message to the external store. Being able to define multiple trace sources allows a single application to define individual sources for various parts of the application. For example, you could have one *TraceSource* for the user interface and another for the data access components

The *System.Diagnostics* namespace also includes a new class named *StopWatch* for easily capturing elapsed intervals. You can start a new timer by calling the shared *StartNew* method, and you can retrieve elapsed intervals by reading the *Elapsed* property, which returns a *TimeSpan* instance.

Walkthrough

The *EmployeeManager* application demonstrates how to implement many of these new framework features. This application loads employee data from an XML file into a collection of *Employee* objects. The data is displayed by binding the collection to a *DataGrid*. The new type improvements are used to ensure that data contained in the XML file is valid employee data. The employee collection is created by implementing one of the provided generic collections. Application exceptions are handled by a centralized exception manager, which uses the new tracing capabilities to output error information to an XML log file using the new *XmlWriter-TraceListener*. Finally, the form's background image is loaded from a strongly typed resource wrapper created by *Resgen*.

Validating and Converting String Data

You can now easily check the existence of a string value and parse it into another data type by using the new *IsNullOrEmpty* and *TryParse* methods. The *CreateEmployee* method of the *EmployeeFactory* class is responsible for reading string values from an XML file, validating that data, and then using it to create *Employee* instances. The following code shows the reading and validation of an employee ID:

```
buffer = empElement.GetAttribute("id")
If String.IsNullOrEmpty(buffer) OrElse _
Not Integer.TryParse(buffer, tempID) Then
  .
  .
  .
End If
```

First, the value is retrieved from the *id* XML attribute and assigned to the buffer variable. The next step is to make sure the buffer contains a value by calling *String.IsNullOrEmpty*. If the buffer contains a value, you can attempt to parse the value into an *Integer* by calling *Integer.TryParse*. In this case, we pass *buffer* as the source value to convert to an integer and we pass *tempID* as the variable to assign the converted integer. If either of these operations returns False, an exception is created. The details of this exception and the handling of it are covered later. The rest of the validation uses a similar pattern to check the employee's name and hire date.

The *Employee* class performs further manipulation of the data by parsing the name passed into its constructor into separate first name and last name values. The XML file stores names as comma-delimited lists of name parts including first, middle, and last names. The middle name, however, is optional. The *ParseName* function uses one of the new *String.Split* overloads to split the delimited name parts into an array of name parts and instructs the *Split* operation to ignore any empty parts. It then determines whether a middle name was provided by checking the length of the resulting array and assigns the appropriate values to the *myFirst-Name* and m*yLastName* variables as shown in the following code:

```
Private Sub ParseName(ByVal fullName As String)

    Dim nameParts() As String
    Dim separators(1) As Char

    separators(0) = Char.Parse(",")
    nameParts = fullName.Split(separators, True)

    Select Case nameParts.Length
        Case 2
            myLastName = nameParts(0)
            myFirstName = nameParts(1)
        Case 3
            myLastName = nameParts(0)
            myFirstName = nameParts(2)
    End Select
End Sub
```

Consuming Generic Collections

The *LoadEmployeeCollection* method of the *EmployeeFactory* class handles the creation and population of the collection of employees. The collection is implemented as an instance of the *System.Collections.Generics.List* class by using the following code:

```
Dim tempList As New List(Of Employee)
```

This code defines a new instance of the *List* generic that will accept only *Employee* instances. Later in the procedure, newly created *Employee* objects are added to the collection with the following code:

```
tempList.Add(tempEmp)
```

Even though this code looks no different than an addition to a normal *ArrayList*, it is significant because while an *ArrayList* would allow any object to be added, this collection will allow only the addition of *Employee* objects.

Monitoring Execution Speed

In addition to returning the populated employee collection, the *LoadEmployeeCollection* method also returns the time it takes to create the collection as an output parameter. The first operation the method performs is to start a new stopwatch using the following code:

```
Dim watch As Stopwatch = Stopwatch.StartNew()
```

Just before the procedure completes, the elapsed time is retrieved and assigned to the *load-Time* parameter with the following code:

```
loadTime = watch.Elapsed
```

This returns a *TimeSpan* instance, which is displayed in the status bar in the user interface.

Tracing Application Events

The *EmployeeManager* application uses a centralized exception handler class named *ExceptionManager*. Whenever an exception is created or caught, the application passes the exception to the *ExceptionManager*'s *HandleException* method, which then passes the exception to the *TraceException* method and then optionally rethrows the exception based on the value of the *rethrow* parameter. The *ExceptionManager* creates a shared *TraceSource* instance when it is first accessed:

```
Private Shared ts As New TraceSource(TRACE_SOURCE_NAME)
```

Every *TraceSource* has a *Name*, which is a string used to identify where events come from. The *TraceSource* being configured here will be used only to trace error information. Other parts of the *EmployeeManager* application could define other *TraceSources* to trace other information such as performance metrics.

This *TraceSource* instance is configured further in the *ExceptionManager*'s shared constructor:

```
Shared Sub New()
    Trace.AutoFlush = True
    ts.Switch.Level = SourceLevels.Error

    Dim outputPath As String
    outputPath = Path.Combine(Directory.GetCurrentDirectory, LOG_FILE_NAME)

    Dim traceListener As New XmlWriterTraceListener(outputPath)

    traceListener.TraceOutputOptions = TraceOptions.DateTime Or _
                                       TraceOptions.ProcessId

    ts.Listeners.Add(traceListener)
End Sub
```

The preceding code begins by setting the shared *AutoFlush* property of the *Trace* class. This ensures that all trace listeners will automatically flush their contents to their underlying stores. The next line specifies that the trace source should trace only messages marked with a source level of *SourceLevels.Error*. Typically, this value would come from a configuration file, so you can easily change what types of trace messages are logged. In fact, most of the configuration in this procedure can also be defined through the application configuration file. Trace sources define what messages to trace, and trace listeners define how to trace the messages. A trace source must have at least one trace listener defined to be useful; however, it can have multiple listeners if you need to output trace information to more than one destination. For example, you might want to output trace messages to the event log and to a local text file.

After defining a text file to log messages to, the preceding code creates an instance of the *Xml-WriterTraceListener*. This framework-provided trace listener outputs messages as XML to the specified file. The next configuration step is to identify which pieces of optional trace information the event builder should output. The *TraceOutputOptions* property of the *TraceListener* class allows you to specify options such as *DateTime*, *ProcessID*, *ThreadID*, and *CallStack*. Listeners use this property to determine what information should be included in the output message they construct. Once the trace listener is configured, it is added to the trace source's *Listeners* collection.

The *TraceException* procedure calls the trace source's *TraceEvent* method with the following code:

```
Dim message As String = x.Message

For Each key As String In x.Data.Keys
    message += vbCrLf & key & ":" & x.Data(key).ToString
Next
ts.TraceEvent(TraceEventType.Error, ERRORCODE_INVALID_EMPLOYEE, message)
```

Before calling the *TraceEvent* method, the procedure builds a custom error message by retrieving information from the *Data* property of the exception. You will see later in this walkthrough how this data was populated. The procedure then calls an overload of the *TraceEvent* method, which allows you to specify the type of event, an arbitrary event *id*, and a message string. The trace source will pass this information on to each of its event listeners, which will then construct the event string and send the event information on to the final store, in this case, the log.txt text file.

In the *EmployeeFactory* class, in the *CreateEmployee* method, you can see that the *ExceptionHandler* is called anytime invalid data is found in the source XML file. For example, the following code is used to parse the employee's hire date:

```
buffer = empElement.GetAttribute("hireDate")

If String.IsNullOrEmpty(buffer) OrElse _
Not Date.TryParse(buffer, tempHireDate) Then

Dim x As New ApplicationException( _
"Unable to create Employee object. Invalid 'hireDate' attribute.")

x.Data.Add("id", tempID)
x.Data.Add("fullName", tempName)
x.Data.Add("hireDate", buffer)

ExceptionManager.HandleException(x, False)
Return Nothing
End If
```

If the data in the *hireData* XML attribute cannot be converted into a valid *DateTime*, a new *ApplicationException* is created and the values from the XML file are added to the exception's *Data* property. This allows the relevant business data that caused the error to travel with the exception.

Using Typed Resources

The *EmployeeManager* makes use of one other framework enhancement. It uses a strongly typed resource wrapper to provide simple access to embedded application resources. If you show all files in Solution Explorer, under My Project, you will find a resource file named MyResources.resx. If you double-click this file, Visual Studio will open the file in the resource editor. A single resource named *FormBackgroundImage* of type *System.Drawing.Bitmap* is defined. Visual Studio maintains a code-behind file for each resource file. This code-behind file contains the generated strongly typed resource wrapper class. You can view the wrapper class by expanding MyResources.resx in Solution Explorer and double-clicking *MyResources.vb*. Access to this class is automatically provided to you through the *My* namespace. The form's *LoadResources* method uses this to load the form image into the *BackgroundImage* property of a *Panel*.

```
Panel1.BackgroundImage = My.Resources.FormBackgroundImage
```

Conclusion

The .NET Framework enhancements presented in this application are not limited to desktop scenarios. Any application—be it a desktop, Web, or service application—can use these enhancements for improved string manipulation, quicker collection generation, more flexible tracing, and easier implementation of resource files.

Application: Console Enhancements

This application demonstrates many of the enhancements to the *System.Console* class that allow you to create more powerful console applications

New Concepts

The *System.Console* class provides the primary user interface services for interacting with a user through a console window, such as displaying text messages and accepting user input through the keyboard.

User Interface Manipulation

A console application's visual interface consists of three main components: the console window itself, the text displayed inside the window, and the cursor. In previous versions of the .NET Framework, you had little control over this interface except for the ability to send messages to the bottom of the screen, using the *Write* and *WriteLine* methods, and to read user input either one character at a time or one line at a time, using the *Read* and *ReadLine* methods. There were no facilities for formatting text, nor could you control where text should be output on screen. It always appeared at the bottom of the console window. In the .NET Framework 2.0, you can now specify interface colors with properties such as *ForegroundColor* and *BackgroundColor*, both of which accept values from the new *ConsoleColor* enumeration. You also have greater control over where text should be output because you can now explicitly set the cursor position using the *SetCursorPosition* method. Color can provide emphasis to important information, and setting the cursor position allows you to easily create more informative displays that use alternative layouts such as columns and tables. You can also now manipulate the size of the console window through code using the *SetWindowSize* method.

Text Capture

You can now read input from a user through three different methods: *Read*, *ReadLine*, and *ReadKey*. *Read* and *ReadLine* operate the same way they always have, by reading one character at a time or one line at a time, respectively. Both of these methods simply return a string containing the character or characters that were entered. The new *ReadKey* method, however, returns a *ConsoleKeyInfo* object that contains much more information about the user entry. Through *ConsoleKeyInfo*, you can determine whether a modifier key is also pressed using the *Modifiers* property, which returns an instance of the *ConsoleModifiers* enumeration. The *Key* property returns an instance of the *ConsoleKey* enumeration, and the *KeyChar* returns a *Char* object containing the actual character that was pressed. Using comparisons against these properties, you can create user input processing code that is very readable and easy to maintain while simultaneously providing more input options for your users.

Buffer Manipulation

The console window is actually just a view onto a character buffer. Previously, this buffer was not directly accessible, but you can now control the size of the buffer with the *SetBufferSize* method. The default buffer size is 80 columns by 300 rows, but you can set this to any custom size depending on your application requirements. For example, a common concern among console users is that once the buffer is full, the oldest data is pushed out of the buffer and lost. If a user attempts to scroll back to that old data, she finds that she can access only the last 300 lines of information. If your application frequently displays large amounts of data that users need to be able to revisit, you could consider increasing your buffer size. You can also override the default buffer input and output streams by using the *SetIn* and *SetOut* methods. Using these methods allows you to redirect where commands such as *ReadLine* get their data from and where methods such as *WriteLine* send their data to.

Walkthrough

The ConsoleEnhancements application shows how to use these new formatting and user input features of the *Console* class to create a rich user interface using the console window. The application allows you to create ASCII art (pictures created through creative arrangement of standard ASCII characters) in the console window. You can move the input cursor with the Arrow, Home, End, Page Up, and Page Down keys. Pressing any character or number key will input that character to the screen at the current cursor location. You can change the current text color by pressing F1 and entering a color name at the prompt. Your color name must be a member of the *System.ConsoleColor* enumeration and it must be case sensitive. All other entries are ignored. Some valid colors are: Red, Blue, Green, and Yellow. You can exit the application at any time by pressing Escape. The application uses most of the features outlined previously in this chapter to provide cursor navigation, color output, window and buffer manipulation, and character input and evaluation.

Manipulating the Console Window

When the application starts, it resizes both the character buffer and console window to be 100 columns wide by 50 rows tall using the following code. This is done by first setting the buffer size using the *SetBufferSize* method and then setting the window size using the *SetWindowSize* method.

```
Console.SetBufferSize(BUFFER_WIDTH, BUFFER_HEIGHT)
Console.SetWindowSize(Console.BufferWidth, Console.BufferHeight)
```

If you attempt to set the window size first, you would encounter an exception because windows cannot be set to a size larger than the underlying buffer. You should notice that the scroll bars are not visible with these settings. This is because the window is large enough to display the full contents of the buffer. There is no way to explicitly show or hide the scrollbars or to prevent users from resizing the window.

Capturing Key Information

The application captures key presses in its *Main* method by using the *Console.ReadKey* method:

```
userKeyInfo = Console.ReadKey(True)
While userKeyInfo.Key <> ConsoleKey.Escape
```

The call to *ReadKey* is blocked until a key press is recognized. It then returns a *ConsoleKeyInfo* object containing information about the key press. *ReadKey* contains one optional parameter named *intercept*, which determines whether or not key presses are automatically sent to the console window. If you want to have complete control over the handling of user input, you can set this parameter to True and handle the display of the character manually. The captured key information is then passed to the *ProcessKey* method, which determines what action to take by interrogating the *Key* property of the *userKeyInfo* parameter. It then employs the help of some utility procedures, depending on what key was pressed.

The *SetDrawLocation* procedure moves the cursor to a particular location in the window by calling *Console.SetCursorPosition*. If you want to keep track of cursor locations so that you can return to a particular spot on screen, you will need to manually store the position before changing it. This applications calls *SetDrawLocation*, which updates the *drawX* and *drawY* variables to contain the current cursor drawing position values every time the cursor moves on the drawing surface.

The application maintains two distinct areas in the console window, the drawing surface and the prompt area. The prompt area is used to display messages to the user and request input from them. The *RequestInput* method outputs messages in this area by setting the cursor location and using *Console.Write* to display the text.

```
Private Function RequestInput(ByVal prompt As String) As String
    Console.ForegroundColor = promptColor

    Console.SetCursorPosition(0, promptLine)
    Console.Write(prompt)
    Dim input As String = Console.ReadLine()

    ClearInputLine()

    Console.ForegroundColor = drawColor

    Return input
End Function
```

It then retrieves the user's response by using *Console.ReadLine* and finishes by clearing the prompt area and returning the console's *ForegroundColor* property to the proper drawing color. When a user presses F1, the application calls the *PickColor* method, which displays a prompt using *RequestInput*:

```
Private Sub PickColor()
    Dim colorInput As String = RequestInput("Enter your color by name: ")
    Dim consoleColorType As Type = Console.ForegroundColor.GetType()

    If [Enum].IsDefined(consoleColorType, colorInput) Then
        Dim tempColor As ConsoleColor = _
CType([Enum].Parse(consoleColorType, colorInput), ConsoleColor)
        SetDrawColor(tempColor)
    End If
End Sub
```

The returned user response string is then parsed into a *ConsoleColor* instance and then assigned to the *Console.ForegroundColor* property by the *SetDrawColor* method.

Conclusion

The improvements to the *Console* class are significant, and they allow you to create much more descriptive interfaces by using features such as absolute positioning, buffer manipulation, and text color. For example, administration tools can now easily present data in tabular formats on much larger window surfaces with color coding for various levels of emphasis.

Application: Security Enhancements

This application demonstrates two improvements that have been made to code access security.

New Concepts

Code access security allows a code entity—such as an assembly, class, or method—to demand that calling code pass a set of permissions before the call will execute. For example, a component that writes to the file system could demand that a caller has been given permission to modify the file system. You demand permissions on a code entity by applying the corresponding permission attribute to the entity declaration. The following code shows a method named *SaveFile* that demands the caller have permission to write to the root directory of the C drive. If the caller passes the permission check, the method will execute; otherwise, the call will fail and a security exception will be thrown.

```
<FileIOPermission(SecurityAction.Demand, Write:="C:\")> _
Public Sub SaveFile(ByVal data As String)
.
.
.
End Sub
```

The framework provides many code access permission classes in the *System.Security.Permissions* namespace, some of which are listed in Table 7-1.

Table 7-1   Framework Permission Classes

Name	Description
EnvironmentPermission	Read or write environment variables
EventLogPermission	Read or write access to event log services
FileIOPermission	Read, append, or write files or directories
OdbcPermission	Access an ODBC data source
PrintingPermission	Access printers
RegistryPermission	Read, write, create, or delete registry keys and values
SocketPermission	Make or accept connections on a transport address

StrongNameIdentityPermission

In some cases, you might want to restrict access to your code based on the identity of the calling code. For example, you might have a utility assembly that is only meant to be called by two other specific assemblies. To do this, your utility assembly must be able to confirm the identity of the calling code and determine whether it has one of the authorized identities. An assembly has a verifiable identity if it was compiled as a strong-named assembly. Strong-named assemblies use a public/private key pair at compile time to establish an identity that can be used by other assemblies at run time to identify them. The utility class would use the *StrongNameIdentityPermission* to specify which identities have access to it. In previous versions of the .NET Framework, you could authorize only one identity to access your code. However, you can now allow multiple identities access because of the addition of new security actions that allow multiple instances of a permission attribute to be applied to an entity. Table 7-2 lists some of the security actions and when to use them.

Table 7-2 Framework Security Actions

Name	Description
Demand	All callers in the call stack must pass the permission check.
DemandChoice (new)	Multiple instances of the permission can be applied. All callers in the call stack must pass at least one of the permissions.
LinkDemand	The immediate caller must pass the permission check.
LinkDemandChoice (new)	Multiple instances of the permission can be applied. The immediate caller must pass at least one of the permissions.

Secutil.exe Command-Line Tool

When you apply the *StrongNameIdentityPermissionAttribute* to a type, you need to be able to specify what identity is allowed. You do this by providing the public key of the authorized identity. You can extract the public key from a strong-named assembly by using the Secutil.exe command-line tool. Secutil.exe is installed with the .NET Framework SDK and can be found in Program Files\Microsoft Visual Studio .NET Whidbey\SDK\v2.0\Bin. This tool allows you to retrieve strong name and certificate information from a compiled assembly. There are a number of options for specifying the format of the returned information. The *StrongNameIdentityPermissionAttribute* class requires the public key to be provided as a hex string. The following command-line instruction retrieves the public key as a hex string from a strong-named assembly named foo.dll.

```
secutil -hex -s foo.dll
```

You can then copy the resulting string into your code or a configuration file.

GAC Identity Permission

There might also be times when you are less interested in a caller's specific identity, but you want to ensure that calling code comes from an assembly in the global assembly cache (GAC). A new permission, the *GACIdentityPermission*, has been added to address exactly this requirement. The *GACIdentityPermission* class can be applied to an assembly, class, or member and verifies that the call is originating from the global assembly cache. The following code show this permission applied to a class declaration:

```
<GacIdentityPermission(SecurityAction.LinkDemand)> _
Public Class Foo
End Class
```

The permission specifies the *LinkDemand* security action, which requires that only the immediate caller be installed in the assembly cache. If you wanted to require that all code in the call stack be in the global assembly cache, you would use the *Demand* security action.

Walkthrough

The SecurityEnhancements application demonstrates how to use the *GACIdentityPermission-Attribute* and *StrongNameIdentityPermissionAttribute* classes to apply their respective permissions to your types. The application is comprised of seven projects. Table 7-3 lists the name, type, whether the assembly has a strong name, and whether the assembly is installed in the global assembly cache.

Table 7-3   Security Enhancement Projects

Name	Type	Strong Name	Installed in GAC?
SecurityEnhancementsUI	EXE	NO	NO
ProtectedCode	DLL	YES	YES
LocalAssembly	DLL	NO	NO
GACAssembly	DLL	YES	YES
TrustedAssembly1	DLL	YES	NO
TrustedAssembly2	DLL	YES	NO
UntrustedAssembly	DLL	YES	NO

The SecurityEnhancementsUI project provides the user interface for testing the permissions applied to the code in the *ProtectedCode* assembly. The interface uses *LocalAssembly* and *GACAssembly* to test the *GACIdentityPermission*, and it uses *TrustedAssembly1*, *TrustedAssembly2*, and *UntrustedAssembly* to test the *StrongNameIdentityPermission*. The following walkthrough details each of these tests and explains why each succeeds or fails. Before you can run the application, you will need to install the ProtectedCode.dll and GACAssembly.dll assemblies into the global assembly cache. The easiest way to do this is to open two instances of Windows Explorer. In one, navigate to SecurityEnhancements\SecurityEnhancementsUI\bin. In the other, navigate to Windows\assembly. Copy ProtectedAssembly.dll and GACAssembly.dll from SecurityEnhancementsUI\bin into Windows\assembly. The assemblies are now installed in the GAC. This placement is required to test the *GACIdentityPermission*.

Enforcing the GACIdentityPermission

In the SecurityEnhancementsUI project, the *MainForm* form contains two buttons for testing the *GACIdentityPermission*. The *btnLocalCall_Click* and *btnGacCAll_Click* event handlers initiate calls that ultimately result in a call to the *GACIdentityTest* class in the *ProtectedCode* assembly. This class is protected by an instance of the *GACIdentityPermission* attribute that demands that the immediate caller be installed in the global assembly cache:

```
Imports System.Security.Permissions

<GacIdentityPermission(SecurityAction.LinkDemand)> _
Public Class GACIdentityTest
    Public Function DoOperation()

    End Function
End Class
```

The *btnLocalCall_Click* event handler uses an instance of the *LocalAssembly.LocalClass* to make the call, while the *btnGacCall_Click* event handler uses an instance of the *GACAssembly.Class-InGAC*. The call from *LocalAssembly.LocalClass* results in a *SecurityException* because this assembly is not installed in the global assembly cache. However, the call from *GACAssembly.ClassInGAC* succeeds because it is installed in the global assembly cache. If you remove *GACAssembly* from the global assembly cache, you will find that this call will also fail.

Enforcing the StrongNameIdentityPermission

The *btnTrustedIdentity1_Click*, *btnTrustedIdentity2_Click*, and *btnUntrustedIdentity_Click* event handlers are used to initiate calls that ultimately result in a call to the *StrongNameIdentityTest* class in the *ProtectedCode* assembly. This class is protected by two instances of the *StrongNameIdentityPermission* attribute. Each instance specifies a public key identity that is authorized to make calls to this class. These keys were extracted from the TrustedAssembly1.dll and TrustedAssembly2.dll assemblies using the Secutil.exe tool. The UntrustedAssembly.dll also has a strong name; however, it is not trusted by the *StrongNameIdentityTest* class.

```
<StrongNameIdentityPermission( _
SecurityAction.LinkDemandChoice, _
PublicKey:="0024000004800000940000000602000000240000525341310004000001000100049AAFA961210D12A
66600C3B569DD010A733B24A6D44C980585EE22608CB2D30379CBA61970ECBEAC7D84C25AF3BF8635A1994DE4DC2
343BE4E4EEA1012EC514763C6C89FBB5A6F290B65B4E9CEFF94F3EECD6E9E9D429D2410301D0E18679AB0C03BF49
EA7E3B8392A5CEC7EAC139FF7E593C10FD4FE70CC2C3E51BA2B680CD")> _
```

```
<StrongNameIdentityPermission( _
SecurityAction.LinkDemandChoice, _
PublicKey:="00240000048000009400000006020000002400005253413100040000010001000B78C8D572199C64E
C19B8DD7D44C73F6248436F8D159F41B9D692565640D2BA0C3D354DE3FD2A41B4CDF07BEDC131D15C12965F3ECF8
71AE8D1DDCCF85961BF7565CB339C80688244119C5E4160301F44383D71724CE0679E5CC9135D1C0C11F67BD6129
6F30222706C4233089086036A130C412B6FABEEB94A6B778F039BFC1")> _

Public Class StrongNameIdentityTest
    Public Sub DoOperation()
    End Sub
End Class
```

It is important to note that the two attribute instances use the *LinkDemandChoice* action, not the *LinkDemand* action. Using *LinkDemandChoice* allows you to specify more than one identity. The *btnTrustedIdentity1_Click* and *btnTrustedIdentity2_Click* event handlers use classes in the *TrustedAssembly1* and *TrustedAssembly2* assemblies to make calls to the protected class. These calls succeed because their identities each match one of the authorized identities. However, the *btnUntrustedAssembly_Click* event handler uses a class in the *UntrustedAssembly* assembly that is not authorized, so the call fails. If you want to test this further, you can use Secutil.exe to extract the public key from UntrustedAssembly.dll and add another *StrongNameIdentityPermission* attribute that authorizes that public key to access the *StrongNameIdentityTest* class.

Other Improvements and Additions

A number of other improvements and additions to the .NET Framework 2.0 are beyond the scope of the chapter but are certainly worth mentioning. There is new support for sending data by means of the File Transfer Protocol (FTP) or through a computer's serial port. The *System.Net* namespace's WebRequest/WebResponse framework now provides support for FTP communication through the *FtpWebRequest* and *FtpWebResponse* classes. The *System.IO.Ports* namespace provides a *SerialPort* class that supports full RS232 communication with devices. In addition, Visual Basic .NET exposes opened ports through the *MyServices* class with methods such as *MyServices.MyPorts.OpenSerialPort*. The *System.IO.Compression* namespace provides two new streams, *DeflateStream* and *GZipStream*, for compressing and decompressing data. These classes allow you to easily compress data before you persist it or send it over the wire. Finally, the *System.Xml* namespace has undergone significant redesign, resulting in dramatic improvements in security, performance, usability, and standards compliance.

> **Note**   For more information on the changes to the System.Xml namespace, go to *http://msdn.microsoft.com/xml/default.aspx?pull=/library/en-us/dnxml/html/sysxmlVS05.asp.*

Conclusion

The .NET Framework 2.0 provides many new features that improve both the developer and end-user experience. Generic collections, in particular, promise to greatly reduce the time spent developing custom collection classes, and the new type improvements make data validation simpler and more efficient. The addition of trace sources and new trace listeners affords you greater control of the content and format of your application's trace messages, resulting in an improved ability to troubleshoot problems in development and production. Administrative tool and other console application end users will benefit from a more informative interface that incorporates improved positioning and color formatting. Finally, you have more flexible options for securing your code by using identity-based permissions and disjunctive demands.

Chapter 8

Deploying Applications

As an application developer, you know the challenges of deploying an application. For that reason, you'll be pleasantly surprised by the new tools as well as the improved tools included in Microsoft Visual Studio 2005 for deploying applications. In this chapter, you'll focus specifically on how to use the new ClickOnce deployment technology. You'll also review how to build Microsoft Windows Installer packages by using the setup project templates and tools included in Visual Studio 2005. Along the way, you'll also learn how to choose the right method for deploying applications given the variety of scenarios you'll face as a Microsoft Visual Basic .NET application developer.

Application: User-Initiated Updates with ClickOnce

This application demonstrates how to add a user-initiated updating capability to a Windows Forms application by using the ClickOnce application programming interfaces (APIs).

New Concepts

In Visual Studio 2005, you have a choice of three primary deployment options: Web, Click-Once, and Windows Installer packages. Using the MS-DOS XCopy command to move application files from one place to another is another option, and it remains the simplest and most direct deployment method. It is also the least flexible and is really appropriate only in a few situations—for example, when updating a Web application (and even that should be qualified to mean only deployments that don't require updates to the IIS metabase) or for installing private .NET assemblies.

ClickOnce is an integrated deployment technology introduced in Visual Studio 2005 that allows you to install and run Windows applications from a Web server with little or no user interaction. *Windows Installer* is an installation and configuration service that ships as a part of Microsoft Windows Server 2003, Windows XP, Windows 2000, and Windows Me (and it is also available for Windows 9x and Windows NT 4.0 as a separate download). You'll find the deployment tools in Visual Studio 2005 build on the foundation of Windows Installer, providing you with rich capabilities for rapidly deploying and updating applications.

Background

The collection of services that make up ClickOnce represent the evolution of technologies that began to emerge in the first version of the .NET Framework known as *No-Touch deployment*. When version 1.0 of the .NET Framework was released, it immediately solved a number of problems faced by developers. Managed applications built on the .NET Framework could benefit from application isolation and low-impact deployment (also known as XCopy deployment). The .NET Framework 1.0 also remedied the problem of "DLL Hell" (where the installation breaks existing software and potentially future software installations) by providing a new approach to sharing and versioning components. Eliminating DLL version problems also opened the door to new ways of thinking about deploying Windows desktop applications that can provide more features and deliver a richer user experience than a Web-based application.

No-Touch deployment emerged as a Web-based deployment method that allowed users equipped with Internet Explorer 5.01 or later to download and install Windows desktop applications from a URL and run them on their local machine without running a typical Setup.exe. Also known as "href-exes," this deployment mechanism allowed you to combine the power of rich desktop applications with the deployment simplicity of Web applications.

Unfortunately, running applications directly from a Web location also has its limitations. First, by their very nature, applications launched from a Web page are available only online and are therefore at the mercy of network connectivity. Another significant problem with href-exes exists in the area of security. To run, applications more likely than not require changes to the default security policy on the client. In earlier versions of Visual Studio, it was virtually impossible for developers to determine the permissions needed for an application at design time. And no doubt many No-Touch deployments were dashed against the rocks of unforeseen security restrictions that rendered them unusable in production. An additional limitation of No-Touch deployments was that it provided no standard mechanism for managing versions of releases.

ClickOnce protects the user's machine and applications. When ClickOnce downloads and installs a program, it does not modify any files other than its own. You can set an update policy, and updates are managed using the .NET Framework versioning mechanism. In this section, you'll look at an application that illustrates using the ClickOnce deployment APIs to allow users to automatically update a Windows desktop application. But before examining the implementation details, let's review what's new with ClickOnce and how it fits within the spectrum of deployment capabilities you have to choose from with Visual Studio 2005. You'll also look in detail at how easy it is to implement ClickOnce deployment and automatic updating declaratively.

Note   As you'll learn in more detail when we discuss ClickOnce security, the tools provided in the Visual Studio 2005 IDE remove the guesswork from calculating and configuring security requirements for a Web-distributed rich-client application. This is a huge step forward in realizing the early promise of No-Touch deployment.

Code Access Security

Code Access Security (CAS) is a feature of the common language runtime (CLR) that enforces security based on the identity of code. As a developer, you probably won't work with CAS as part of your daily routine because the infrastructure for securing code is built in to the .NET Framework libraries. However, to make the right decisions about the security requirements for your applications, it is essential that you understand CAS—particularly how the .NET Framework handles evidence, permissions, and code groups. Equally important is that you address security issues early and often during the life cycle of a development project. A thorough discussion of CAS is beyond the scope of this book. To learn more, visit the MSDN Web site (see *http://msdn.microsoft.com/library /default.asp?url=/library/en-us/cpguide/html/cpconcodeaccesssecurity.asp*), which contains a number of articles on security issues in general and CAS in particular; or read any of a number of books specifically devoted to .NET Framework security, such as *Writing Secure Code, 2nd Edition*, by Michael Howard and David LeBlanc (Microsoft Press, 2003) or *.NET Framework Security*, by Brian A. LaMacchia, et al. (Addison-Wesley, 2002).

Advantages of ClickOnce

Building on the foundation of this earlier initiative, ClickOnce has been designed to address a number of obstacles associated with other deployment methods.

- **Automatic / Self-Service Updating**   No-Touch Deployment introduced Web-based installation of desktop applications. ClickOnce extends this capability to provide a mechanism for automatically updating applications or for allowing users to update their applications at their own discretion. Updates are also applied without requiring the user to reinstall the entire application.

- **Self-Contained Applications**   To avoid the versioning conflicts sometimes associated with applications using shared components, ClickOnce deploys applications as self-contained entities that won't interfere with other applications. This means that applications installed through ClickOnce won't be broken by later application installs.

- **Nonadministrator Installs**   Windows Installer applications will run only under administrative permissions. ClickOnce applications can be installed under accounts with reduced permissions, and they are granted rights only as required to run the application.

■ **Offline Access**   Applications deployed using ClickOnce can be installed either to run online or locally. In the latter case, they are integrated with the Windows Shell, which includes adding a Start Menu shortcut to the application. This provides access anywhere and anytime to Web-deployed applications.

> **Note**   For versions 1.0 and 1.1 of the .NET Framework, Microsoft provides the *Updater Application Block for .NET* as a way to further extend the benefits of No-Touch deployment. Developed and released by the Microsoft Patterns and Practices group, this application block is available as a free download from MSDN, and includes documentation and custom .NET assemblies (with source code) for developers to add self-updating capabilities to their applications. (See *http://msdn.microsoft.com/library/default.asp?url=/library/en-us/dnbda/html/updater.asp* for more details.)

ClickOnce deployment also offers significant cost benefits in terms of money, time, and effort. Imagine how such savings can positively influence a critical decision point in your application designs: How many times have you built solutions as Web-based applications because you needed a way to easily deliver that application to a wide audience and you needed to be able to update the application quickly and easily? And if you're a developer working in a managed network environment, you face the additional obstacle of network administrators who are either unwilling or unable to support deploying updates that require an installation program to run on every client system on the network.

The bottom line is that for several good reasons, building solutions as Web-based applications has been the path of least resistance. Although advanced features and a rich user interface were sacrificed, Web applications were easier and cheaper and less of a headache to deploy and update. ClickOnce removes the need to make a tradeoff between functionality and ease-of-deployment because it brings the simplicity and reliability of Web-application deployment to rich-client applications.

None of this suggests that Web-based applications will become obsolete. They still provide the broadest reach for solutions that need to run on a wide variety of operating systems. A Windows Installer package remains the best choice for a full-featured client installation. In many scenarios, however, one can now look forward to delivering rich-client applications to users without having to face the deployment constraints that made that deployment modality an impractical option in the past.

At its core, ClickOnce is a set of new deployment features built into the .NET CLR. These features include a programmable interface as well as design-time support that are integrated into the Visual Studio 2005 IDE. Moreover, ClickOnce deployment functionality can be built directly into applications themselves, freeing you from the need to build a separate installation program.

Publishing a ClickOnce Application

ClickOnce technology is integrated in the Visual Studio 2005 IDE in two primary areas. The first place is in the Build menu, which includes a Publish menu item. The same command is also available from solution and project context menus in Solution Explorer. A third option for publishing within the Visual Studio 2005 IDE is to use command buttons available in the Publish pane of the Project Designer. (This represents the second key area of Visual Studio 2005 IDE integration with ClickOnce.) Selecting the Publish menu command (or clicking the Publish Wizard button in the Publish pane) launches a Publish Wizard (shown in Figure 8-1), a tool that guides you through the necessary steps required for publishing.

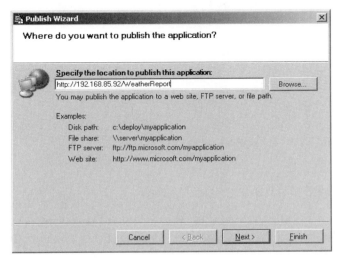

Figure 8-1 Publish Wizard.

The first page of the Publish Wizard asks you to select a location for the application. The other steps in the wizard similarly allow you to change other deployment settings (for example, install mode and how users will install the application, as well as selecting a public/private key required for signing the application and deployment manifests). If you need to make a change, click the Next button to advance through the wizard. Once you're finished updating the settings, click Finish.

> **Note** The *deployment manifest* is an XML file that describes a ClickOnce application deployment, including the current version of the deployment, update configuration settings, and most importantly, the current version of the ClickOnce application's application manifest.

> **Note** The *application manifest* is an XML file that identifies the application being deployed using ClickOnce, including the identity of the application's primary assembly, its security requirements, a list of nonassembly files used by the application, as well as any dependencies necessary for the application to run.

When you publish an application for the first time, Visual Studio 2005 creates a new folder in the solution named *publish* and stores the files necessary to install the application in that directory, including the deployment manifest and a bootstrapper program containing the application prerequisites. It also generates a Web page with links to the program installation and the prerequisites. If you specified a Web site as the publish location, the ClickOnce publish engine creates a virtual directory on the target Web server and copies the files from the local publish folder to that location. Finally, ClickOnce opens the publish page in a Web browser as shown in Figure 8-2.

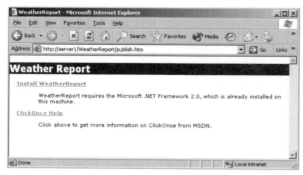

Figure 8-2   Publish page.

Installing and Running a ClickOnce Application

If the application is deployed for offline use (this is the default install mode), clicking the application link begins an installation of the application on the user's machine. If the application is configured for online use only, it will be launched directly from the publish page. Figure 8-3 shows the security confirmation message you receive when you attempt to install the application.

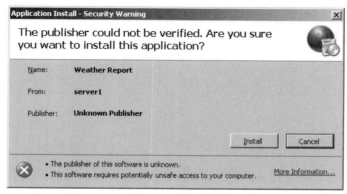

Figure 8-3   Installation confirmation dialog box.

After a user clicks the *Install* button, the application is installed to a local folder on the user's machine. Following successful installation, the ClickOnce subsystem then automatically runs the application from the local installation directory.

Updating a ClickOnce Application

To deliver updates to your application, the procedure is the same as it is for publishing the original version of an application. The only thing you need to do prior to publishing the update is increment the version number of your application. You can increment the publish version automatically or manually. By default, the publish version is set to automatically increment the revision number every time you publish the application. As illustrated in Figure 8-4, however, you can clear the Automatically Increment Revision With Each Release check box to set this value manually.

Figure 8-4   Publish Version.

It is important to note that the publish version is entirely independent from the version number of the application assembly. If the application is configured to automatically increment the version with each release, the easiest way to publish the new version of a ClickOnce application is to click the Publish Now button in the Publish pane of the Project Designer. The publishing subsystem compiles the updated application and stores the assembly and its associated application manifest in a new folder in the publish location. It also updates the deployment manifest to point to the new application manifest. The next time a user opens the application (and assuming the application is configured to check for updates), the ClickOnce run time on the user's machine finds the new version and either notifies the user that an update is available or installs it automatically.

Figure 8-5 shows a typical update notification dialog box. In this example, you have the option to either install the updated version of the application or skip the update. You can control whether a user has the option to reject updates in the update configuration settings for the ClickOnce application.

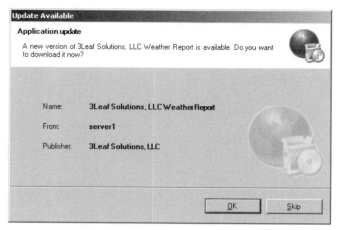

Figure 8-5 Update notification.

To better understand how a ClickOnce application knows when an update to your application is available, examine the files and folders shown in Figure 8-6. This illustrates a typical update scenario where the original version of the application, stored in the folder *WeatherReport_1.0.0.0*, has been updated with a newer version stored in the folder *WeatherReport_1.0.0.1*.

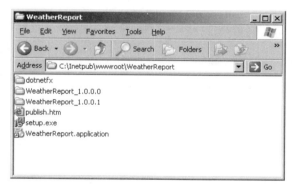

Figure 8-6 Published application files.

The deployment manifest (the file WeatherReport.application shown in Figure 8-6) contains an entry for the latest version of the application. When an application checks for updates, Click-Once looks at the deployment manifest and compares that to the current version of the application. If the available version is newer than the current version of the application, and depending on how you configure the update application settings, ClickOnce either displays a message prompt informing the user that an update is available or automatically updates the application.

Figure 8-7 illustrates this process. The server includes the application files for both the original version of the application and an updated version (1.0.0.1). The deployment manifest shows that a newer version of the application is available. When the installed application performs an update check, it will read the deployment manifest and know that an update is available.

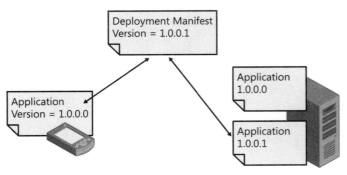

Figure 8-7 Update check.

Configuring ClickOnce Properties

While the default ClickOnce settings might be appropriate in some situations, you will need to become familiar with the Publish pane of the Project Designer to control different deployment scenarios. The settings in the Publish pane allow you to configure advanced deployment options, configure a variety of update scenarios, add application prerequisites to the ClickOnce application, and manage how the files included in the application itself are treated within the application manifest.

> **Note** For more information on the Visual Studio 2005 Project Designer, see Chapter 3, "Visual Studio 2005 Integrated Development Environment."

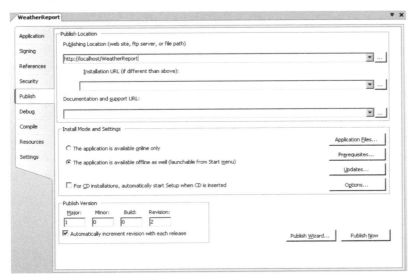

Figure 8-8 Publish pane of the Project Designer.

Publishing Location

The publishing location can be a Web site, an FTP site, a file share, or the path to a disk. Selecting a disk path would be an appropriate option if your intention is to distribute the application on removable media such as a CD. Using a network file share or ftp server as the publishing location is a good alternative in cases where the target Web server is not configured to use Microsoft Front Page server extensions (a requirement for publishing to a Web site).

If the installation URL is different than the publishing location, in the Publish pane specify that address in the Installation URL text box. For example, if you publish to an internal Web site and the application is intended for Internet users, this would be the place to specify the external address. Another scenario in which you will need to specify a separate installation URL is if the publishing location is a file share or an ftp server.

You can also include a reference to Web-based help or other supporting documentation for the application by setting the URL in the Documentation And Support URL text box contained in the Publish pane. If you enter an address for this property, it appears as a link on the publish page generated when you publish the application.

Install Mode

Install mode defines the deployment as either an *installed* application or a *launched* application. Table 8-1 summarizes the primary characteristics of each option.

Table 8-1   Install Mode Options

Installed	Launched
Installed from Web, CD/DVD, or Network share	Runs directly from Web or Network share
Shell integration (entry added to Add or Remove Programs, Start menu presence)	No shell integration
Available offline	Available online only
Variety of application update strategies	Always runs the most recent version of the application

A ClickOnce installed application has the same basic properties as a traditionally installed Windows application. ClickOnce adds a program shortcut to the Start menu, and the application appears in the local Add or Remove Programs applet; therefore, it can be uninstalled like any other program or rolled back to a previous version.

You can set the Install Mode either in the Publish Wizard or in the Publish pane of the Project Designer. In the Publish pane, the section titled Install Mode And Settings contains two options. Select one of these options:

- The Application Is Available Online Only
- The Application Is Available Offline As Well

Note Support for version rollback is limited to one prior version of the ClickOnce application.

A ClickOnce launched application executes from its published Web page. This gives it the "feel" of an href-exe—no shortcuts are added to the Start menu, and the application does not appear in Add or Remove Programs. However, while it might seem to users that applications deployed in this way are running from the source Web location, they are actually cached locally in a fashion similar to Web page caching and toward the same goal of reducing network traffic to improve application performance. This type of application caching was first introduced with No-Touch deployments, where the application executable is downloaded to the local machine's assembly download cache.

Publish Options

The Install Mode And Settings section of the Publish pane includes four button controls to access dialog boxes for manipulating additional publishing properties. If you click the bottommost button, Options, this opens a Publish Options dialog box, which is shown in Figure 8-9.

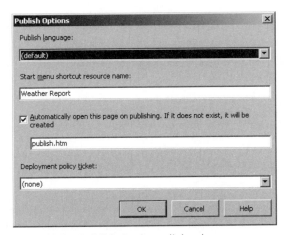

Figure 8-9 Publish Options dialog box.

Publish Language The Publish Language property controls the language of user interface items displayed during installation of the ClickOnce application. If this property is set to Default, the installation uses the culture and language settings on the user's computer. If you are publishing a localized version of the ClickOnce application, change this property to the language and culture matching the localization settings for the application.

Start Menu Name   As noted above, applications *installed* locally enjoy Windows shell integration that includes a presence on the Start menu. You can specify the name that appears in the Start menu item for the application in the Start Menu Shortcut Resource Name text box. If you leave this property blank, ClickOnce uses the title of the underlying application assembly.

Publish Page   When you publish the first version of a ClickOnce application, the publishing engine creates an HTML page called publish.htm. The page displays the name of the Click-Once application and links for installing the application and (if specified) any prerequisites or supporting documentation, as well as a link to an MSDN ClickOnce help topic. This page is copied along with the ClickOnce application files to the publish location as part of the publishing process.

If you publish subsequent versions of the application, the publish page is not overwritten. That means you can customize the page after you have published it by using any HTML editor without having to worry about losing those changes later on.

The Publish Options dialog box allows you to change the name of the publish page from the default publish.htm. You can also disable opening this page in a Web browser after publishing by clearing the Automatically Open This Page On Publishing check box.

Deployment Policy Ticket   If you plan to deploy your application in a managed network (for example, if you are a corporate developer deploying applications over an intranet), you can use ClickOnce for what is known as *Trusted Application Deployment*, which describes a model for safe and reliable deployment of applications requiring a high level of trust without having to prompt your users. System administrations in an organization can enable this type of deployment by distributing a ClickOnce deployment policy to client machines that defines specific application publishers as trusted. (These publishers are also known as trust issuers.) Once this policy has been installed, any ClickOnce application signed by one of these publishers receives a higher level of trust.

> **Note**   Trusted Application Deployment is not practical for deployment to unmanaged networks. Instead, you must use Permission Elevation, which is discussed in detail in the "Click-Once Security" section of this chapter.

As an application developer, you need to perform the following two basic steps to take advantage of this security model:

1. Obtain a trust license file (.tlic) from the trust license issuer for your organization, and add it to your project.

2. Set the Deployment Policy Ticket property of your ClickOnce application to the trust license file.

Once you have added a trust license file to the project, use the Publish Options dialog box to select the Deployment Policy Ticket property. The license file will appear in the drop-down list provided in the dialog box.

> **Note** A detailed discussion of security policy management and creating trust licenses is beyond the scope of this book. For more information about these topics, see the MSDN Library for Visual Studio 2005.

Determining Application Update Requirements

Give careful thought to update requirements before deploying version 1 of your application because the choices you make will be in effect when it comes time to release version 2. For example, if you configure version 1 of a ClickOnce application to check for updates in the background while the application is running and then, when you're preparing version 2 of the application, you decide you'd rather check for updates before the application launches, the change will not be applied until after version 2 is successfully installed.

Or consider how you might address a common update scenario by asking the question, "Do I need users to always have the most recent version of my application?" Depending on how you answer that question for any particular application, you can choose an update strategy that is relaxed in how it delivers updates or use a more rigorous approach that ensures users always have the most recent version of your application.

By default, a ClickOnce application looks for updates in the background while the application is running. If an update is in fact available, the next time a user runs the application, a prompt appears asking her to install the update. This is an example of a fairly relaxed approach to updating because the user continues to use the application after the update is discovered. You can change this behavior to check for updates before the application starts. In this case, when an update is available the update prompt appears *before* the application runs. This approach still allows the user to control whether or not she installs the update, but it at least gives her the chance to make that decision before the application is running.

Configuring Automatic Update Options

While prompting a user might work in some cases, other situations will arise where updates are mandatory. An obvious example is if your application is sending data to a server and the data model is later modified on the server side; an out-of-date client runs the risk of sending bad data to the server. You can solve this problem by configuring your application for automatic updates as outlined in the following steps:

1. Click the Updates button on the Publish pane of the Project Designer. This opens the Application Updates dialog box, shown in Figure 8-10.

2. Select The Application Should Check For Updates check box.

3. To choose when the application should check for updates, select Before The Application Starts.

4. Clear the Allow The Users To Choose Whether To Accept The Update check box.

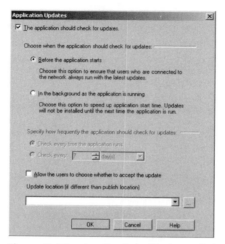

Figure 8-10   Applications Updates dialog box.

> **Note**   Remember, configuring application updates is necessary only for locally installed ClickOnce applications. If the application is configured to launch online, updates are by definition automatically delivered (that is, they work exactly the same way as Web page updates).

Setting Update Check Intervals

Unless configured otherwise, a ClickOnce-enabled application checks for updates every time it runs. You can change this behavior to a specified time interval—every two weeks, for example. This is a sensible option if the application doesn't require users to immediately receive the latest application update. Spacing automated update checks over longer time periods can be a good strategy if you also implement user-initiated updating to allow users to check for updates from within the application itself. (You'll look at how to implement user-initiated update checking later in the "Walkthrough" section of this chapter.)

> ### Consider Your Bandwidth
>
> The quality of the network connection used by your ClickOnce application should be a factor in determining a strategy for checking for updates. If your network has high-bandwidth, it is appropriate to check for updates before the application starts. On the other hand, if the network is slow, this can lead to very slow load times for your application. In this case (and if it is acceptable for users to temporarily use an outdated version of the application), a better option is to check for updates while the application is running to allow the .NET Framework to perform the update check on a background thread.

Application Prerequisites

ClickOnce applications require that the correct version of the .NET Framework be installed on a computer before they will run. Additionally, as with a standard installation program, a ClickOnce application might require additional software components. If the application uses the latest version of Microsoft Data Access Components (MDAC) or Microsoft DirectX, for example, you can include them in the ClickOnce deployment as a separate installation program that gets published with the ClickOnce application. Providing a separate installation program for application prerequisites is commonly referred to as *bootstrapping*. A bootstrapper has the following key features:

- It's a lightweight installation program that installs only the components that are needed on the target machine.

- It supports standard setup EXEs and Windows Installer installation packages (.msi files).

- It supports automatic rebooting and resumption.

- It's easy to add redistributable packages to the list of available prerequisites.

The bootstrapper bridges the gap between ClickOnce and higher impact software installations. The bootstrapper can also be useful in a corporate setting where you have .NET components built in-house that are shared across various applications and need to be installed in the global assembly cache (GAC). Because ClickOnce application files can be installed only to the local application cache, assemblies destined for the GAC must be installed using a Windows Installer installation package (.msi file) added to the application prerequisites. A caveat to bear in mind is that the bootstrapper requires Full Trust permissions. Your users will need administrative permissions to install components included in the bootstrapper regardless of the security level specified by the ClickOnce application itself.

To configure which installation components to include in the bootstrapper, use the Prerequisites dialog box, which provides a list of available redistribution packages. (See Figure 8-11.) By default, the Microsoft .NET Framework 2.0 redistributable package (Dotnetfx.exe) is preselected. This is a bootstrapper utility that will automatically download and install the .NET Framework if it is not present on the user's machine. The dialog box lets you choose to download the prerequisites from the same location as the application (the default) or specify another location for download. Using a different location would be a good choice if your organization uses a common set of prerequisites and you want to conserve disk space on your deployment server as well as make sure every application receives the same version of the prerequisites.

Note   Prerequisites are extensible—you can add your own Windows Installer .msi files or other third-party redistribution packages to the bootstrapper program. For details, see the MSDN Library for the Visual Studio 2005 article "How to: Add Your Own Prerequisites to a ClickOnce Application."

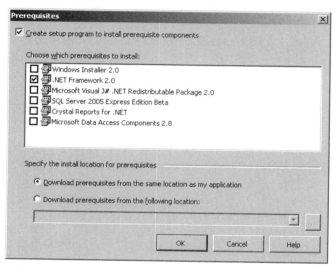

Figure 8-11   Prerequisites dialog box.

When you publish the application, the prerequisites are bundled together into the bootstrapper setup program. The resulting publish Web page contains separate links for installing the ClickOnce application and the bootstrapper program.

Warning   Prerequisites cannot be updated using the auto-update feature of ClickOnce. Only the application itself is a candidate for updates.

Application Files

When you publish a ClickOnce application, all the files in the project get published along with the application. In certain situations, the project might contain files necessary for development but that you don't want to include in the deployment. In other cases, you might want to maximize application performance and installation time by specifying that certain files will be installed based only on conditions you can control. Using the Application Files dialog box in the Publish pane, you can exclude files, mark files as data files or as prerequisites, and create groups of files that download only when they are needed by the application.

Figure 8-12 illustrates how the Application Files dialog box can be used to group required and optional files. The file located at the top of the list (OnDemand.exe) is identified as the entry point to the application and is a required component of the deployment. The application icon file (App.ico) is also categorized as a required item. The assemblies OrderListControl.dll and OrderLibary.dll, however, are assigned to a group titled "OnDemand". These files will be marked as optional in the application manifest and will not be installed when the application is first used.

> **Note** To install items that are marked as optional, you must include code in your ClickOnce application that recognizes when optional assemblies or other files are requested by the application. Your code must then call either the *DownloadFiles* or *DownloadFilesAsync* method of the *System.Deployment.ApplicationDeployment* class to install the needed files. For more information, see the "Walkthrough: Downloading Assemblies On Demand with the ClickOnce Deployment API" topic in the Visual Studio 2005 documentation.

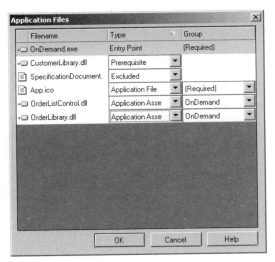

Figure 8-12 Application Files dialog box.

When you first open the Application Files dialog box, the type column will show all files as application files, except .dll files, which are listed as application assemblies. As shown in Figure 8-12, you can change the type of some of the files. The type options available in the drop-down list of the dialog box vary depending on the file type of the associated file. For example, .dll files can be designated as either an Application Assembly or as a Prerequisite. (They cannot be explicitly excluded.) Text files, on the other hand, can be marked as an Application File, Data File, or Excluded.

The third column in the Application Files dialog box lists the file groups for the application. Initially, the only group listed is [Required]. If you need to identify files that should be included in the deployment but downloaded only under certain conditions (that is, installed optionally), you should create additional file groups and assign files to them.

To add a new group, follow these steps:

1. In the Application Files dialog box, select a file that you want to include in the new group.

2. Click the drop-down list under the Group field and choose New. This causes a New Group dialog box to display.

The new group name is thereafter available for you to assign to other files in the list within the Application Files dialog box.

ClickOnce Security

Before you get too far along in thinking about using ClickOnce as a new way to deploy rich-client applications, you might start having concerns about what this means for security. ClickOnce provides a simplified deployment model for full-featured desktop applications. These applications could come from a variety of sources, and you might trust these sources to varying degrees. (For example, you probably trust applications on your intranet more than applications from the Internet.) In fact, ClickOnce has been engineered for deploying applications that are extremely safe and secure.

ClickOnce Applications Run in a Sandbox

By default, ClickOnce applications execute in a security *sandbox*. A sandbox is determined based on the .NET security policy installed on a particular user's machine and the location from which the ClickOnce application is installed or run. Table 8-2 lists the default permissions for ClickOnce applications based on the publish location.

Table 8-2   Security Zones for Publish Locations

Publish Location	Security Zone
Launched from Internet Web site	Internet Zone
Install from Internet Web site	Internet Zone
Install from intranet Web Site	Intranet Zone
Install from network file share	Intranet Zone
Install from CD-ROM	Full

The default security policy in the .NET Framework is highly restrictive. An application running under the default Internet Zone, for example, does not have access to local file resources, cannot connect to databases, and cannot communicate with outside Web resources, to cite just a few restrictions. As a practical matter, before you deploy a ClickOnce application you'll need to determine what Code Access Security (CAS) permissions the application requires to do its work. And then you'll need to configure the application to request those permissions on install.

Configuring ClickOnce Code Access Security

The Security pane in the Project Designer of the Visual Studio 2005 IDE provides an interface for configuring permissions for a ClickOnce application. If it is deployed over the Internet, it has default Internet security permissions. If it is deployed within an intranet, it has Local Intranet permissions. If it is deployed via any other means, it has Full Trust permissions. As described in the previous section, you can deploy a ClickOnce application using the default permissions, in which case you don't need to make any changes in the Security pane. In Internet or intranet deployment scenarios, the default permissions might be too limiting. Conversely, applications deployed with Full Trust enjoy unrestricted system access. In either case, however, as a best practice the application should contain only permissions that it actually needs to run. To help you achieve this goal, the Security pane provides an interface for customizing ClickOnce security settings, as shown in Figure 8-13.

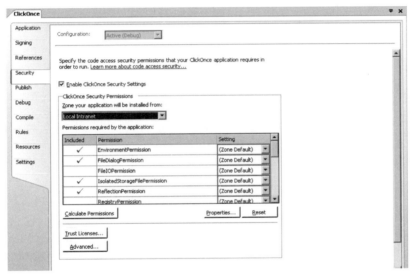

Figure 8-13 Security pane of the Project Designer.

Before you can begin customizing security settings for ClickOnce, you need to select the Enable ClickOnce Security Settings check box. This activates a group of security-related controls in the Security pane. Begin the customization process by selecting one of four zones from which the application will be installed: Local Computer (Full Trust), Local Intranet, Internet, and Custom. Because your objective in customizing security settings is to define the minimum permissions necessary to run the application, you could select the zone that most closely matches the permissions required by your application and use this zone as a starting point for your permission set. Then, working in the table of permissions provided in the Security pane, you should further modify the permission set by either enabling or disabling individual permissions as necessary.

To modify a particular permission in the table, scroll to the row in which it is listed. The Setting column contains a drop-down list with three options: Include, Exclude, and Zone Default. Select Include to add the permission or Exclude to remove the permission. Selecting Zone Default resets the permission to its default state for the selected zone.

Figure 8-14 illustrates an example of manual configuration of permissions. The setting for the FileDialogPermission has been explicitly excluded from the permission set, while the FileIO-Permission has been included. Notice the information icon appearing in the Included column; this icon indicates that the FileIOPermission requires a level of trust that is higher than that provided by the selected security zone (in this example, Local Intranet).

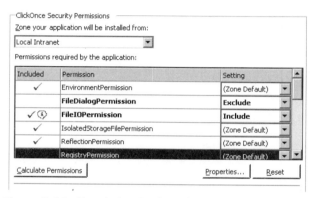

Figure 8-14   Permission Settings dialog box.

If you include a permission that isn't included by default in the selected zone, an information icon appears in the permission row. This indicates that the application will require elevated permissions to run in the selected zone.

You can further modify individual permissions by modifying their particular properties. This allows you to define permissions for specific files or directories, registry keys, or individual Web sites, to name just a few examples.

To illustrate, Figure 8-15 shows the Properties page for the FileIOPermission. The available properties displayed in this window will vary depending on the underlying permission. In the case of the FileIOPermission, for example, you can specify which files or folders require file access, and further define the type of access required to Read, Write, Append or Path discovery using the check boxes provided in the grid. To request unrestricted access to the file system, select the Grant assemblies unrestricted access to the file system radio button.

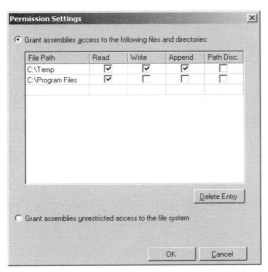

Figure 8-15 Defining properties for the FileIOPermissions.

Manually tailoring security permissions works fine if you know precisely what permissions are necessary for your application. Evaluation of the security requirements for an application should absolutely be an integral part of a project's development life cycle, and therefore you should know what permissions you need to configure. For many reasons, however, that might not always be the best approach. You might not be certain about the permission requirements for your application or how a particular permission influences application behavior. And in a situation of uncertainty, it is far more likely that you will request more permissions than are necessary, violating the primary goal of ensuring that the application has only permissions it needs to run. Fortunately, the Visual Studio 2005 IDE includes two additional tools—the Permissions Calculator and a facility that allows you to debug the application using the configured security settings—that help you accurately identify the security requirements for your ClickOnce application.

Permissions Calculator

The Permissions Calculator is available from the Security pane of the Project Designer. If you aren't sure about the code access security requirements for your application, use the Permissions Calculator tool to perform a static analysis of the code in your project. When the analysis is complete, the tool automatically updates the ClickOnce security permissions for the project as a custom set of permissions.

> **Caution** Because the Permissions Calculator does a static analysis of your code, in some cases the tool might not be 100-percent accurate. If your application requires dynamic file system access, for example, you will need to configure this permission manually.

Debugging in a Security Zone

As a companion to the Permissions Calculator, you can run your application in the debugger by using the currently defined ClickOnce security settings. This approach lets you test your application using the exact permissions granted when the application is deployed. Recall from the discussion earlier in this chapter about the limitations of No-Touch deployment that developers would build and debug applications in an environment with Full Trust and then have those applications throw security exceptions when they were deployed over the Internet or an intranet. Using the currently defined ClickOnce security settings to run your application in the debugger allows you to entirely remove the guesswork in determining whether an application will have sufficient permissions to work when it is actually deployed.

To configure a project for debugging in the sandbox, click the Advanced button on the Security pane to display a dialog box for configuring the application to run with the currently selected ClickOnce security settings. You can also specify the URL from which the ClickOnce application will be downloaded.

Figure 8-16 shows the Advanced Security Settings dialog box with a typical configuration. The Debug This Application With The Selected Permission Set check box is selected. The URL value entered in the text box will determine the level of trust granted to the application while executing in the debugger.

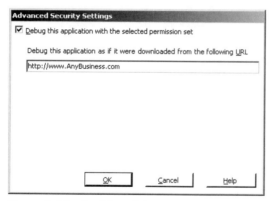

Figure 8-16   Enabling debugging in the sandbox.

Once the application is configured for debugging in the sandbox, simply run the application in the debugger and exercise its functionality. If you attempt to perform a task for which the application does not have the required permission in the selected security zone, a run-time security error displays as it would if the application were actually deployed.

Elevating Permissions

Now consider what happens after you have established the security settings for a ClickOnce application. When you publish a ClickOnce application, the permissions defined in the Security pane of the Project Designer get written to the *trustInfo* element of the application manifest.

When a user launches or installs the application, the ClickOnce subsystem reads the permissions requested from the application manifest and notifies the user if they are beyond the permissions provided by the default security zone. For example, if you have deployed a ClickOnce application over the Internet that requires local file system access and you have followed good security practice by configuring the application to request the minimum set of permissions, when a user installs the application from its publishing location he will be presented with a prompt stating that the application requests a higher level of trust than the Internet Zone.

Figure 8-17 shows the security warning message that appears when a user attempts to install a ClickOnce application requesting a higher level of trust. A message at the bottom of the message window warns that the application requires potentially unsafe access to the computer.

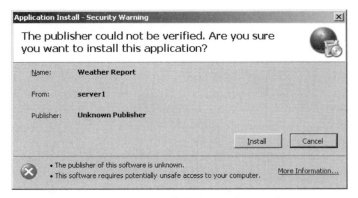

Figure 8-17   Application installation security warning.

Improved Security Policy Model

As described earlier in the "Deployment Policy Ticket" section, for organizations using ClickOnce deployment within a managed network, Visual Studio 2005 introduces a new security policy model whereby network administrators can establish a deployment authority for applications distributed across the enterprise. This requires a one-time only installation of a policy ticket on a local system granting the entity identified by the policy special rights to distribute ClickOnce applications. On computers with this policy installed, elevated permissions are granted automatically and the user won't be prompted.

Authenticode Signing

Finally, a security policy can also grant permissions based on the publisher of a ClickOnce application. Digital certificates provide information about a software publisher that is verified by a trusted third-party. For commercial software distribution, you would likely obtain a certificate from a company such as Thawte or VeriSign. You can use a digital certificate to sign a deployment manifest. The .NET Framework SDK includes a tool for file-signing called SignCode.exe.

Windows Installer Enhancements

Microsoft Windows Installer is an installation and configuration service that ships as a part of Windows Server 2003, Windows 2000, and Windows XP. As of this writing, most systems use Windows Installer version 2.0 (including Windows 9x and Windows NT 4.0, where Windows Installer can be installed as a separate download). Visual Studio 2005 will support Windows Installer version 3.0, and we'll look at some enhancements provided in this release in the sections that follow.

> **Warning**   While Windows Installer version 2.0 can be used on Windows 9x and Windows NT 4.0, Windows Installer version 3.0 is not available to these older operating systems.

Earlier types of setup programs used a procedural model, providing scripted instructions for application installations. An installation package file (characterized by its .msi extension) uses structured storage to organize resources and custom actions associated with a particular installation. At installation time, the Windows Installer engine parses the data in the installation file to build both the installation script and a rollback script that is available for uninstalling the program at a later date. To prevent uninstalls from breaking other applications, a local database tracks information about all the applications on a computer, such as registry settings and installed files. On uninstall, Windows Installer reads this database to confirm that no other applications are relying on files or registry settings that it is removing.

Windows Installer also provides a self-repair facility, which allows applications to automatically reinstall missing files that might have been deleted by the user. A related feature is installation rollback; if a fatal error occurs midway through an installation, Windows Installer can abort the installation and return the computer to its original state.

Windows Installer 3.0 Enhancements

Version 3.0 of Windows Installer includes a number of enhancements to the existing Windows Installer feature set and adds new areas of functionality. Among the improvements in Windows Installer 3.0 is better author control and resource management, including improvements to the interfaces for querying a computer for users and other software products installed on the machine.

The most significant improvement in Windows Installer 3.0 is the addition of a software-patching capability. Whereas in the past application updates might have required a full reinstall of a particular application, patch installation packages (or .msp files) allow developers to deploy incremental updates to their applications. Among the key benefits of MSP files is that they allow for smaller and better performing installation packages.

Visual Studio 2005 Integration

Building on the foundation of Windows Installer technology, Visual Studio 2005 includes tools for creating comprehensive and far-reaching installations. That said, you will also find that Visual Studio 2005 does not include all the authoring tools necessary to take full advantage of the capabilities of Windows Installer. Notably absent from the Visual Studio 2005 IDE, for example, is the ability to create Windows Installer 3.0 software update packages.

> **Note**   For comprehensive Microsoft Windows Installer authoring tools, you should investigate products from third-party vendors, such as InstallShield and Wise.

Setup Projects   Visual Studio 2005 includes several project templates for building installation programs based on Windows Installer technology. As shown in Figure 8-18, you have three basic types of installer projects: Setup projects, Web Setup projects, and Smart Device CAB projects. They are distinguished from one another based on where the installer will be deployed: Setup projects will install files into the file system of a target computer; Web Setup projects install files into a virtual directory of a Web server; and Smart Device CAB projects install Pocket PC, Smartphone or other Windows-CE based applications.

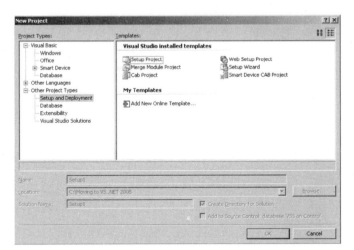

Figure 8-18   Visual Studio 2005 Setup projects templates.

Table 8-3 summarizes each of the various deployment project types and their purpose. In addition to the three primary setup projects discussed above, you will find project templates for building a Merge Module or CAB project.

Table 8-3   Visual Studio 2005 Deployment Project Types

Project Type	Purpose
Setup Project	Builds an installer for a Windows-based application
Web Setup Project	Builds an installer for a Web application
Merge Module Project	Packages components that can be shared by multiple applications
CAB Project	Creates a cabinet file for downloading to a legacy Web browser
Smart Device CAB Project	Builds an installer for a Smart Device application

Another choice in the setup project templates is the Setup Wizard; while not a setup project itself, choosing this item launches a wizard that guides you through the process of choosing the correct deployment project type.

Note   Windows Installer project files (.wip) created with the Visual Studio Installer add-in for Visual Studio 6.0 cannot be opened in Visual Studio 2005.

Merge Modules   Merge modules are a special type of deployment project. They can be used to deliver shared code, files, resources, registry entries, and setup logic to applications as a single file. As a simplified form of an .msi file, merge modules have an .msm file name extension. As such, they cannot be installed directly and need to be merged into a setup project. When a merge module is merged into the .msi file of an application, all the information and resources required to install the components contained in the merge module are incorporated into the application's .msi file. Because all the information needed to install the components is delivered as a single file, the use of merge modules can help reduce version conflicts, missing registry entries, and improperly installed files.

Tip   Merge modules can be incorporated directly into a Setup Project or a Web Setup Project from the Project menu.

Building a Windows Installer Installation Package

If you have worked with setup projects in previous versions of Visual Studio, the tasks you need to perform in building a setup project in Visual Studio 2005 should be familiar to you. In most cases, you'll want to create the installation as a subproject of the solution containing the application you intend to deploy. You can choose either one of the predefined setup projects or the Setup Wizard to create the shell for the project. A key advantage of using a Windows Installer-based installer rather than ClickOnce is the flexibility it provides in customizing the installation. And the Visual Studio 2005 IDE provides editors to work with registry settings and file types and associations. You can also customize the user interface for the installation, specify launch conditions, and define custom actions to be performed after installation.

> **Tip**   Remember, you can include Windows Installer packages with a ClickOnce deployment as a prerequisite.

Installing Files, Folders, and Shortcuts   The basic task of a Setup project is installing files to the target computer. The File System Editor represents the file system on a target computer, and you use this tool to specify where application files will be installed. In most cases, you will want to place application files in the Application Folder or in subfolders you create beneath the Application Folder. When installed on a target computer, files from the Application Folder will be located in the Program Files*Manufacturer**ProductName* folder, where *Manufacturer* is the company name that you used when you installed Visual Studio and *ProductName* is the name that you used for the deployment project. You can override both of these settings in the properties window for the setup project.

Figure 8-19 shows the File System Editor for a setup project that will include the primary output from a project titled "WeatherReport." Note that both this application project and the setup project (WeatherReportMSI) are listed in Solution Explorer. The Application Folder also includes a shortcut to the application being installed and the icon file (CLOUD.ICO) associated with the application. After adding an icon file to the Application Folder, you can use it to set the icon property of shortcuts or the icon associated with the item added to the Add or Remove Programs list on the target computer (set using the *AddRemoveProgramsIcon* property of the Setup project).

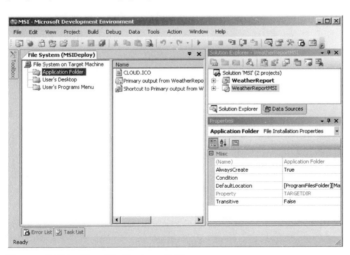

Figure 8-19   The File System Editor.

You can also configure the installation to add items to the desktop and/or Start Menu of the target machine. Most commonly, you will add a shortcut to the installed application. In the File System Editor, add shortcuts in the folders titled User's Desktop and User's Program Menu to install shortcuts on the user's desktop and Start Menu, respectively. In the example shown in Figure 8-19, you could simply cut the shortcut listed in the Application Folder and paste it into the User's Desktop or User's Program Menu, or both.

Creating File Associations   Use the File Types Editor to establish file associations on the target computer by associating file extensions with your application and specifying the actions allowed for each file type. You can also specify the default action for a file type, such as opening or printing the file. The default actions occur when a user double-clicks a file in Windows Explorer. And all the actions you specify appear as commands in the context menu when a user right-clicks a file in Windows Explorer. Figure 8-20 shows an example of using the File Types Editor to add Open and Print actions for a file type of *.wxl*.

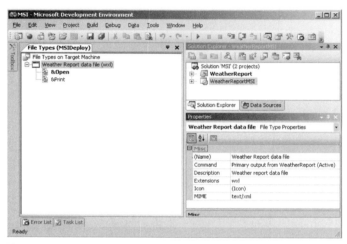

Figure 8-20   The File Types Editor.

Modifying the User Interface   A set of default dialog boxes are provided automatically for display during installation. This set of dialog boxes provided varies based on the type of project you're building. Using the User Interface Editor, you can reorder or delete dialogs.

As shown in Figure 8-21, the dialog tree displayed in the editor contains two sections: Install and Administrative Install. The Install section includes the dialog boxes displayed when an end user runs the installer, while the Administrative Install section contains the dialog boxes displayed when a system administrator uploads the installer to a network location. If you want to build an install with no user interface, simply delete all dialog boxes in the Install section of the dialog tree. Or you can add dialog boxes to the install project from a set of available templates.

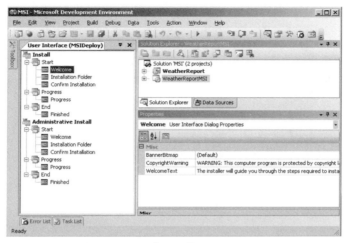

Figure 8-21   The User Interface Editor.

Managing Registry Keys and Values   If the application install requires changes to the registry, use the Registry Editor to add registry keys and values during installation. As illustrated in Figure 8-22, the Register Editor provides a split-pane window for adding registry settings. The left pane displays a hierarchal view of the registry on the installation target machine, which you can use to build paths to one or more registry keys. Use the right pane to add values for the currently selected registry key.

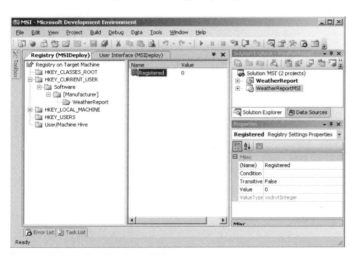

Figure 8-22   The Registry Editor.

Defining Launch Conditions   Use the Launch Conditions Editor to define conditions that must be met to successfully run an installation. For example, you can check for a specific version of an operating system. If a user attempts to install on a system that does not meet the condition, the installation aborts. You can also configure launch conditions to search the target computer for a particular file, registry key, or component. Windows Installer performs searches and conditional evaluations at the beginning of an installation and in the order shown in the Launch Conditions Editor.

Figure 8-23 shows the Launch Conditions editor. This editor contains folders to add search and launch conditions and it shows the default launch condition requiring a specific version of the .NET Framework. For this particular launch condition, the Properties pane allows you to specify the supported runtime.

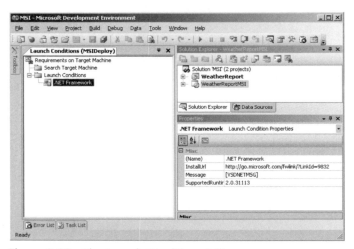

Figure 8-23   The Launch Conditions Editor.

Defining Custom Actions   Custom actions provide a mechanism for performing tasks at the end of an installation. For example, you might want to launch a self-registration program or relay account information to a Web service after an application is installed, or you might want to direct users to a customer satisfaction survey on uninstall. Custom actions are built as separate .dll or .exe files and then added to the project where they can be associated with different phases of the installation by using the Custom Actions Editor. Figure 8-24 shows the Custom Actions Editor, which includes separate folders for placing the binaries used to perform Install, Commit, Rollback, or Uninstall tasks.

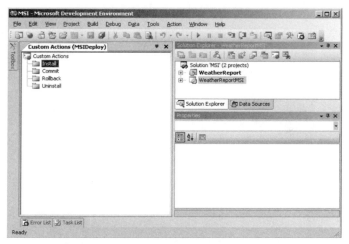

Figure 8-24   The Custom Actions Editor.

Building the Installation Package   Building the installation package is no different than compiling a finished .NET assembly. Selecting Build from the project menu causes the .msi file to be compiled along with the bootstrapper program. You can also test installations directly from the Visual Studio 2005 IDE. When a setup project is active in the IDE, the Project menu includes menu items for Install and Uninstall, making it a very simple matter to safely test installations in development. Figure 8-25 shows the installation package (MSIDeploy.msi), and the bootstrapper programmer (setup.exe) as they appear in the project's bin directory.

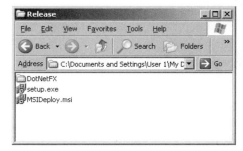

Figure 8-25   The compiled .msi installation file and bootstrapper.

Walkthrough

This example is a Visual Basic .NET Windows Forms application that provides user-initiated updating using the ClickOnce APIs. Before you start, make sure to disable automatic update checking in the project properties; having an application check for updates every time a user launches the application renders user-initiated update checks redundant (unless you expect your users will never close your application!).

> **Important** To use the ClickOnce APIs from code, include a project reference to the *System.Deployment* assembly.

Providing UI Access

Of course you need to provide a way for your users to check for updates from your application. One option is to place a Check For Updates menu item on your application's main form. As Figure 8-26 illustrates, the demo application includes submenus for using either the synchronous or asynchronous version of the ClickOnce API for update checking.

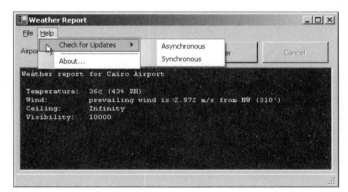

Figure 8-26   Provide the user easy access to updates from the Help menu.

Adding Code to Check for Updates

At the top of the code file for the main form, import the deployment namespace as follows:

```
Import System.Deployment
```

Next, add code to the click event handler for the menu item to check for updates. *Application-Deployment* is a class contained in the *System.Deployment* namespace, and you'll use the properties and methods of this class to programmatically update to the current deployment (you also use this class for on-demand downloads of files). Before creating an instance of this, check the static *IsNetworkDeployed* property, a boolean value indicating whether the current application is a ClickOnce application:

```
If True = ApplicationDeployment.IsNetworkDeployed Then
    ' Update check code goes here.
End
```

As the code snippet illustrates, it is wise to enclose the update checking code within an *If* statement confirming that this is a ClickOnce application. If you attempt to create an instance of *ApplicationDeployment* for an application that is not ClickOnce-deployed, the result is an *InvalidDeploymentException* error. Also, you cannot create an instance of *ApplicationDeployment* directly. Instead, use the static *CurrentDeployment* property, which returns the current *ApplicationDeployment* object for the ClickOnce application:

```
Dim thisDeployment as ApplicationDeployment = _
    ApplicationDeployment.CurrentDeployment
```

Once you have created an instance of the *ApplicationDeployment* object, you can all the *CheckForUpdate* method to determine whether a newer version of the application is available. This method returns a Boolean value of true if an update is available:

```
If True = thisDeployment.CheckForUpdate() Then
    ' New version of application is available.
Else
    ' Application is up-to-date.
End If
```

The asynchronous version of this method is *CheckForUpdateAsync*. To implement this method, you first need to add an event handler for the *CheckForUpdateCompleted* event:

```
AddHandler thisDeployment.CheckForUpdateCompleted, _
    AddressOf CheckForUpdateCompleted

thisDeployment.CheckForUpdateAsync()
```

The method signature for the *CheckForUpdateCompleted* event includes a *CheckForUpdateCompletedEventArgs* object. In the event handler, you need to check the value of the boolean *UpdateAvailable* property of *CheckForUpdateCompletedEventArgs* to determine if a new version of the application is available:

```
Private Sub CheckForUpdateCompleted(ByVal sender As Object, _
    ByVal e As CheckForUpdateCompletedEventArgs)

    If e.UpdateAvailable Then
        ' New version of application is available.
    Else
        ' Application is up-to-date.
    End If
End Sub
```

The *CheckForUpdateCompleted* event is called on the main application thread. So it is perfectly safe to use your application's Windows Forms controls directly within this callback.

The *Update* method of the *ApplicationDeployment* class updates the application to the latest version:

```
thisDeployment.Update()
```

The asynchronous version of this method, *UpdateAsync*, uses the same pattern as the *CheckForUpdateAsync* method. The *UpdateAsync* method raises two separate events: *ProgressChanged* occurs at intervals during download of the updated application files, which can be useful for reporting installation progress for large applications, or updates that execute over a slow network connection; *UpdateComplete* occurs when the update is complete. Before calling the *UpdateAsync* method, first add event handlers for the *UpdateComplete* event and (optionally) the *ProgressChanged* event:

```
AddHandler thisDeployment.UpdateCompleted, AddressOf Update_UpdateCompleted
AddHandler thisDeployment.ProgressChanged, AddressOf Update_ProgressChanged

thisDeployment.UpdateAsync()
```

The method signature for the *ProgressChanged* event handler includes a *DeploymentProgressChangedEventArgs* parameter. You can access the properties of this object to report the status of the application update. In this example, the progress information is written to a panel on the status strip of the application's main Windows form.

```
Private Sub Update_ProgressChanged(ByVal sender As Object, _
    ByVal e As DeploymentProgressChangedEventArgs)
    ' Calculate progress of update and store value in local string.
    Dim updateProgress As String = String.Format( _
        "{0:D}K out of {1:D}K downloaded - {2:D}% complete", _
    e.BytesCompleted / 1024, _
    e.BytesTotal / 1024, e.ProgressPercentage)
    ' Update status bar with update progress.
    Me.StatusStripPanel2.Text = updateProgress
End Sub
```

The method signature for the *UpdateComplete* event handler includes an *AsyncCompletedEventArgs* parameter. The code in the event handler should examine the properties of this object to determine the outcome of the application update. *AsyncCompletedEventArgs* exposes a *Cancelled* property, which signals whether the update was canceled, and an *Error* property, which contains exception information if an error occurred during the update.

```
Private Sub Update_UpdateCompleted(ByVal sender As Object, _
    ByVal e As AsyncCompletedEventArgs

    If Not e.Cancelled Then
        If (e.Error Is Nothing) Then
            ' Update was successful.
```

```
        Else
                ' Error occurred during update.
        End If
    Else
        ' Update was cancelled.
    End If
End Sub
```

Conclusion

With ClickOnce, you can deploy and update rich-client applications as simply and easily as Web applications. Using the tools provided in Visual Studio 2005, it is simple to add ClickOnce functionality to an application. The programming model for building custom updating solutions is powerful and straightforward, and it gives you plenty of room for addressing various deployment scenarios. Finally, and probably most importantly, the security features built into ClickOnce allow you to deliver applications that are not only feature-rich and convenient to deploy and maintain, but which also enjoy the protections provided by the .NET Framework.

Even though Visual Studio 2005 and the .NET Framework 2.0 introduce a simple and easy-to-use declarative model for deploying applications with ClickOnce, this isn't a one-size fits all solution. For more complex application installations that might require deploying shared components or other high-impact changes to a computer system, Microsoft Windows Installer technology, which is tightly integrated into all modern Windows operating systems, gives you the power and flexibility you need to build reliable and highly customizable installation programs.

Index

Number

About the Authors

Sean Campbell, **Scott Swigart**, **Kris Horrocks**, **Derek Hatchard**, **Peter Bernhardt**, **Gerry O'Brien**, and **Oz Rugless** are developers with 3 Leaf Solutions, a firm that provides training and consulting services supporting next-generation Microsoft technologies. 3 Leaf Solutions works closely with Microsoft product groups to develop best-practice reference applications, training courses, and sample applications that demonstrate how to use emerging technology to build real solutions.